IMAGES
of America

DURANT

On the Cover: **DC-3 Air Freight Transport.** This image, dated April 4, 1946, captures a booster trip. Skytrain Air Express was owned by Ed McGee and Roy Paul, and the business was later moved to Tulsa. Pictured are, from left to right, (first row) Rector Swearengin, Garland Harper, Kay Bass, and Ed McGee; (second row) Roy David, C. Rowland, Anna Pappas, Mrs. Loy Fry, Allen Hill, S.W. McGee, Mrs. Frank Dyer, Frank Dyer, Miller Davidge, and Geo. Pendleton Jr.; (third row) David Bates, Jack Foote, Miller Pitts, P.L. Moore, O.W. Davison, Art Holmes, Roy Hamilton, R.W. Fleak, R.W. Reeves, Bennett Story, and Geo. Pendleton Sr. (Courtesy of Matt Swearengin.)

IMAGES
of America

DURANT

Donovin Arleigh Sprague

ARCADIA
PUBLISHING

ISBN 978-0-7385-9098-1

Published by Arcadia Publishing
Charleston, South Carolina

Printed in the United States of America

Library of Congress Control Number: 2012950253

For all general information, please contact Arcadia Publishing:
Telephone 843-853-2070
Fax 843-853-0044
E-mail sales@arcadiapublishing.com
For customer service and orders:
Toll-Free 1-888-313-2665

Visit us on the Internet at www.arcadiapublishing.com

Dedicated with love to Deb, Darrel, and Velda Sprague

Contents

Acknowledgments

My thanks to the following people and organizations that have inspired, supported, or helped in my endeavors and research. Thanks also to all the nice people from Durant and Bryan County who I have worked with!

Bill and Geraldine Anderson; Paula Anderson; John Andrews; Hoyt Axton; Marcia Ball; Lou Ann Barton; Frank Beard; Regina Berna; Doyle Bramhall I; Doyle Bramhall II; Eddie Brigati; Doris Brown; Donna Bullard; Alan Burton; the City of Durant; Eddy Clearwater and Renee Greenman; Jessi Colter; the Confederate Memorial Museum and Cemetery, Atoka, Oklahoma; *Cowboys & Indians Magazine*; Crazy Horse Tiwahe; David L. Crouch; Dottie Davis; Marion Downs; Chris Duarte; James Dunegan; the Durant Chamber of Commerce; the *Durant Daily Democrat*; Durant High School; Juanita Estes; Fort Washita; Denny Freeman; Clyde and Elsie Frost; Lane Frost; Billy Gibbons; Merle Haggard; Harold Harmon; Ted Harvey; Tuff Hedeman; Dusty Hill; the Margaret Hogan family; Jesse Holder; Hump Tiwahe; the Indian Territory Museum, Caddo, Oklahoma; John Inmon; Waylon Jennings; Jones Academy; Calvin Jones; Albert King; B.B. King; Freddie King; Cody Lambert; Bess LeFlore; David and Joanie Lindley; Barbara Logan; Wilma Mankiller; Paul Mauck; Reba McEntire; Susie McEntire; Mike Metheny; Rick Munholland; Michael Martin Murphey; Bobbie Nelson; Lana Nelson; Willie Nelson; Gary P. Nunn; Jill Nunn; Monte Olsen; Iris Lowe O'Riley; Don Parker; Bob Pearson; Nell Pearson; Pinetop Perkins; Kathryn Plunkett; the Pooley family; DeAnn Prince; Dylan Pudwill; Rhianna Pudwill; David Ray; Johnny Smith; Robert Smith; Thomas "Tinker" and Elma Lou Ray; Janet Reed; the Donald W. Reynolds Community Center and Library; George Rains; the Robert L. Williams Library; Crystal Robinson; Jimmy Rogers; the Serfling family; Tommy Shannon; Mark Shillingstad; Joe Sirmans; Southeastern Oklahoma State University; SOSU Intercollegiate Athletics; SOSU Henry G. Bennett Memorial Library; Wanda Shelton; Inez Sitter; Abby Sprague; Ava Pearl Sprague; Brandon Sprague; Deb Sprague; Marcie Sprague; Rylan, Rosie, and Ella Sprague; Hubert Sumlin; Flavia Swearengin; Matt Swearengin; Gene Taylor; B.J. Thomas; Matt Thomas; Steve Thomas; Winnie Timmons; Reba Titsworth; Ben Trent; Casie Trent; Mike and Sandra Trent; the Trent family; the Vance family; Jimmie Vaughan; Stevie Ray Vaughan; Gwen Walker; Jan Wallbaum; Cindy Wallis; Leta Whitaker; James White; Rex White; Tom Williams; and Kim Wilson.

INTRODUCTION

The Durant area, previously been claimed by both Spain and France, officially became part of the United States following the Louisiana Purchase and the Adams-Onís Treaty. During the 1820s and 1830s, the area was designated as part of the Choctaw Nation in the southern Indian Territory.

The name Durant is of French origin. French colonists, interested in the fur trade, explored Canada and the Great Lakes area of the United States and came across what is now called the Mississippi River. French families by the name of Durant (and alternative spellings) made their way southward, and many followed the Mississippi River to New Orleans and the Gulf of Mexico. Many of the French-Canadians settled in present-day Mississippi and the Louisiana Territory, often intermarrying with members of the area's American Indian tribes, including the Choctaw and Chickasaw. In 1830, the US Congress passed the Indian Removal Act, displacing many of people in the southeastern United States. The Durant families and others would accompany these tribes during their forced relocation to Indian Territory. Earlier, more American Indian tribes had vacated the area of Durant as the new tribes arrived.

In the new Indian Territory, the Durants and the Choctaw and Chickasaw tribes were allotted land. Dixon Durant and his brothers Besant and Jesse (sons of Fisher Durant) were one-fourth French Canadian and three-fourths Choctaw by blood. Dixon's cousin William A. Durant became principal chief of the Choctaw Nation. Just prior to the allotment of land, Dixon made a claim on the area that includes most of the present-day city of Durant. He would later be credited as the city's founder and namesake.

The Missouri-Kansas-Texas ("Katy") Railroad reached the area around Durant (present-day Atoka) about 1872, and a station in Durant was approved in 1880. An old boxcar without wheels was placed on the east side of the main track, where Main Street now intersects it, to serve as a depot. A water tank was built on the west side of the tracks, and a waterline was installed to Mineral Bayou Creek. Railroad officials named the depot area Durant Station, which was changed to Durant in 1882. The railroad opened the door for people to move in. In 1873, Dixon Durant built a small store just east of the boxcar depot.

Fort Washita, to the northwest of Durant, was built in 1842. As early as 1843, the Choctaw Nation opened the Armstrong Academy (Chahta Tamaha) for students located northeast of Durant, east of Caddo, and west of Banty.

In 1894, the Dawes Commission urged the Choctaws and Chickasaws to accept statehood. An Act of Congress, approved in 1898, allowed towns in Indian Territory with a population of 200 or more to incorporate, and Durant, having grown to a population of 2,5000, applied. W.H. Hilton was elected as the first mayor of Durant in 1899, and the original 1,319-acre townsite was approved by the secretary of the interior in 1902. Durant is the county seat of Bryan County, which was created from Choctaw lands in 1907 and was named after William Jennings Bryan (a US secretary of state and three-time nominee for president).

In 1900, Durant's population was listed at 2,980; by 1940, it had grown to 10,027 people. Today, Durant is a thriving city with a population of 15,877 (according to the 2010 census). It is home to Southeastern Oklahoma State University and is the headquarters of the Choctaw Nation of Oklahoma. The city is officially known as the "Magnolia Capital of Oklahoma" and is home to the annual Magnolia Festival and the Three Valley Museum. The festival, put on by the Durant Chamber of Commerce and Durant Main Street Program, features music, shopping, shows, and two pageants (the Magnolia Pageant and the Choctaw Princess Pageant). Durant also has a "World's Largest Peanut" monument (two other such monuments exist in Texas and Georgia).

Lake Texoma is Oklahoma's second-largest lake and one of the premier striped bass hot spots in the southwest. Besides fishing and a myriad of water sports, Lake Texoma State Park offers swimming, camping, picnic areas, wildlife-viewing opportunities, and hiking. Golfing and the Two Rivers Nature Center are also popular in the area. Durant is located in a region named Texoma, or Texomaland, because of its short distance from Lake Texoma. In 2004, Durant was ranked as the fastest-growing rural city in Oklahoma, having the fastest growth rate outside of Oklahoma City and Tulsa. Durant and Southeastern Oklahoma State University have produced outstanding athletic teams, players, and coaches, including professional basketball and baseball players—and even an Olympian.

Superstar singer, and recent inductee to the Country Music Hall of Fame, Reba McEntire is an alumna of Southeastern Oklahoma State University. Gail Farrell, a cast member of *The Lawrence Welk Show*, has a street named in her honor in her hometown of Durant. Actor Jose Ferrer and actress/singer Rosemary Clooney were married in Durant in 1953. Other notable people from Durant include Ralph Faudree, mathematician and provost of the University of Memphis; Sen. Jay Paul Gunn; author Billie Letts (formerly a professor at SOSU); Pulitzer Prize– and Tony Award–winning playwright and actor Tracy Letts; first chief justice of the Oklahoma Supreme Court and third governor of Oklahoma Robert L. Williams; and television host Jack Wyatt.

Durant currently leads the state in economic development, with tourism being one of the city's strongest industries. The largest employer in Durant (with over 5,400 employees) is the Choctaw Nation of Oklahoma. The *Durant Daily Democrat*, a vital resource for connecting with people during this book project, published its first issue on June 1, 1910, and still exemplifies its mission of serving the community of Durant.

One

Indian Territory

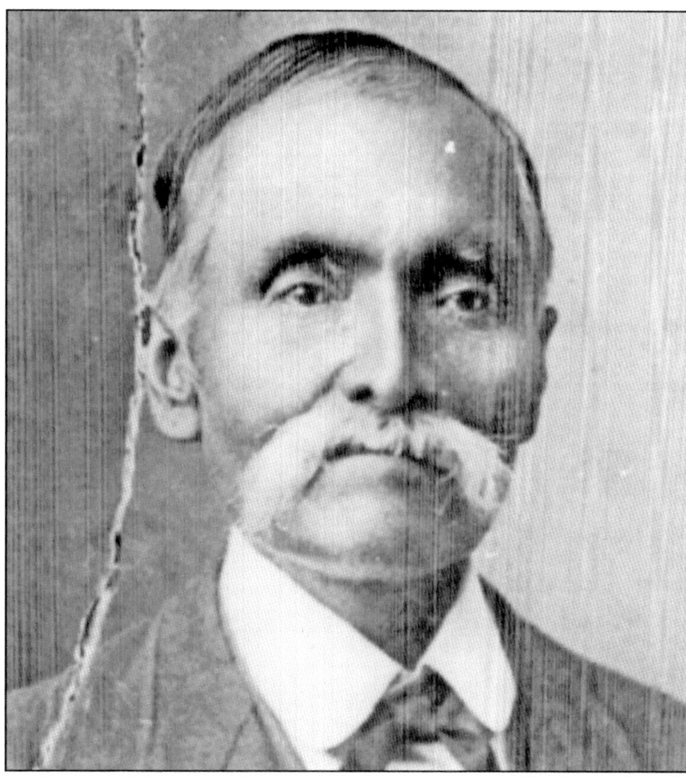

Dixon Durant. Dixon was the founder of the city of Durant. He was one of three sons of Fisher Durant and is generally considered to be the origin for the city's name. He was a father, farmer, businessman, and minister before his death in 1906. His paternal grandfather, Pierre Durant, had come to the area on the Trail of Tears route traveled by the Five Civilized Tribes from the southeastern United States. In 1832 or 1833, Dixon's father built the first log-house structure in what is now Durant, located between North Eighth and Ninth Avenues in what became Northside City Park. (Courtesy of David L. Crouch and the *Durant Daily Democrat*.)

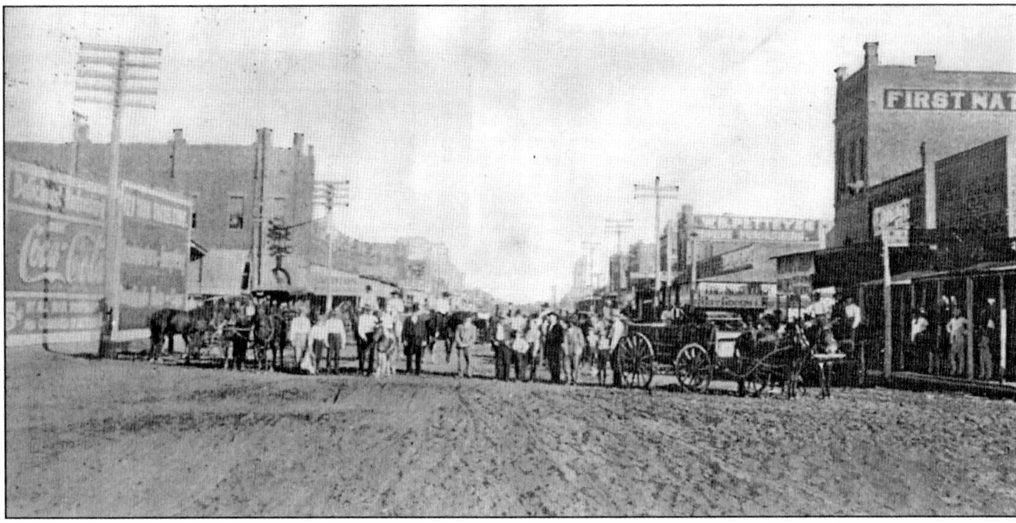

MAIN STREET, INDIAN TERRITORY. This is an early photograph of Main Street in Durant, Indian Territory, before statehood. (Courtesy of Don Parker.)

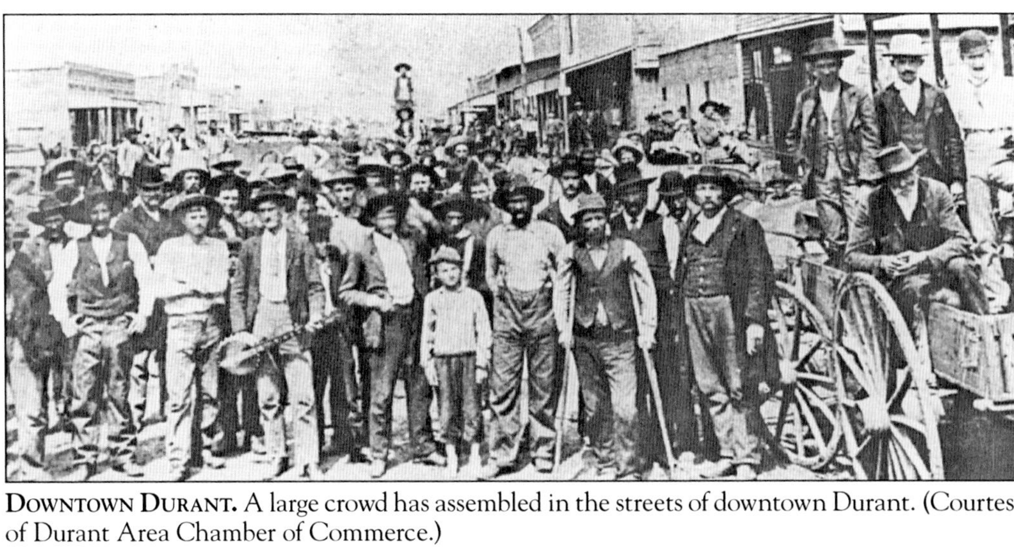

DOWNTOWN DURANT. A large crowd has assembled in the streets of downtown Durant. (Courtesy of Durant Area Chamber of Commerce.)

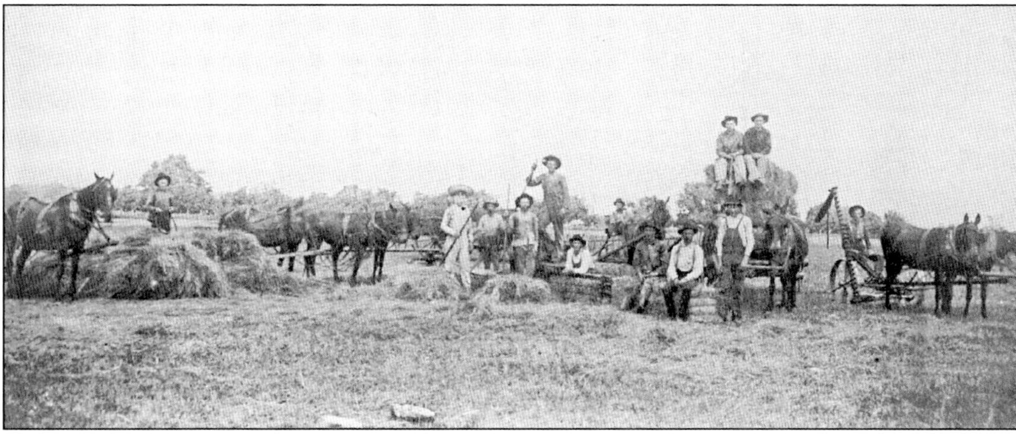

FARM HAYING CREW. This is a haying crew on a farm near Durant. (Courtesy of Marion Downs.)

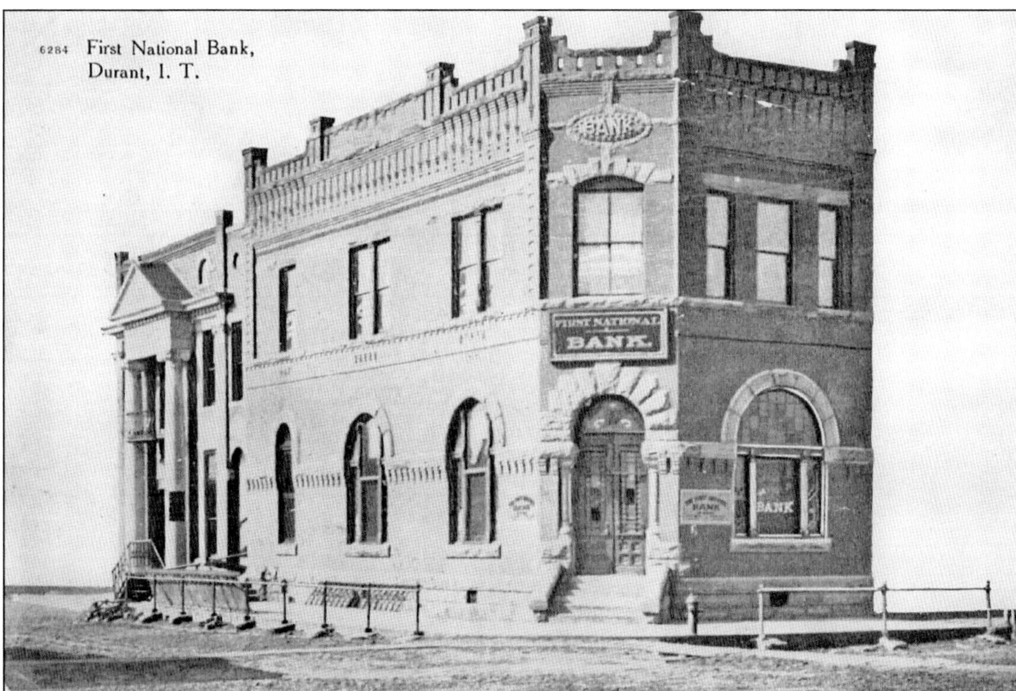

LANDMARK BUILDING. Constructed between 1897 and 1898, this redbrick building at the southeast corner of Third Avenue and Main Street at one time (until 1918) housed the First National Bank; it was later occupied by the First State Bank, Indian Territory Building & Loan, Lee Insurance, and Swearengin Insurance Company. The pillars now stand at the entrance to Southeastern Oklahoma State University. (Courtesy of Don Parker.)

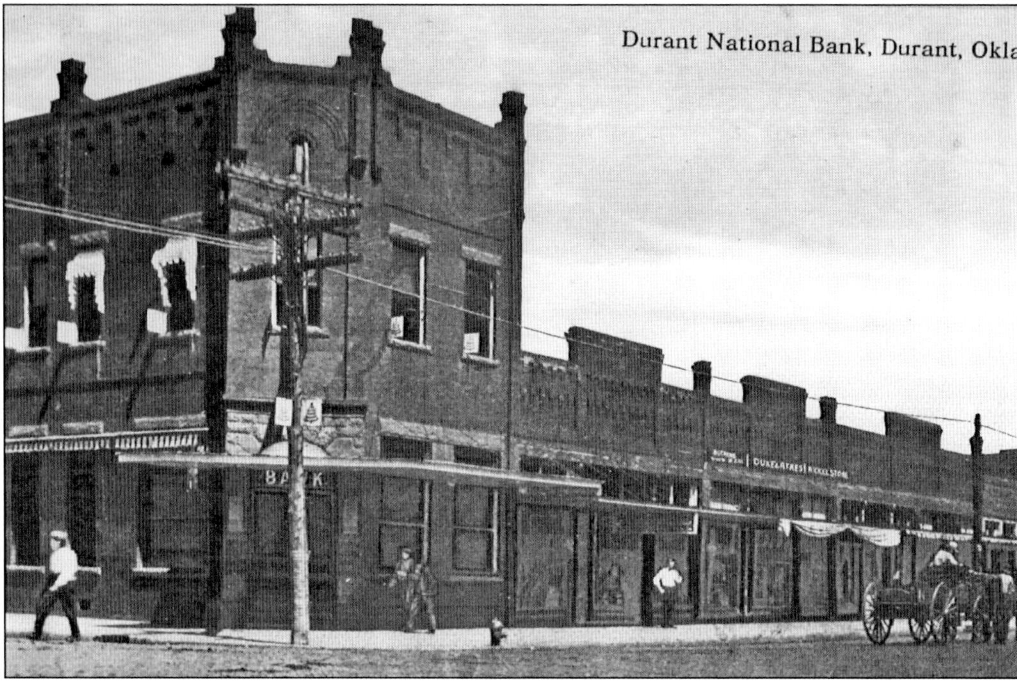

Durant National Bank. Pictured is the Durant National Bank. (Courtesy of Don Parker.)

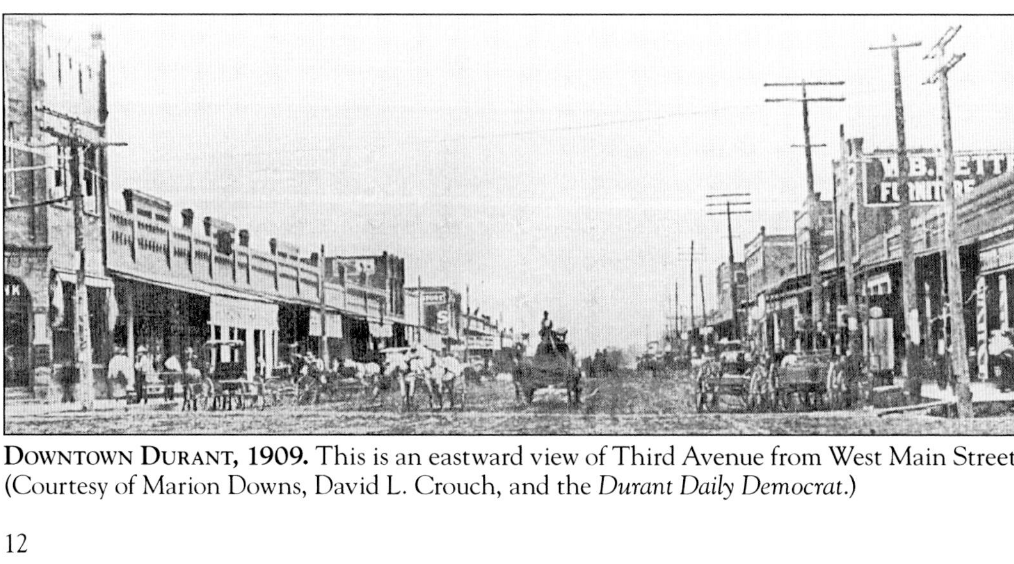

Downtown Durant, 1909. This is an eastward view of Third Avenue from West Main Street. (Courtesy of Marion Downs, David L. Crouch, and the *Durant Daily Democrat.*)

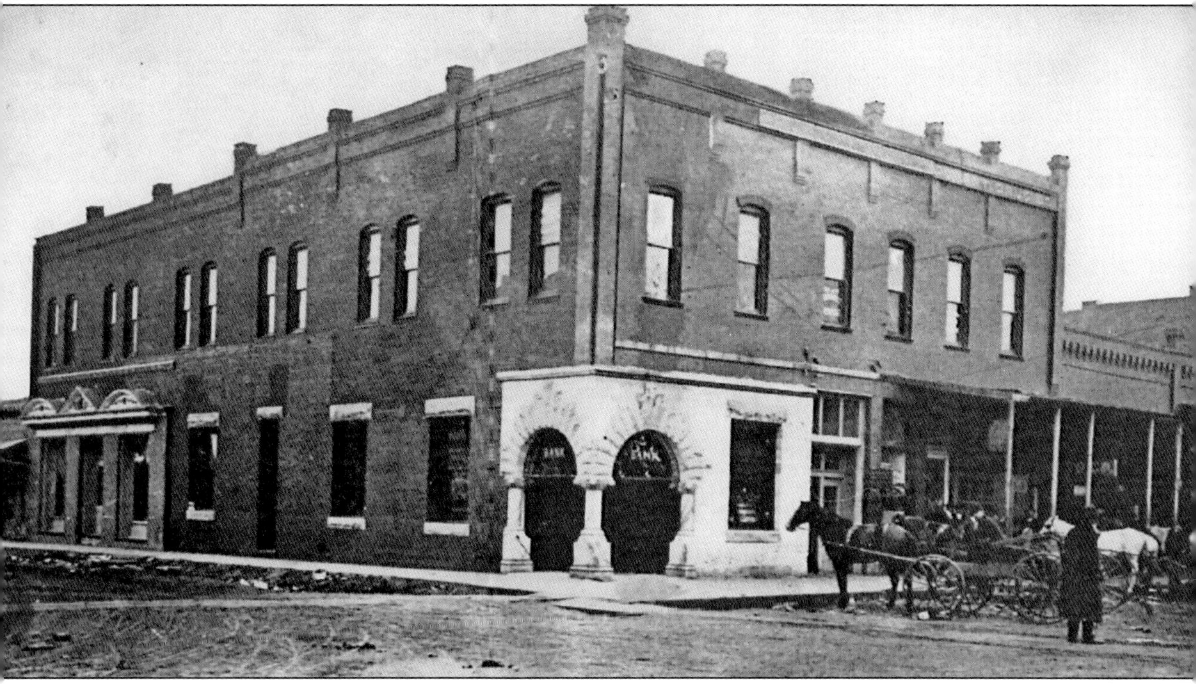

Farmers National Bank. In 1918, the First National Bank moved into its second home on the southwest corner of Second Avenue and Main Street. This two-story, double-entrance building was constructed around 1900 and later housed Curtis Jewelry & Personal Touch. (Courtesy Matt Swearengin.)

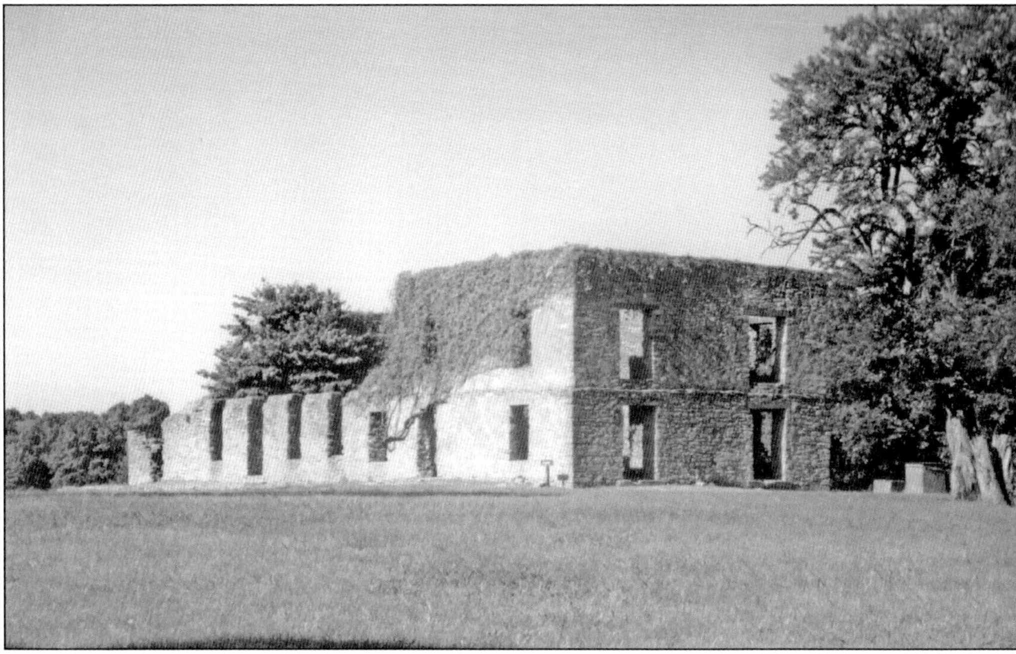

FORT WASHITA. This fort, established in 1842, is 17 miles northwest of Durant. Its purpose was to protect Chickasaw and Choctaw Indians from the Plains Indians. The Indian Removal Act put these tribes into a territorial conflict with each other. During the Civil War, the fort was occupied by Confederate forces. The image shows the West Barracks area, which was built in 1856 of native limestone. The structure also served as a home for the Colbert family, but it was destroyed by fire in 1917. (Author's collection.)

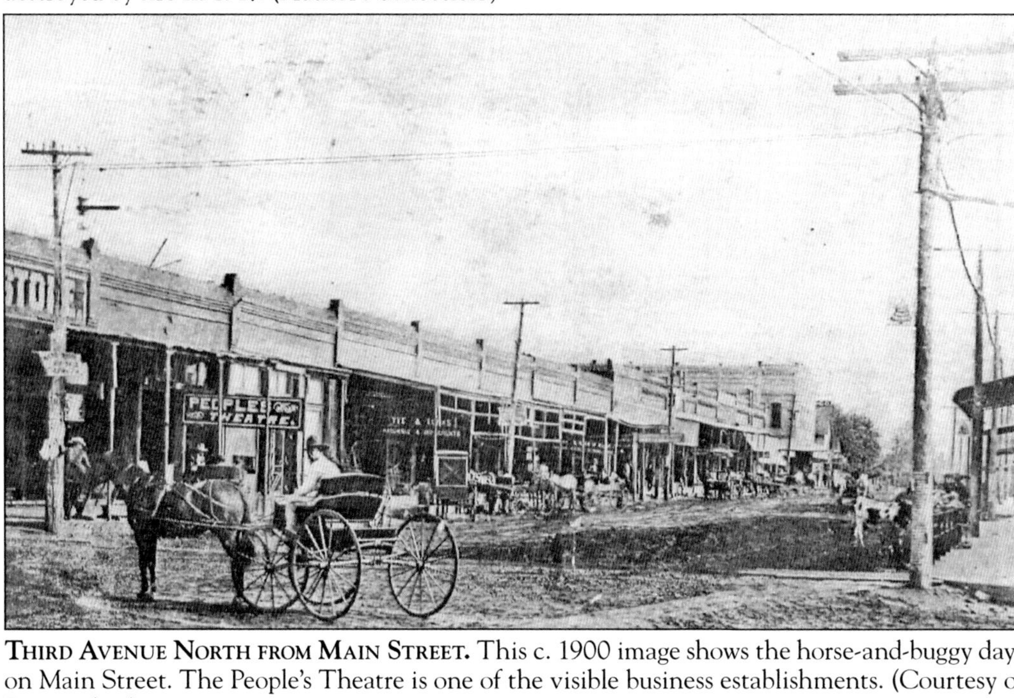

THIRD AVENUE NORTH FROM MAIN STREET. This c. 1900 image shows the horse-and-buggy days on Main Street. The People's Theatre is one of the visible business establishments. (Courtesy of Don Parker.)

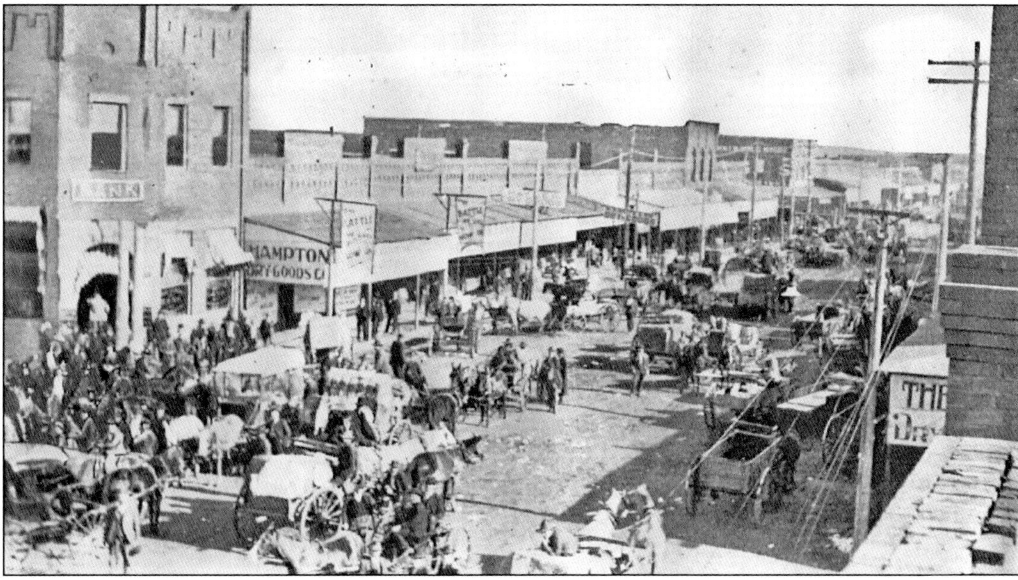

Durant, Indian Territory, before 1907. A bank and Hampton Dry Goods are visible on the left side of the street. (Courtesy of Don Parker.)

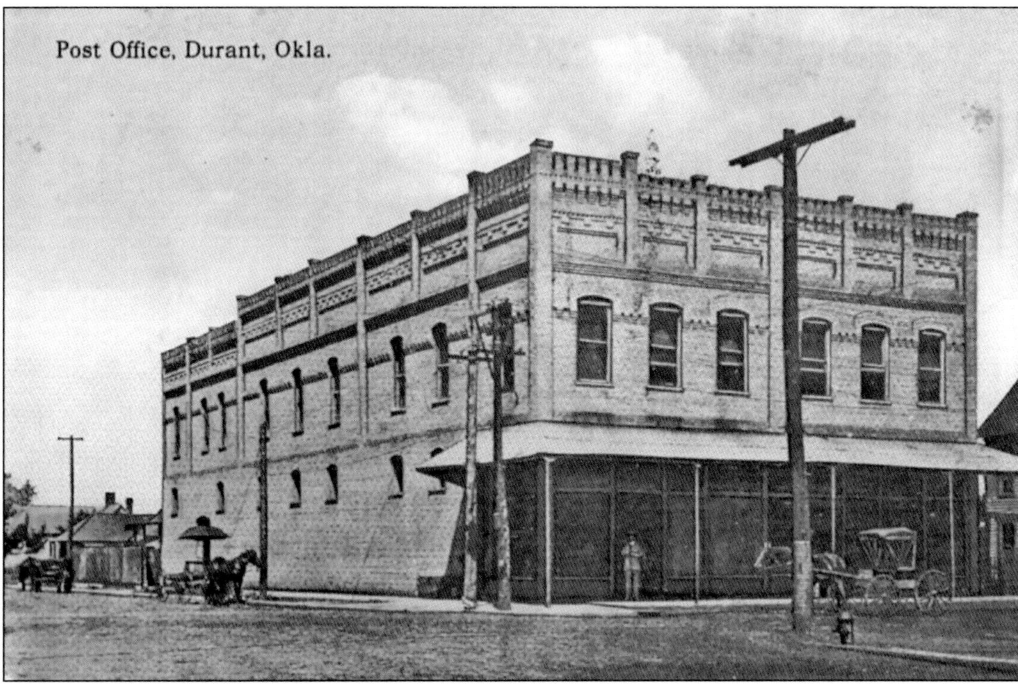

US Post Office. Beginning in 1858, the Butterfield Overland Mail Company operated a stage line, carrying mail on a "southern route" from St. Louis, Missouri, to California. Post offices in the area were listed as being in Arkansas until 1875, when the designation was changed to Indian Territory. An order established the first post office in Durant in 1879, and records show that a permanent post office was established in 1882. It was housed in various buildings until 1905. A contract was let in 1917 to build a new post office. The addition of a second story was delayed by the war in France but was finally completed in 1919. (Courtesy of Don Parker.)

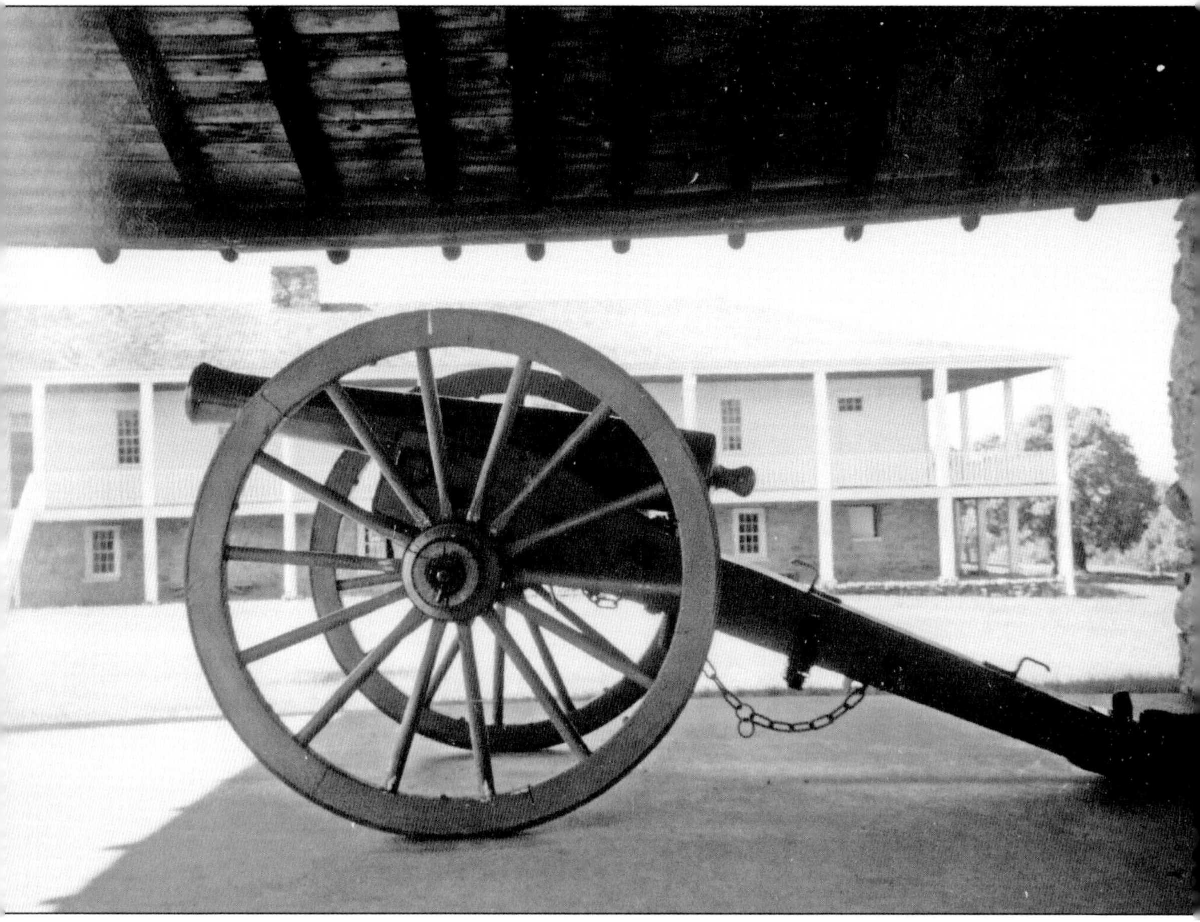

Fort Washita Cannon Pavilion. The fort served as a quarters for the US Indian Agency and was abandoned by US forces on April 16, 1861. The next day, Confederate forces occupied it for use during the Civil War. In 1853, only one battery of light artillery was assigned to the post. Pictured here on the cannon pavilion is a Napoleon 12-pound howitzer, which, widely used in the Civil War, had a maximum range of 1,680 yards. (Author's collection.)

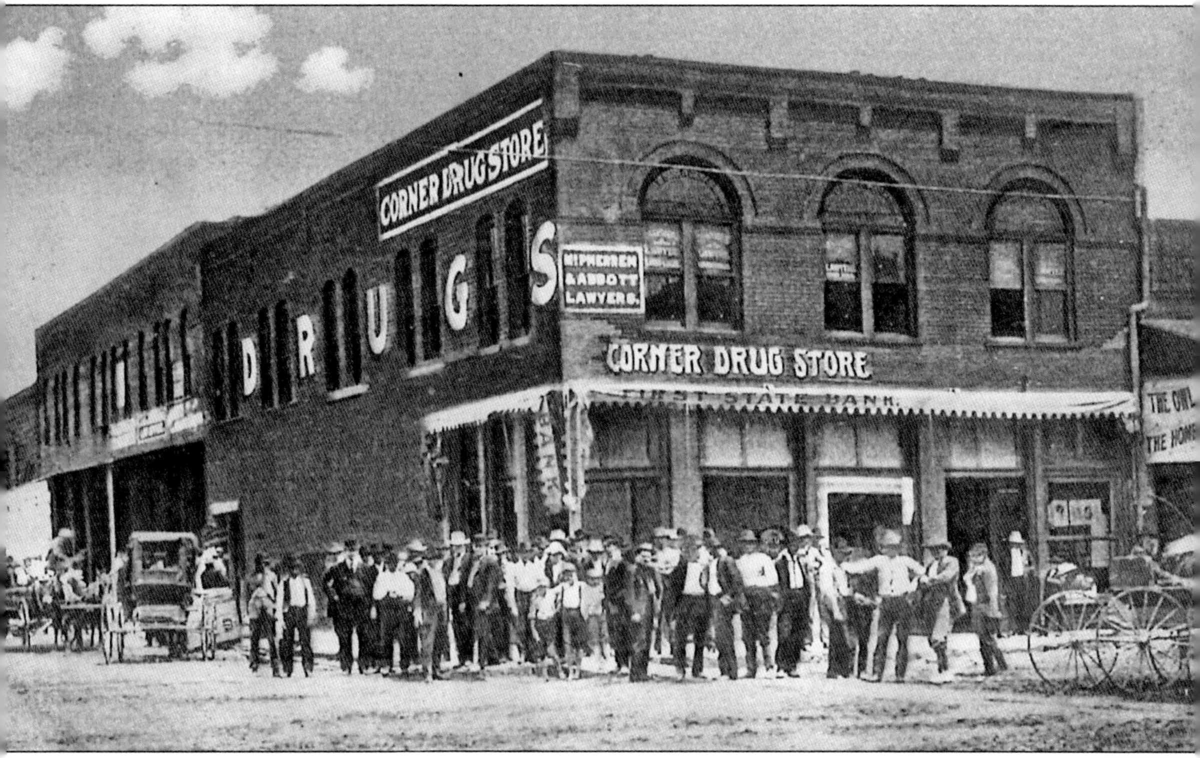

Corner Drug Store. A large number of people have gathered at the Corner Drug Store. (Courtesy of Don Parker.)

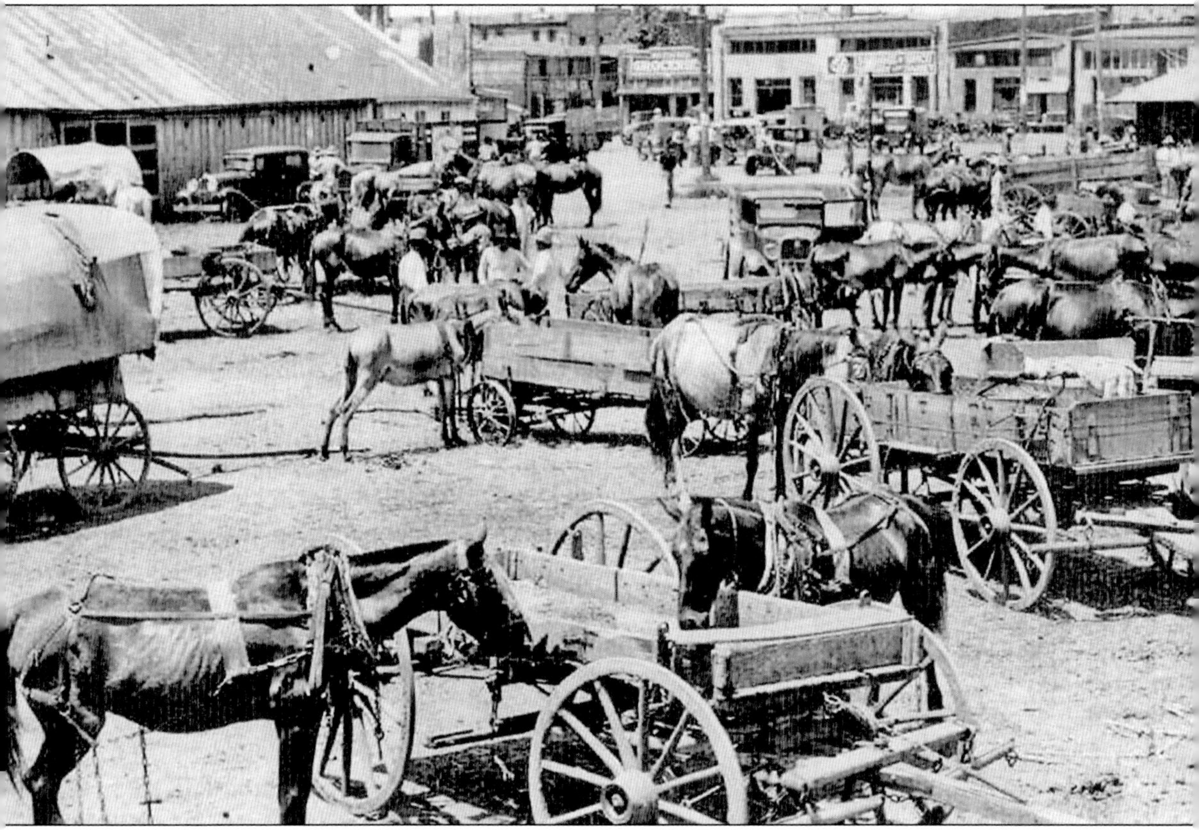

DOWNTOWN DURANT, 1932. This photograph captures a busy day in Durant, possibly where Market Square is today, with many horses, mules, and wagons; there are very few cars. (Courtesy of David L. Crouch and the *Durant Daily Democrat*.)

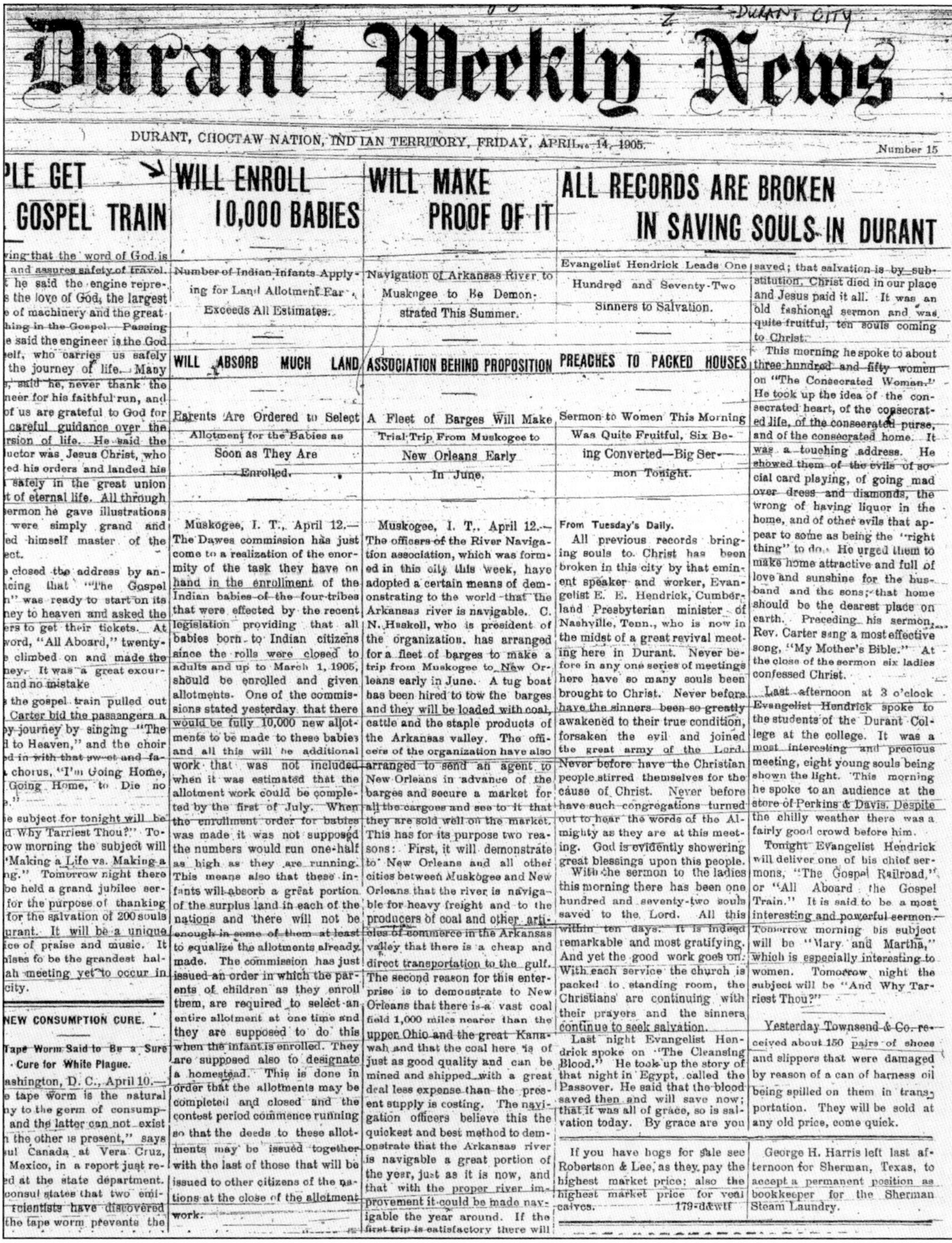

Durant Weekly News

DURANT, CHOCTAW NATION, INDIAN TERRITORY, FRIDAY, APRIL 14, 1905. Number 15

[PEO]PLE GET GOSPEL TRAIN

[...]ing that the word of God is [...] and assures safety of travel. [...] he said the engine repre[sent]s the love of God, the largest [...] of machinery and the great [...]hing in the Gospel. Passing [...]e said the engineer is the God [him]self, who carries us safely [through] the journey of life. Many [...], said he, never thank the [engi]neer for his faithful run, and [few] of us are grateful to God for [His] careful guidance over the [...]rsion of life. He said the [cond]uctor was Jesus Christ, who [obey]ed his orders and landed his [...] safely in the great union [depo]t of eternal life. All through [the s]ermon he gave illustrations [that] were simply grand and [show]ed himself master of the [subj]ect.

[H]e closed the address by an[noun]cing that "The Gospel [Trai]n" was ready to start on its [jour]ney to heaven and asked the [...]ers to get their tickets. At [the] word, "All Aboard," twenty-[...] climbed on and made the [jour]ney. It was a great excur[sion] and no mistake.

[...] the gospel train pulled out [Rev.] Carter bid the passengers a [...]y journey by singing "The [Roa]d to Heaven," and the choir [...]d in with that sweet and fa[miliar] chorus, "I'm Going Home, [I'm] Going Home, to Die no [More]."

[Th]e subject for tonight will be "[An]d Why Tarriest Thou?" To[m]orrow morning the subject will [be] "Making a Life vs. Making a [Livi]ng." Tomorrow night there [will] be held a grand jubilee ser[vice] for the purpose of thanking [God] for the salvation of 200 souls [in D]urant. It will be a unique [serv]ice of praise and music. It [prom]ises fo be the grandest hal[lelu]jah meeting yet to occur in [the] city.

NEW CONSUMPTION CURE.

Tape Worm Said to Be a Sure Cure for White Plague.

[W]ashington, D. C., April 10.—[Th]e tape worm is the natural [ener]ny to the germ of consump[tion] and the latter can not exist [whe]n the other is present," says [Cons]ul Canada at Vera Cruz, Mexico, in a report just re[ceiv]ed at the state department. [The c]onsul states that two emi[nent s]cientists have discovered [that] the tape worm prevents the

WILL ENROLL 10,000 BABIES

Number of Indian Infants Applying for Land Allotment Far Exceeds All Estimates.

WILL ABSORB MUCH LAND

Parents Are Ordered to Select Allotment for the Babies as Soon as They Are Enrolled.

Muskogee, I. T., April 12.—The Dawes commission has just come to a realization of the enormity of the task they have on hand in the enrollment of the Indian babies of the four tribes that were effected by the recent legislation providing that all babies born to Indian citizens since the rolls were closed to adults and up to March 1, 1905, should be enrolled and given allotments. One of the commissions stated yesterday that there would be fully 10,000 new allotments to be made to these babies and all this will be additional work that was not included when it was estimated that the allotment work could be completed by the first of July. When the enrollment order for babies was made it was not supposed the numbers would run one-half as high as they are running. This means also that these infants will absorb a great portion of the surplus land in each of the nations and there will not be enough in some of them at least to equalize the allotments already made. The commission has just issued an order in which the parents of children as they enroll them, are required to select an entire allotment at one time and they are supposed to do this when the infant is enrolled. They are supposed also to designate a homestead. This is done in order that the allotments may be completed and closed and the contest period commence running so that the deeds to these allotments may be issued together with the last of those that will be issued to other citizens of the nations at the close of the allotment work.

WILL MAKE PROOF OF IT

Navigation of Arkansas River to Muskogee to Be Demonstrated This Summer.

ASSOCIATION BEHIND PROPOSITION

A Fleet of Barges Will Make Trial Trip From Muskogee to New Orleans Early In June.

Muskogee, I. T., April 12.—The officers of the River Navigation association, which was formed in this city this week, have adopted a certain means of demonstrating to the world that the Arkansas river is navigable. C. N. Haskell, who is president of the organization, has arranged for a fleet of barges to make a trip from Muskogee to New Orleans early in June. A tug boat has been hired to tow the barges and they will be loaded with coal, cattle and the staple products of the Arkansas valley. The officers of the organization have also arranged to send an agent to New Orleans in advance of the barges and secure a market for all the cargoes and see to it that they are sold well on the market. This has for its purpose two reasons: First, it will demonstrate to New Orleans and all other cities between Muskogee and New Orleans that the river is navigable for heavy freight and to the producers of coal and other articles of commerce in the Arkansas valley that there is a cheap and direct transportation to the gulf. The second reason for this enterprise is to demonstrate to New Orleans that there is a vast coal field 1,000 miles nearer than the upper Ohio and the great Kanawah and that the coal here is of just as good quality and can be mined and shipped with a great deal less expense than the present supply is costing. The navigation officers believe this the quickest and best method to demonstrate that the Arkansas river is navigable a great portion of the year, just as it is now, and that with the proper river improvement it could be made navigable the year around. If the first trip is satisfactory there will

ALL RECORDS ARE BROKEN IN SAVING SOULS IN DURANT

Evangelist Hendrick Leads One Hundred and Seventy-Two Sinners to Salvation.

PREACHES TO PACKED HOUSES

Sermon to Women This Morning Was Quite Fruitful, Six Being Converted—Big Sermon Tonight.

From Tuesday's Daily.

All previous records bringing souls to Christ has been broken in this city by that eminent speaker and worker, Evangelist E. E. Hendrick, Cumberland Presbyterian minister of Nashville, Tenn., who is now in the midst of a great revival meeting here in Durant. Never before in any one series of meetings here have so many souls been brought to Christ. Never before have the sinners been so greatly awakened to their true condition, forsaken the evil and joined the great army of the Lord. Never before have the Christian people stirred themselves for the cause of Christ. Never before have such congregations turned out to hear the words of the Almighty as they are at this meeting. God is evidently showering great blessings upon this people.

With the sermon to the ladies this morning there has been one hundred and seventy-two souls saved to the Lord. All this within ten days. It is indeed remarkable and most gratifying. And yet the good work goes on. With each service the church is packed to standing room, the Christians are continuing with their prayers and the sinners continue to seek salvation.

Last night Evangelist Hendrick spoke on "The Cleansing Blood." He took up the story of that night in Egypt, called the Passover. He said that the blood saved then and will save now; that it was all of grace, so is salvation today. By grace are you saved; that salvation is by substitution, Christ died in our place and Jesus paid it all. It was an old fashioned sermon and was quite fruitful, ten souls coming to Christ.

This morning he spoke to about three hundred and fifty women on "The Consecrated Woman." He took up the idea of the consecrated heart, of the consecrated life, of the consecrated purse, and of the consecrated home. It was a touching address. He showed them of the evils of social card playing, of going mad over dress and diamonds, the wrong of having liquor in the home, and of other evils that appear to some as being the "right thing" to do. He urged them to make home attractive and full of love and sunshine for the husband and the sons; that home should be the dearest place on earth. Preceding his sermon, Rev. Carter sang a most effective song, "My Mother's Bible." At the close of the sermon six ladies confessed Christ.

Last afternoon at 3 o'clock Evangelist Hendrick spoke to the students of the Durant College at the college. It was a most interesting and precious meeting, eight young souls being shown the light. This morning he spoke to an audience at the store of Perkins & Davis. Despite the chilly weather there was a fairly good crowd before him.

Tonight Evangelist Hendrick will deliver one of his chief sermons, "The Gospel Railroad," or "All Aboard the Gospel Train." It is said to be a most interesting and powerful sermon. Tomorrow morning his subject will be "Mary and Martha," which is especially interesting to women. Tomorrow night the subject will be "And Why Tarriest Thou?"

Yesterday Townsend & Co. received about 150 pairs of shoes and slippers that were damaged by reason of a can of harness oil being spilled on them in transportation. They will be sold at any old price, come quick.

If you have hogs for sale see Robertson & Lee, as they pay the highest market price; also the highest market price for veal calves. 179-d&wtf

George H. Harris left last afternoon for Sherman, Texas, to accept a permanent position as bookkeeper for the Sherman Steam Laundry.

DURANT WEEKLY NEWS, FRIDAY, APRIL 14, 1905. This is a copy from the archives of the Chickasaw, Cherokee, and Creek tribes. (Courtesy of Bryan County Archives.)

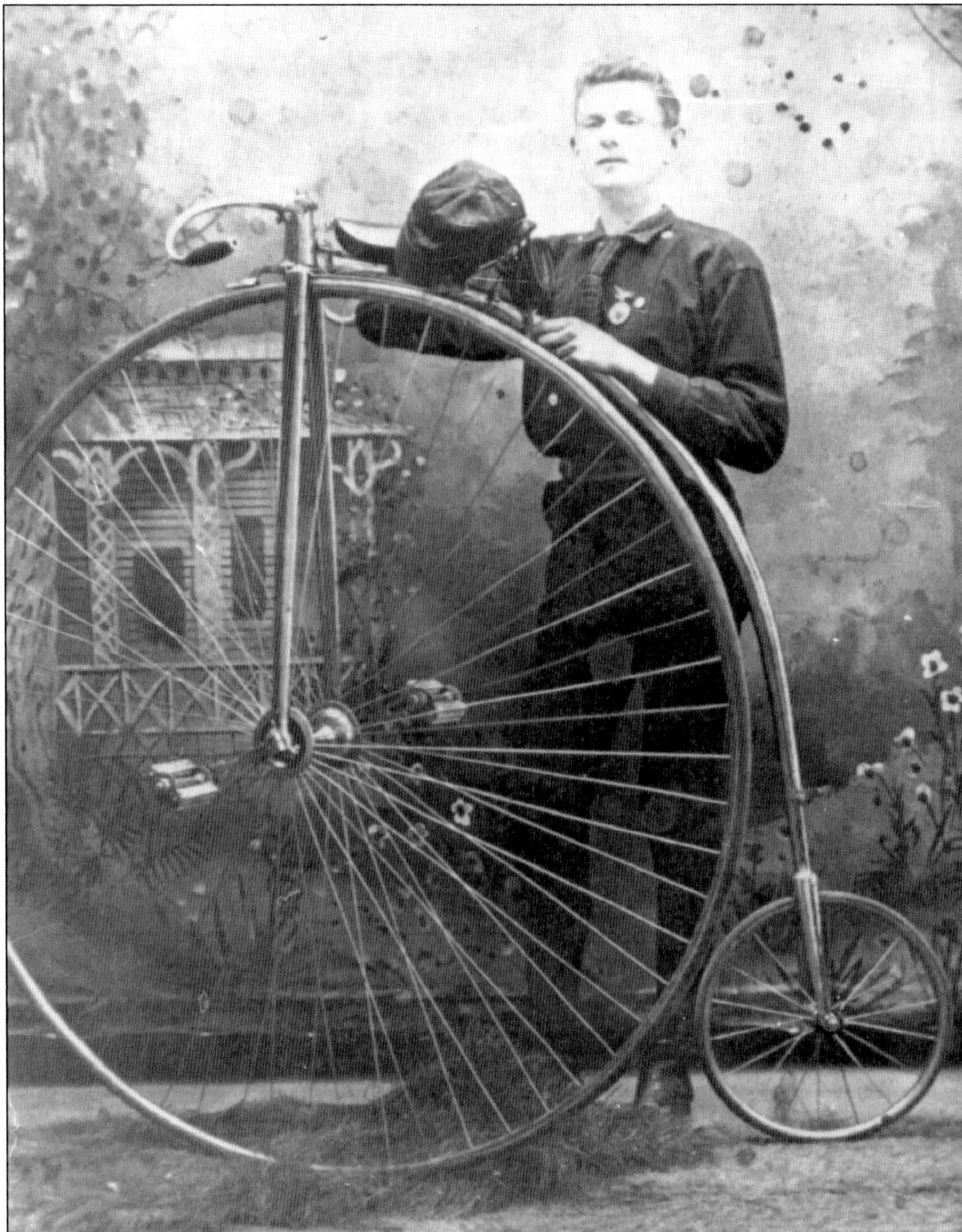

Horace Marshall. Marshall displays the first bicycle in Durant. The exact date is uncertain; the year 1890 is written on the photograph, but another source dates it to 1895. Marshall was a city alderman in 1917, 1919, and 1925. (Courtesy of First Texoma National Bank.)

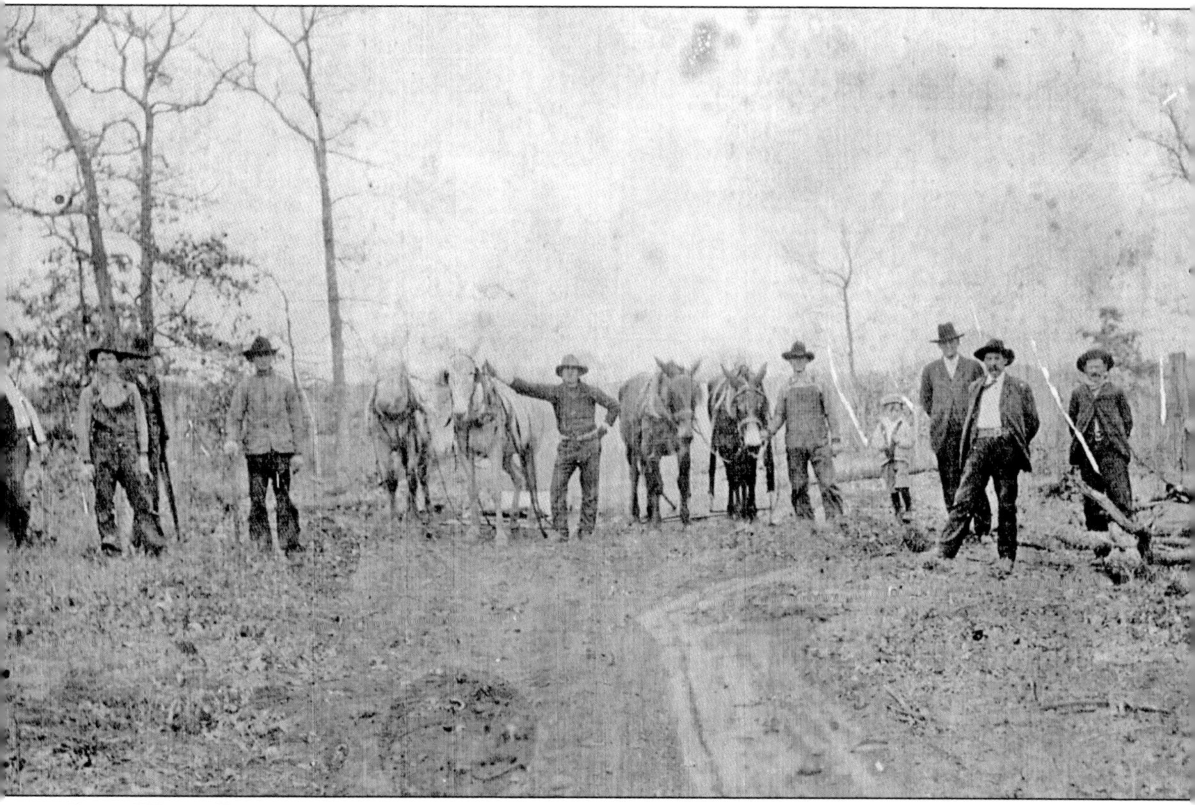

JOHN WILLIS PARKER WITH PRISONERS. John Parker (second from the right) was a guard who is seen watching over prisoners doing roadwork north of Kingston. This undated photograph was taken before Oklahoma statehood. Parker lived in Kingston and owned Parker-Faulk General Merchandise store in Cliff, Indian Territory. He and his wife, Lela Parker, were grandparents of Don Parker, who owns and operates Rick's Boots in Durant. (Courtesy of Don Parker.)

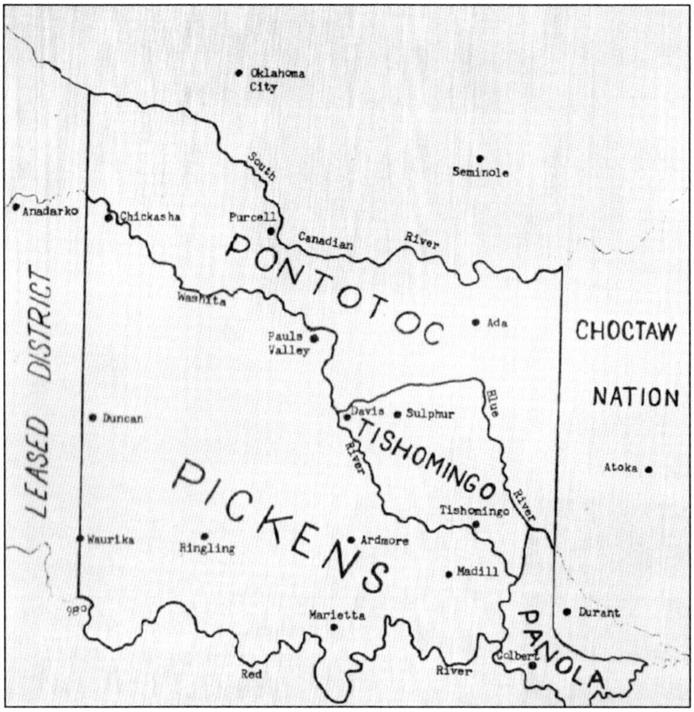

1867 Map of Chickasaw and Choctaw Nation. The Durant area was originally Indian Territory, and as the Five Civilized Tribes were removed from the southeastern United States, their new homeland included Choctaw land at Durant and Chickasaw land to the west. The other Five Civilized Tribes included Cherokee, Creek (Muscogee), and Seminole. Oklahoma became the 46th state on November 16, 1907, formed from Oklahoma Territory and Indian Territory. (Author's collection.)

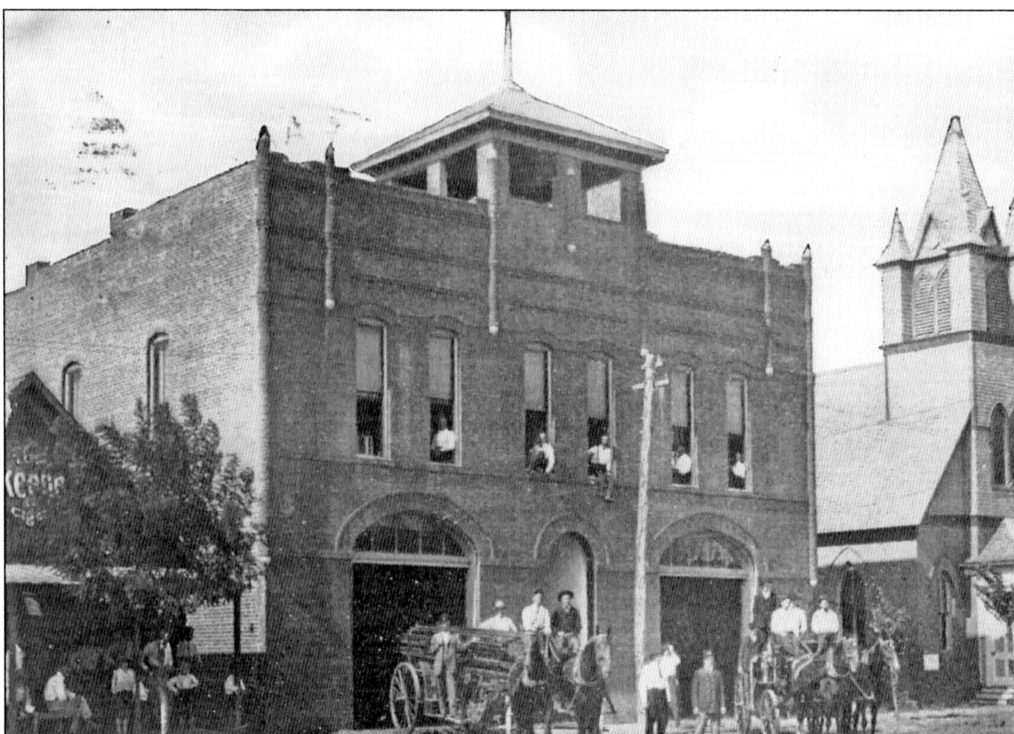

Durant Fire Headquarters. This image of the Durant Fire Department predates the use of motorized vehicles. (Courtesy of Don Parker.)

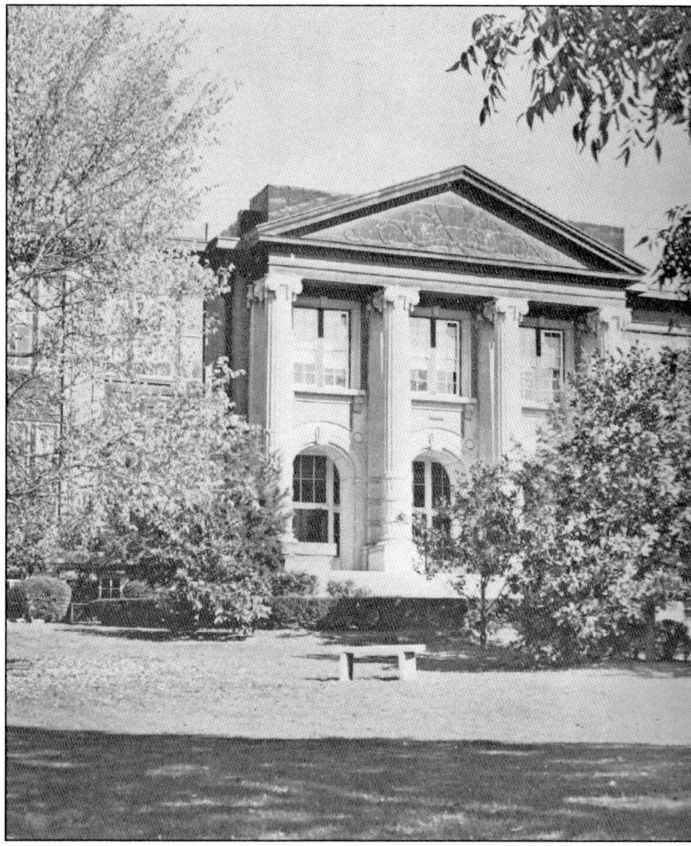

Southeastern State College. This c. 1955 photograph shows the administration building on the campus of Southeastern State College. (Courtesy of Southeastern Oklahoma State University.)

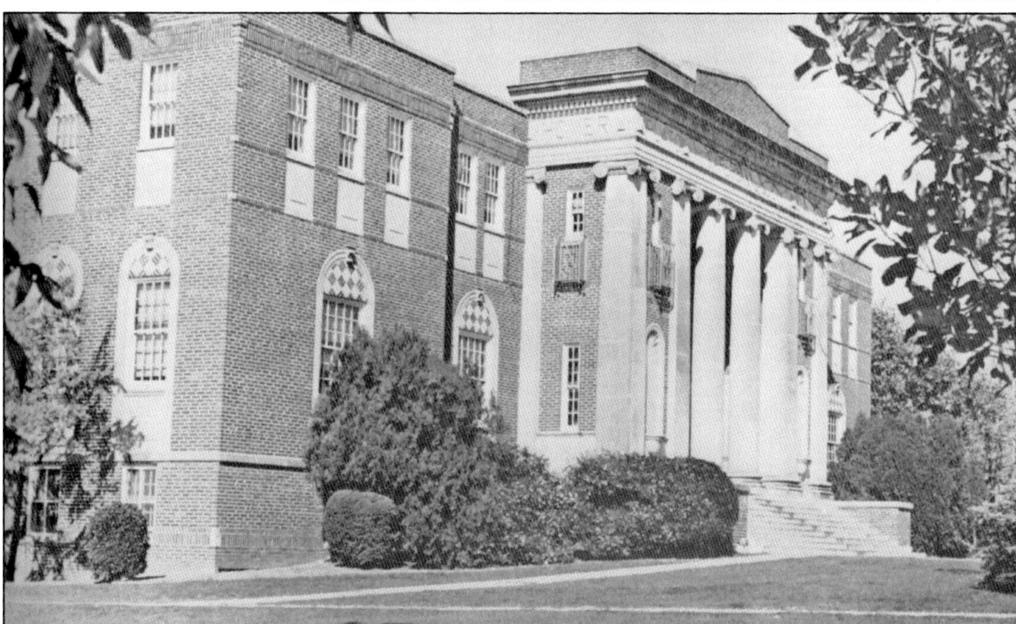

Library at Southeastern State College. Also from 1955, this photograph shows the library at Southeastern State College. (Courtesy of Southeastern Oklahoma State University.)

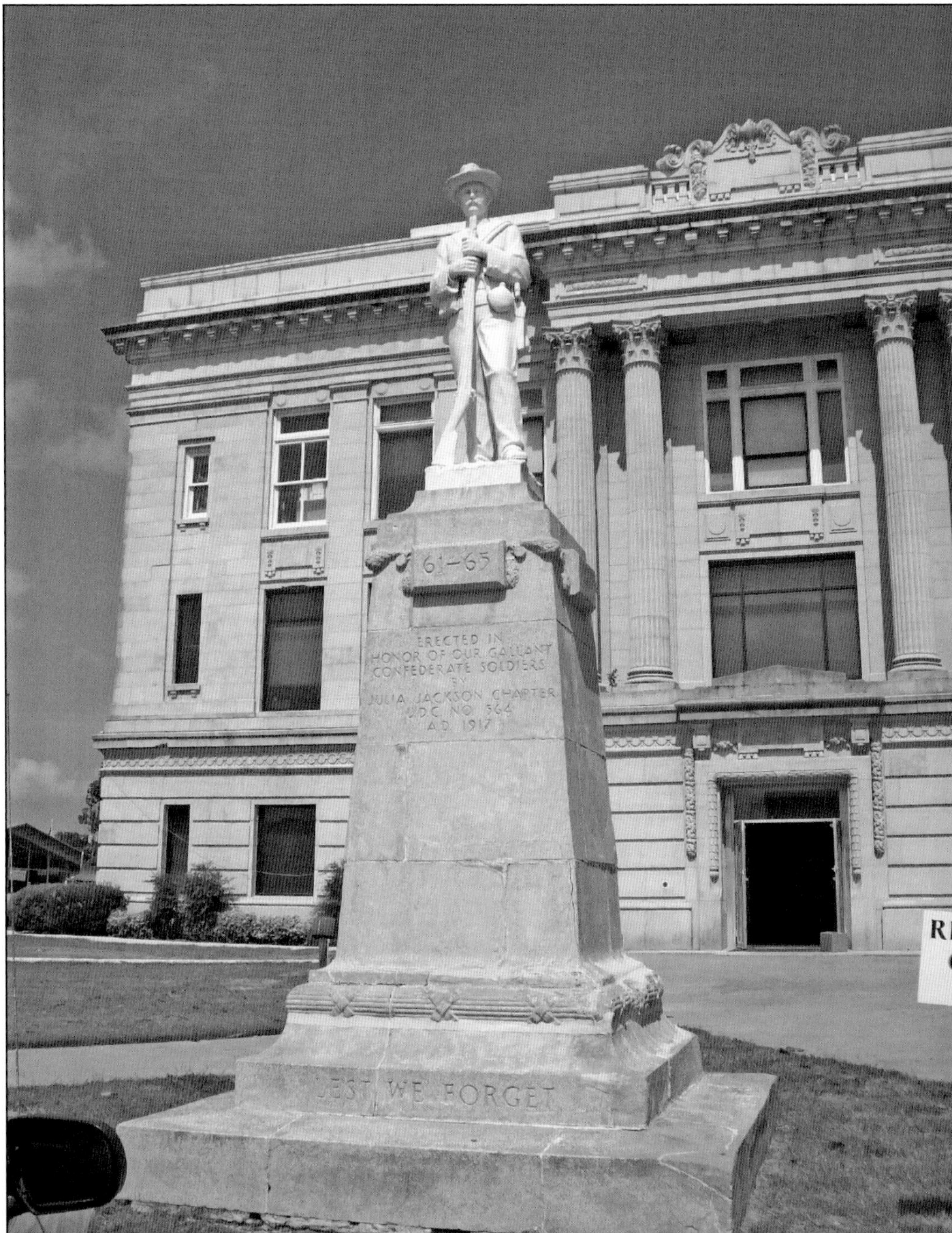

Bryan County Courthouse. This statue, erected in 1917 by the Julia Jackson Chapter of the United Daughters of the Confederacy No. 564 memorializes Confederate soldiers. Gov. Robert Lee Williams was on hand to on July 4, 1917, for the laying of the cornerstone, and the completed project was unveiled by Stonewall Jackson's daughter in 1918. (Author's collection.)

Lillie May Atwell Phillips. Lillie May was active in church, civic, and lodge work in Durant. She was recognized on her 90th birthday by the First Presbyterian Church for her services, especially as church historian. Lillie May was born in 1890 in Lowry City, Missouri, and attended Oklahoma Presbyterian College in Durant from 1912 to 1914. She married Sheriff John A. Phillips Sr. and was a schoolteacher for many years. (Courtesy of Bryan County Archives.)

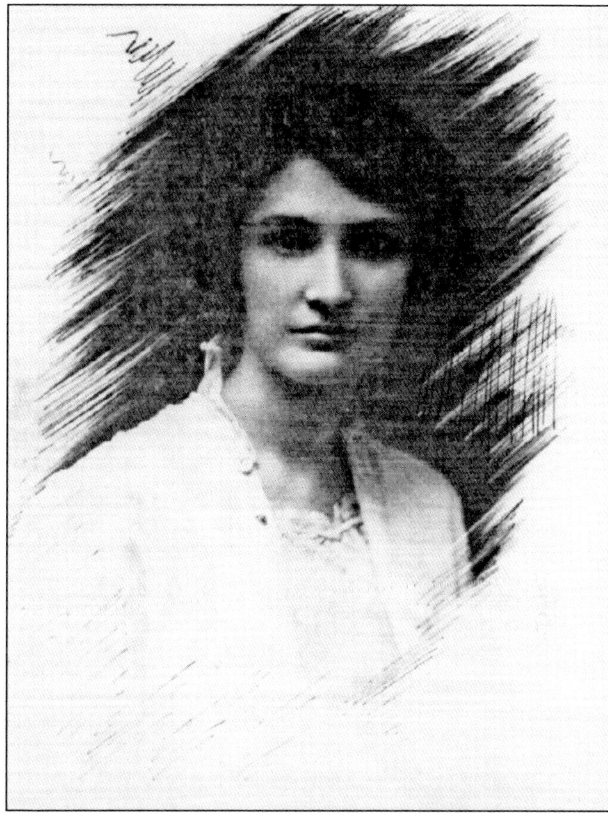

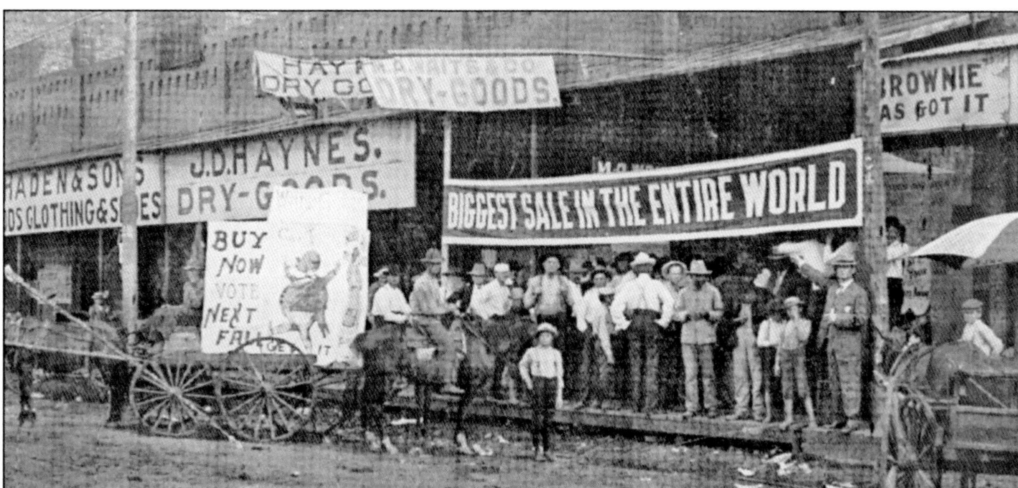

"Biggest Sale in the Entire World," around 1900. Downtown business M.A. Waits & Co. Dry-Goods, located on the north side of Main Street between First and Second Avenues, advertises the "biggest sale in the entire world." Also visible in this image are the store's neighbors, J.D. Haynes Dry-Goods and Haden & Sons; a political advertisement is also in the street. The store was owned and operated by Mitton C. Waits, grandfather of Addylou Haggerty and great-grandfather of Tommy Jean Edwards, David Waits Thornton, and William Mack Thornton. (Courtesy of Marion Worth, David L. Crouch, and the *Durant Daily Democrat*.)

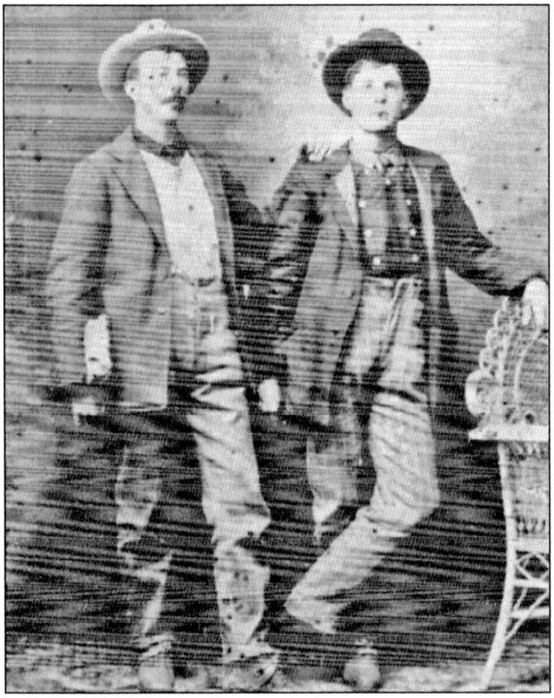

Ed M. Sliger. Ed M. Sliger (left), the father of Thurman Sliger of Durant, is pictured around 1900 with an unidentified friend. (Courtesy of Bryan County Archives.)

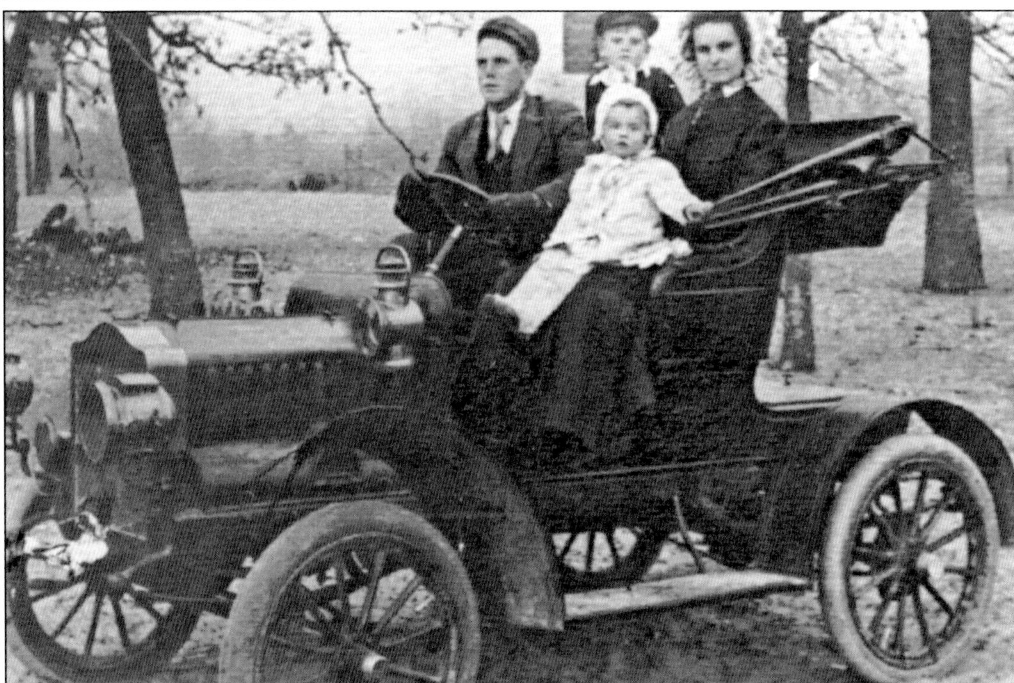

Walter M. Johnson, MD, and Family. Dr. Walter Johnson is pictured driving this automobile about 1908; his wife, Lola, is in the backseat with their son Paul, while daughter Ruth (later Ruth Potter) sits in the front with her father. Paul later owned the Johnson Motor Co. in Durant; he was also appointed by President Eisenhower as US marshal for the Eastern District of Oklahoma. (Courtesy of David L. Crouch and the *Durant Daily Democrat*.)

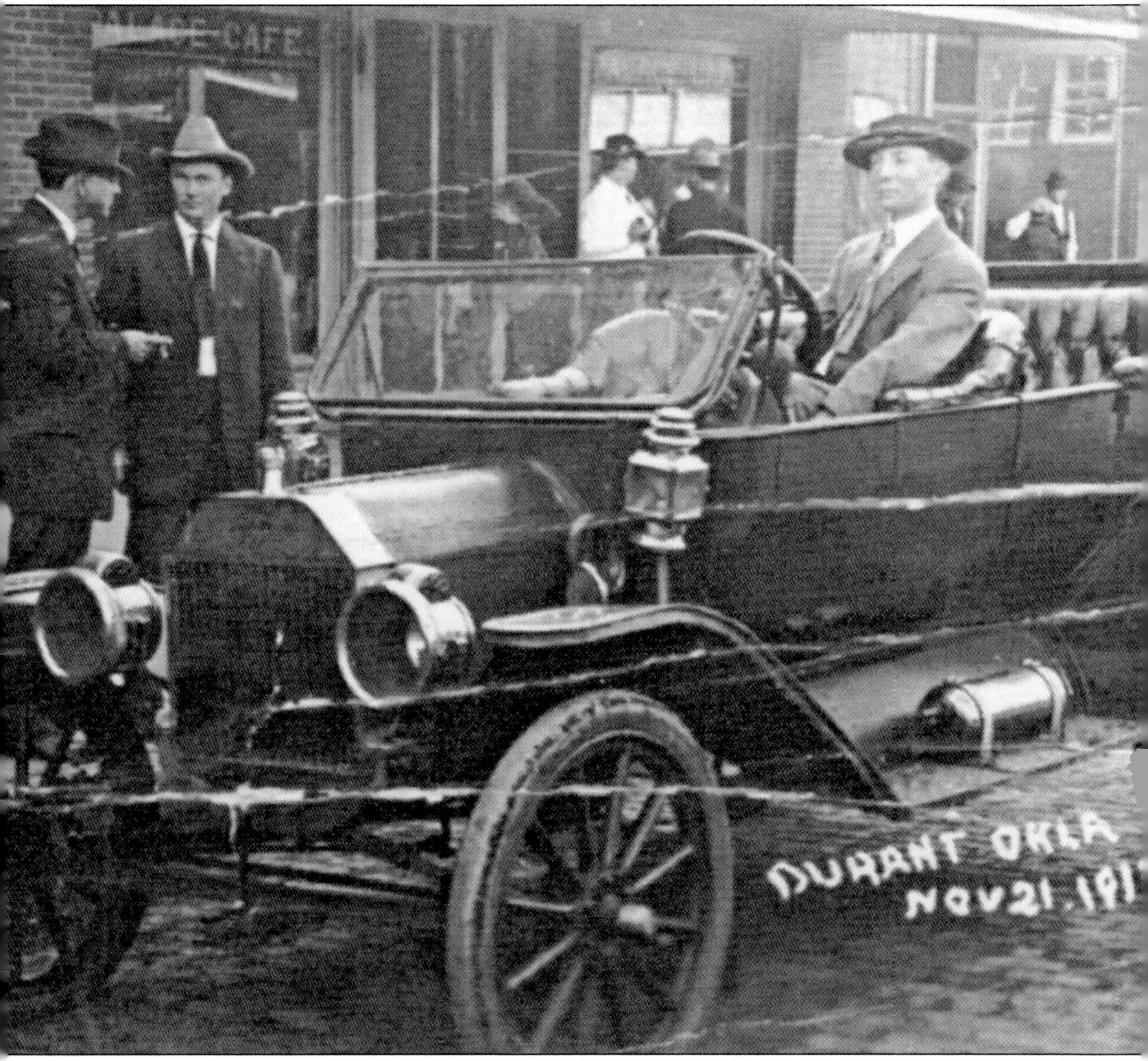

EARLY AUTOMOBILE IN DOWNTOWN DURANT. This photograph was taken on November 21, 1913, on the 100 block of West Main Street in front of the Palace Café (later occupied by Rick's Shoe Center). This early car, driven by Laute England, features carbide headlights. Ben Blanchard and Dave Wright are standing to the left. (Courtesy of David L. Crouch and the *Durant Daily Democrat*.)

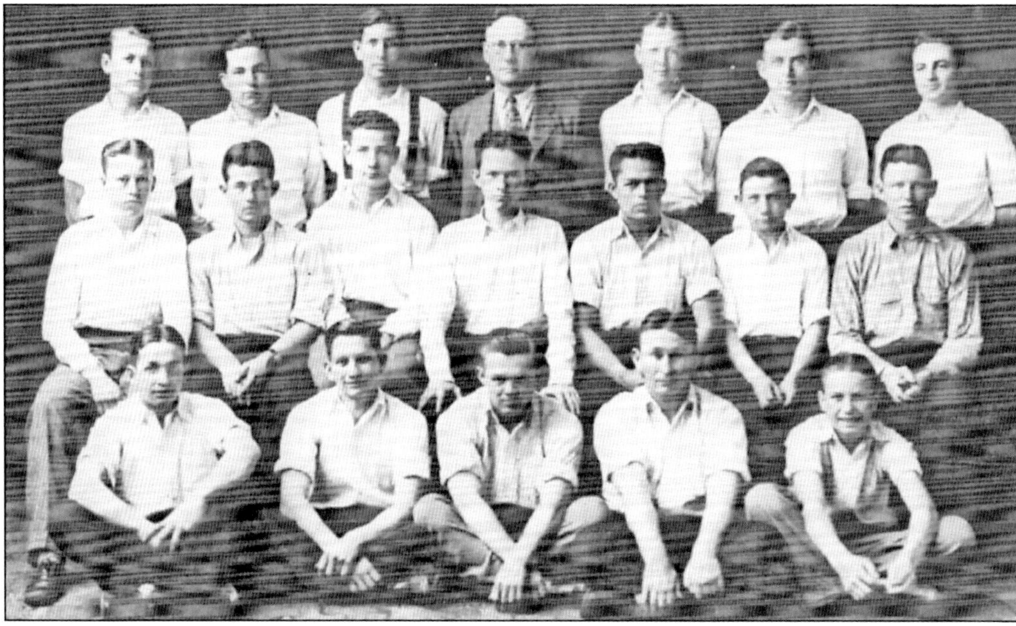

DURANT HIGH SCHOOL DEMOLAY ORGANIZATION. This photograph was taken during the 1926–1927 academic year. School principal H.S. Bates is seen in the center of the back row. Also pictured in no particular order are John Gibson, Cleo Dodson, Hezzie Simpson Bates, Jack Oliver, Lonnie Factor, Red Kennedy, Floyd Bryant, and Jack Crutchfield. (Courtesy of David L. Crouch and the *Durant Daily Democrat*.)

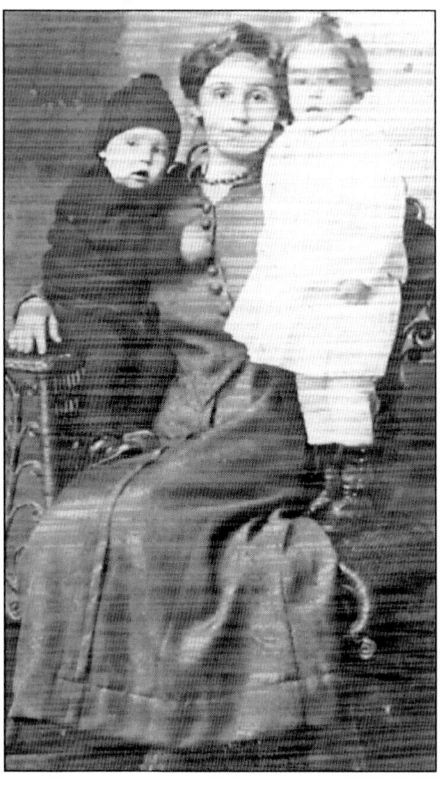

MAUDE HULL AND CHILDREN. Maude Hull is pictured here with children Lodie and Beatrice Hull. Another child of Maude's was Jerri McKinney of Durant. (Courtesy of David L. Crouch and the *Durant Daily Democrat*.)

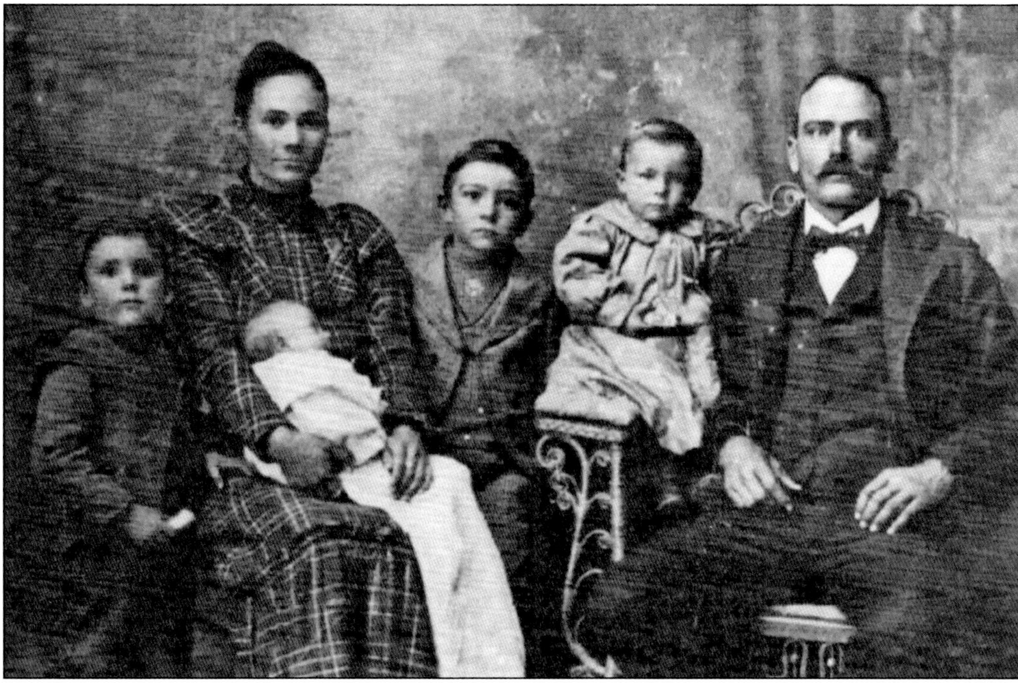

Hiram Alexander McMillin Family. In this c. 1900 photograph are, from left to right, Arthur Otto, Mary Isabella (mother), Bertha (in her mother's lap), Ira Wheeler, Hiram Alexander, and George William McMillin (father). Hiram was born in 1898 at Telephone, Texas, in Fannin County. In 1903, when he was five, his family moved to the Creek Nation, Indian Territory, in covered wagons and on horseback. They later camped at Blue and Caddo Creeks. (Courtesy of Bryan County Archives.)

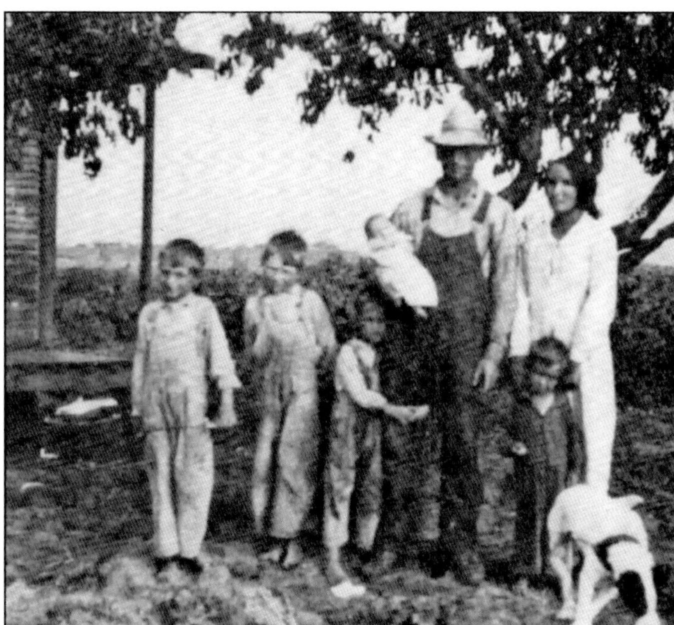

Frank A. Rodgers Family. Pictured in 1926 are, from left to right, John, Frank Jr., Leon, Byron (baby), Frank Sr., Leland, and Ora Rodgers. Frank A. Rodgers had a farm south of Durant, and other family members also lived there. Frank and wife Ora McDonald Rodgers moved to Bryan County by wagon in 1921. Frank trained himself to be an electrician, mechanic, and refrigerator-repair engineer. His son Leon was also engaged in business with him until Frank's death in 1953 at age 55. (Courtesy of Bryan County Archives.)

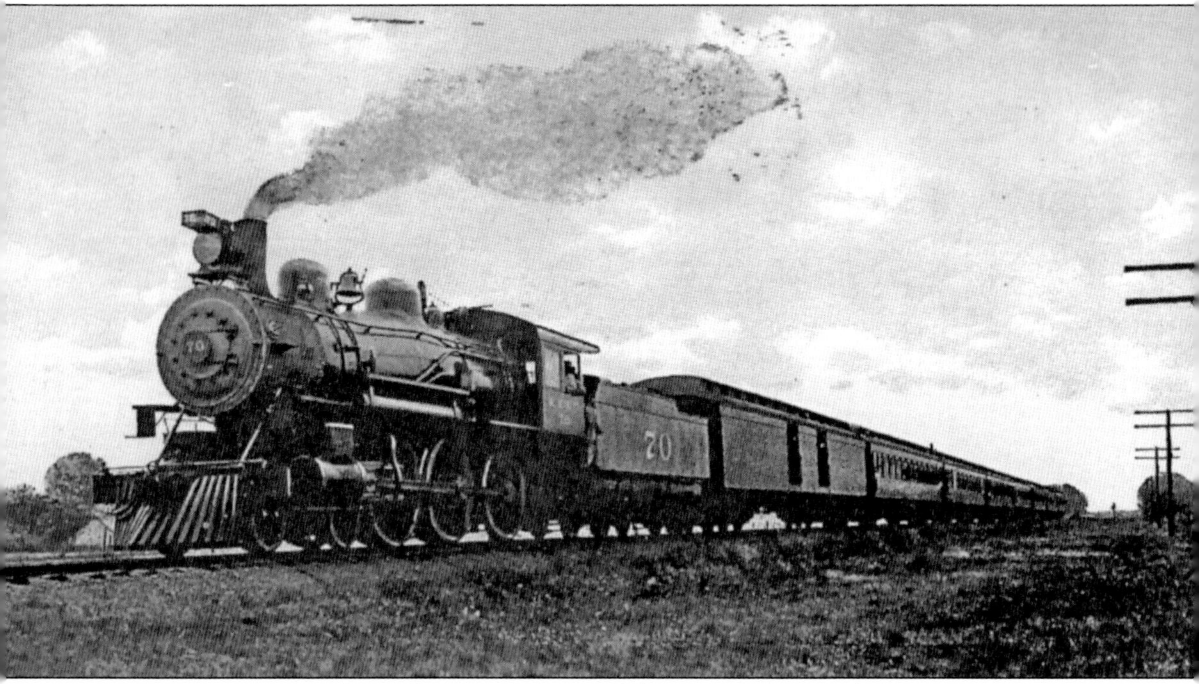

THE *KATY LIMITED*. This is the train that served the Durant area on the Missouri-Kansas-Texas Railroad. The "Katy" was completed through Choctaw Nation, which included Durant, sometime between 1872 and 1874. In 1916, the city built a Union Station. (Author's collection.)

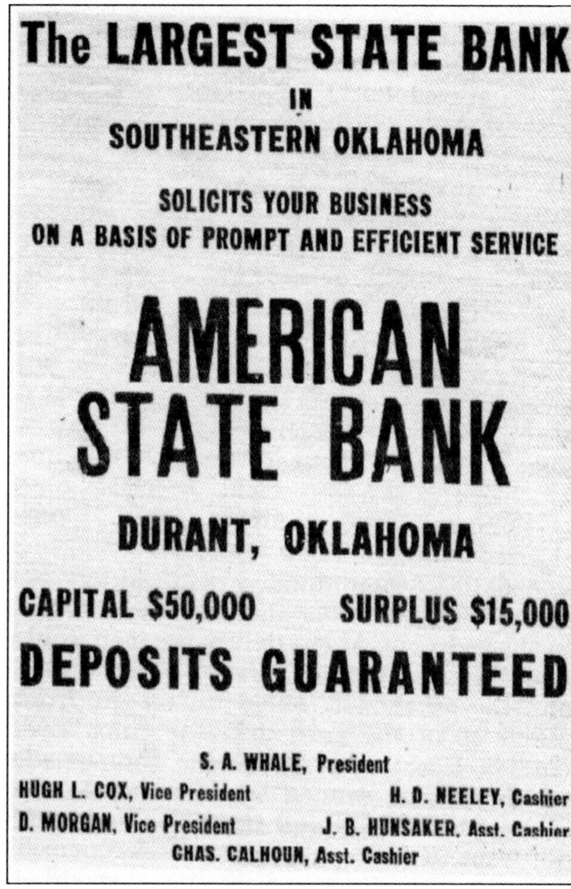
The LARGEST STATE BANK
IN
SOUTHEASTERN OKLAHOMA
SOLICITS YOUR BUSINESS
ON A BASIS OF PROMPT AND EFFICIENT SERVICE
AMERICAN
STATE BANK
DURANT, OKLAHOMA
CAPITAL $50,000 SURPLUS $15,000
DEPOSITS GUARANTEED
S. A. WHALE, President
HUGH L. COX, Vice President H. D. NEELEY, Cashier
D. MORGAN, Vice President J. B. HUNSAKER, Asst. Cashier
CHAS. CALHOUN, Asst. Cashier

Poster Advertisement for American State Bank in Durant. This advertisement promotes the bank as the largest in southeastern Oklahoma. (Courtesy of Bryan County Archives.)

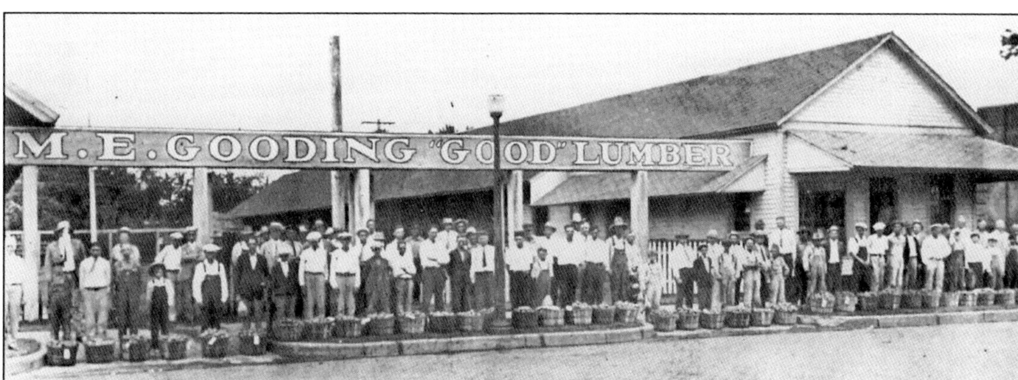

M.E. Gooding "Good" Lumber. A crowd has gathered along the street in front of this business for the Potato Festival in Durant around 1910. Bushel baskets of potatoes are lined up in front. This lumberyard was at 314 North Fourth Avenue and later became Rockwall Bros. & Company. (Courtesy of Marion Downs, David L. Crouch, and the *Durant Daily Democrat*.)

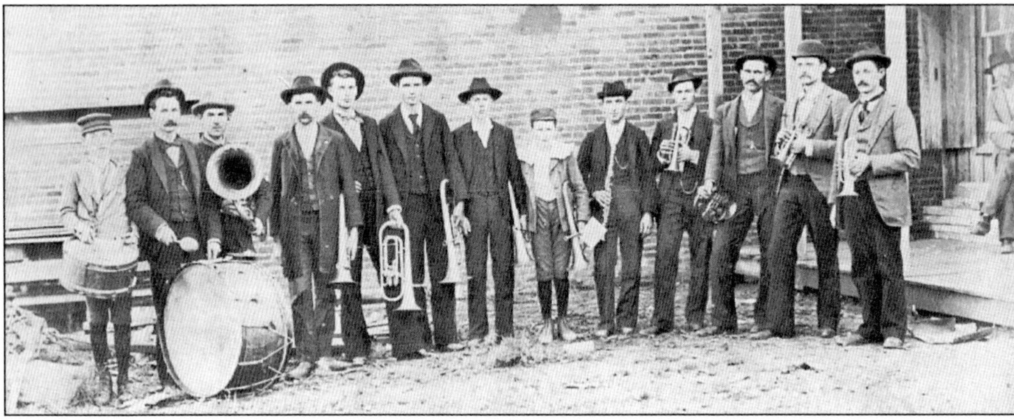

Band of Musicians. This was the first organized band in Durant, forming in 1894. They are photographed about six years later by Barnes & Turney, Photo Artists. Ron Waits stands sixth from the left. (Courtesy of Durant Area Chamber of Commerce.)

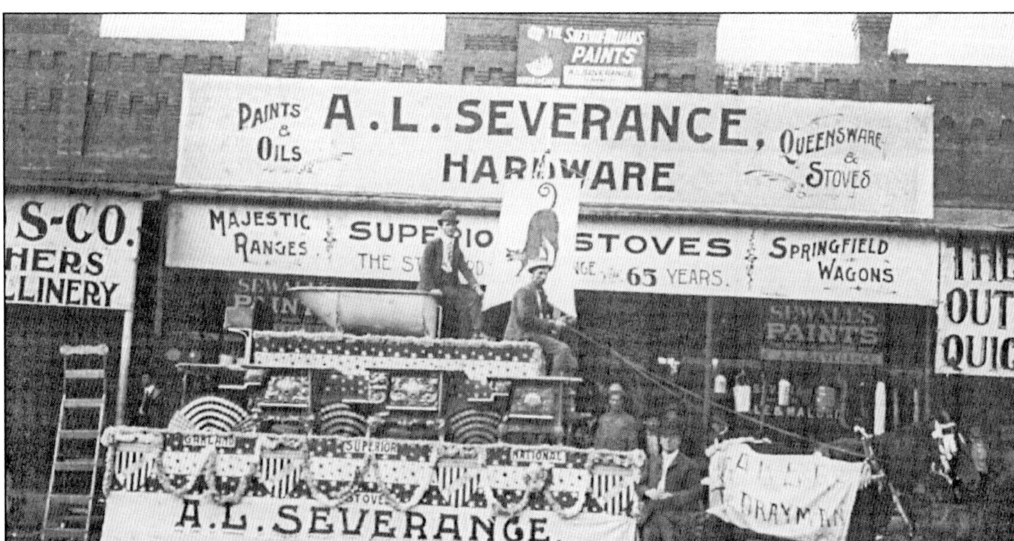

A.L. Severance Hardware, 1909. This downtown Durant business sold hardware, Springfield wagons, Queensware Stoves, Sherwin-Williams Paints, Sewall's Paints, Majestic Ranges, and Superior Stoves. The store opened in 1900 and was located at 209 West Main. The Severance family home was built about 1898 by Tom Hale at Third Avenue and Locust Street. (Courtesy of Durant Chamber of Commerce, David L. Crouch, and the *Durant Daily Democrat*.)

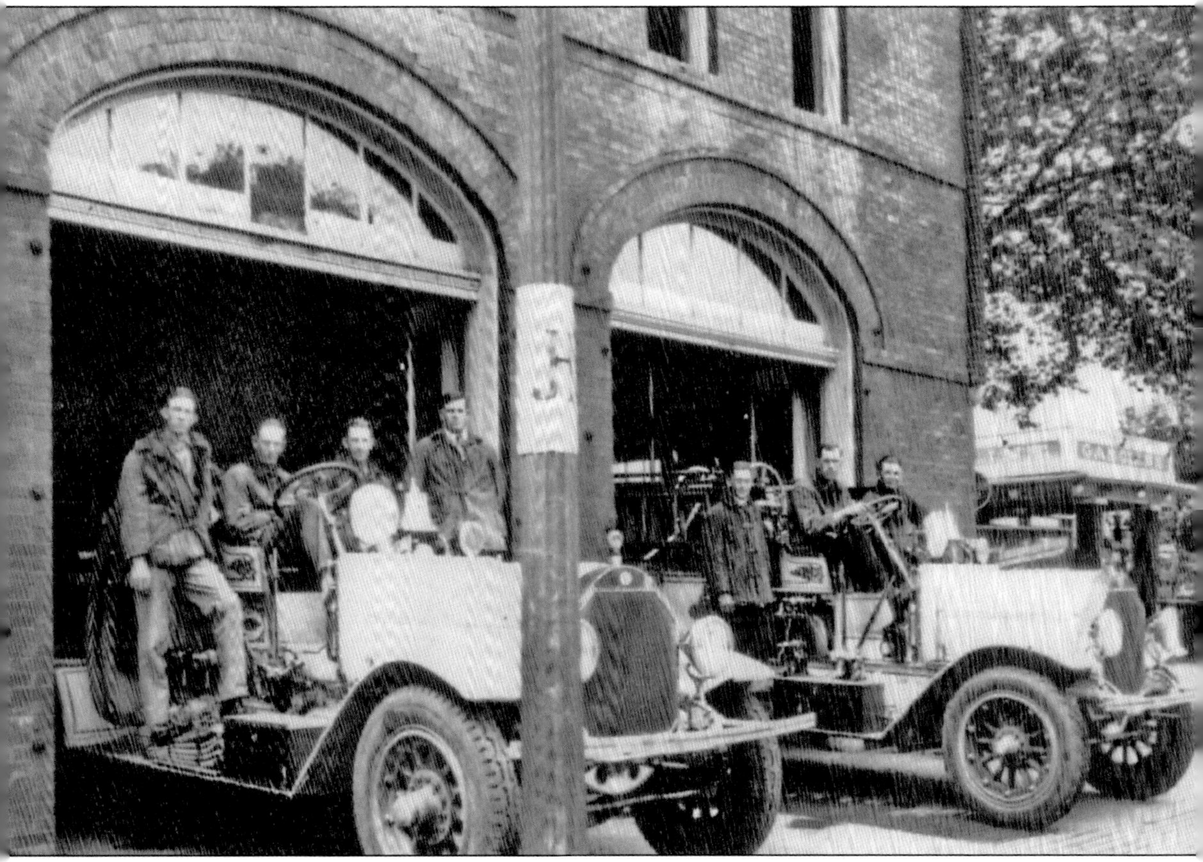

Durant Fire Department. Pictured at the fire department in the 400 block of West Main Street are, from left to right, Troy Tomlin, Henry Clover, Bill Sammon, Bud Wyatt, Jake Helback, Grover Bradford, and fire chief Doc Moore. The fire trucks are 1928 models. (Courtesy of David L. Crouch and the *Durant Daily Democrat*.)

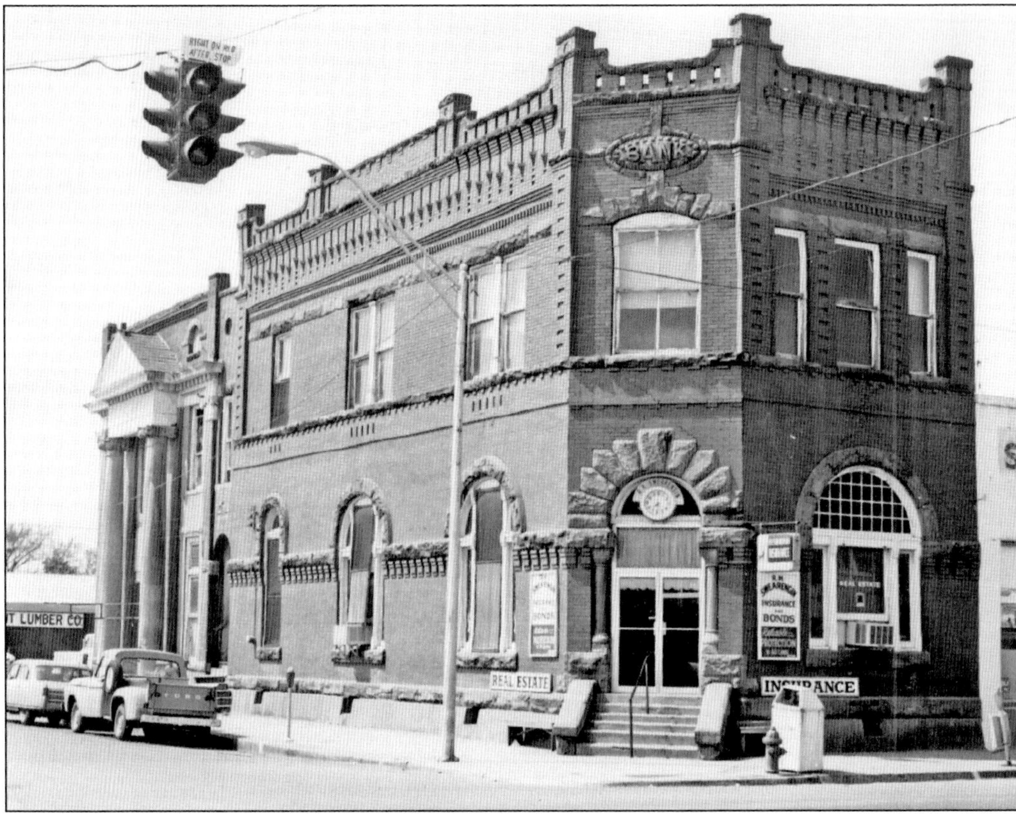

SWEARENGIN INSURANCE. This building was the original location of First National Bank, which opened in 1898; it also housed Swearengin Insurance. (Courtesy of Matt Swearengin.)

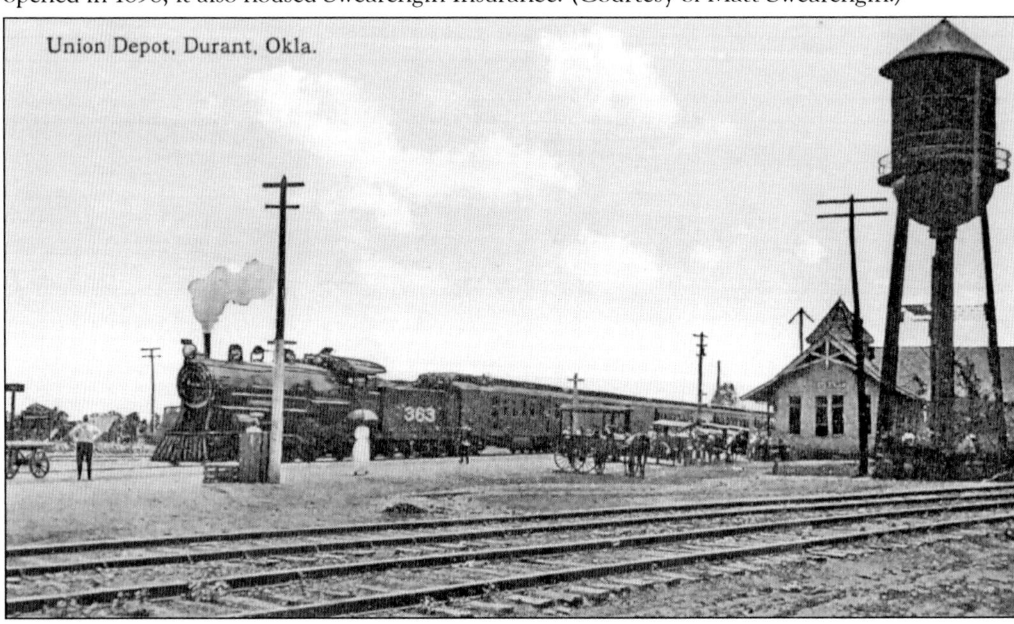

UNION DEPOT, DURANT. This is the Union Depot, with horses and buggies waiting at the station. (Author's collection.)

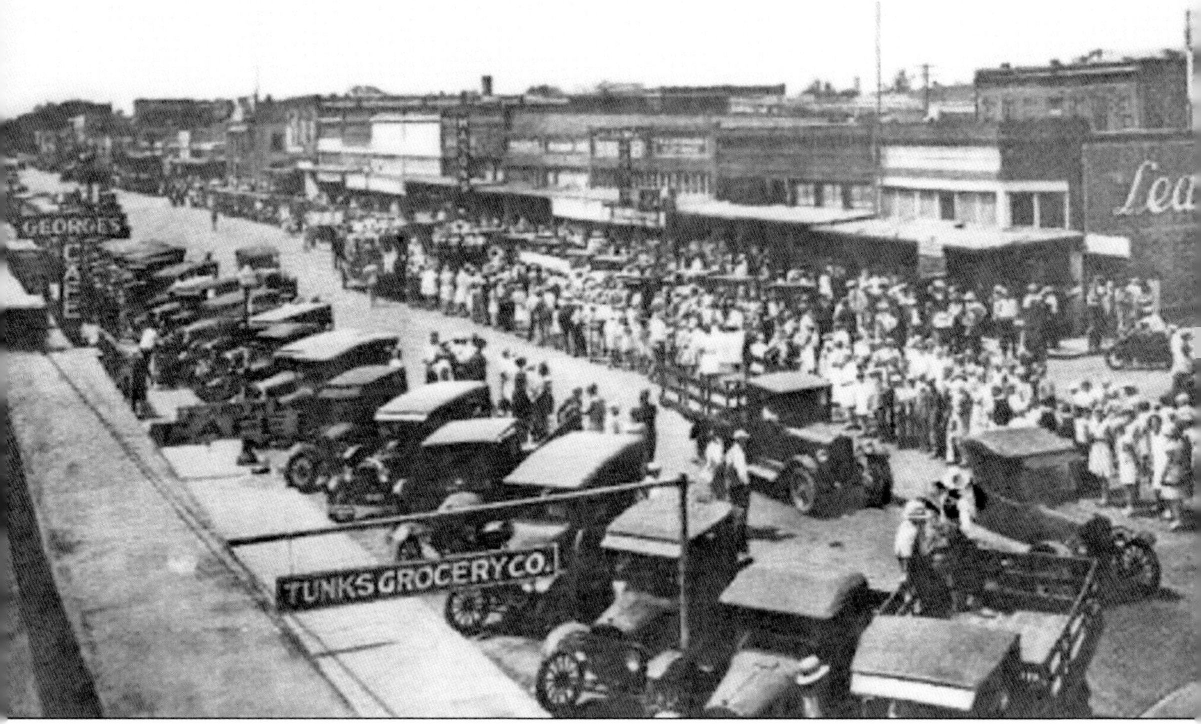

Downtown Durant. This image documents a busy day downtown, with a large procession of people in the street. Tunks Grocery Co. is shown in the foreground at left. Next to it are two cafés. (Courtesy of Marion Downs.)

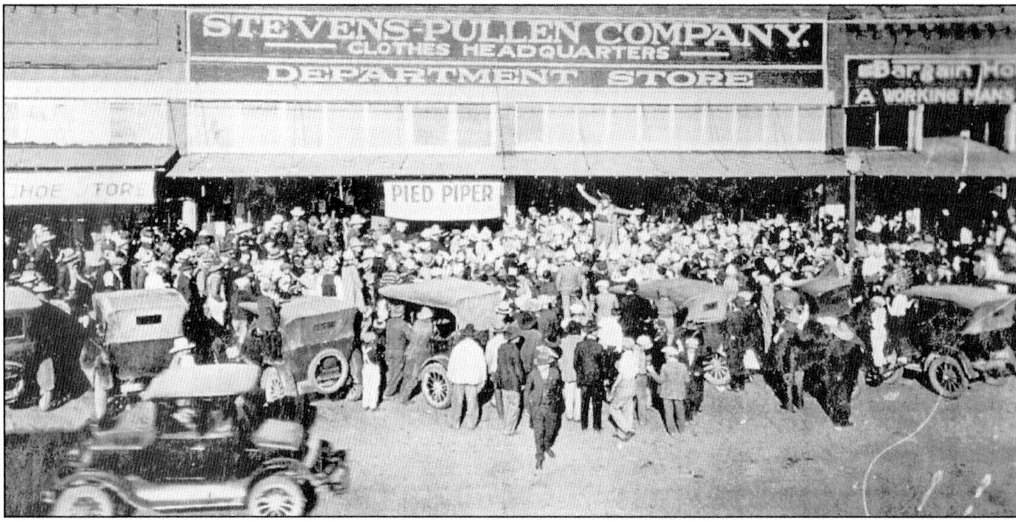

Stevens-Pullen Company. This downtown department store, on Main Street between First and Second Avenues, had a shoe store next to it. A sign advertises the "Pied Piper," promoting a line of children's "health shoes." An automobile giveaway, sponsored by local merchants, helped draw this crowd. (Courtesy of Marion Downs, David L. Crouch, and the *Durant Daily Democrat.*)

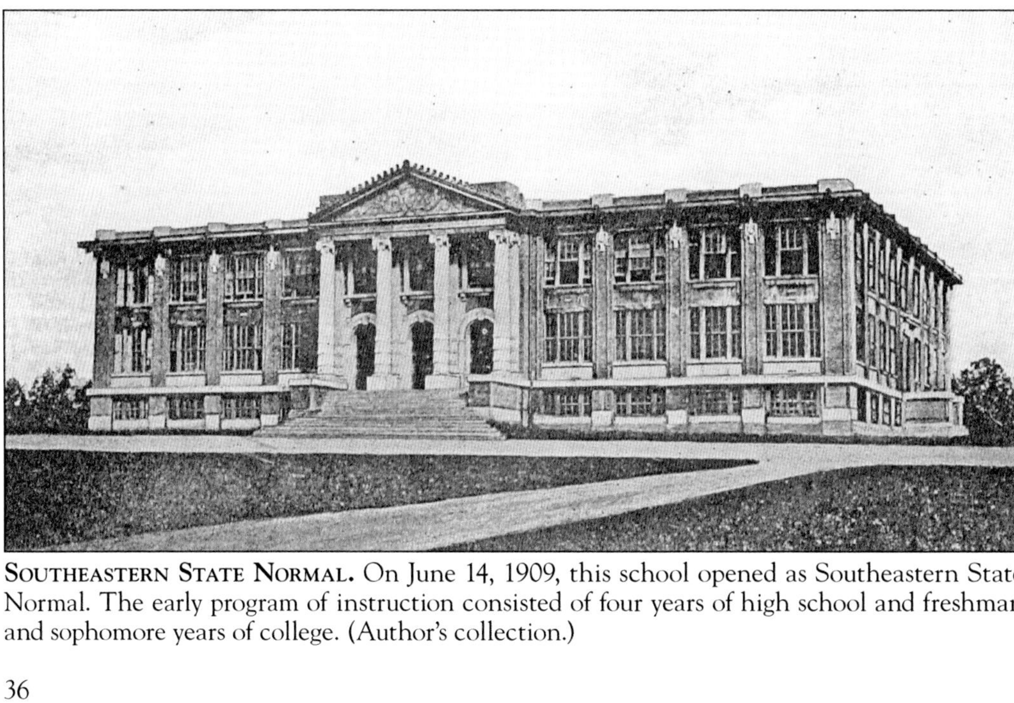

Southeastern State Normal. On June 14, 1909, this school opened as Southeastern State Normal. The early program of instruction consisted of four years of high school and freshman and sophomore years of college. (Author's collection.)

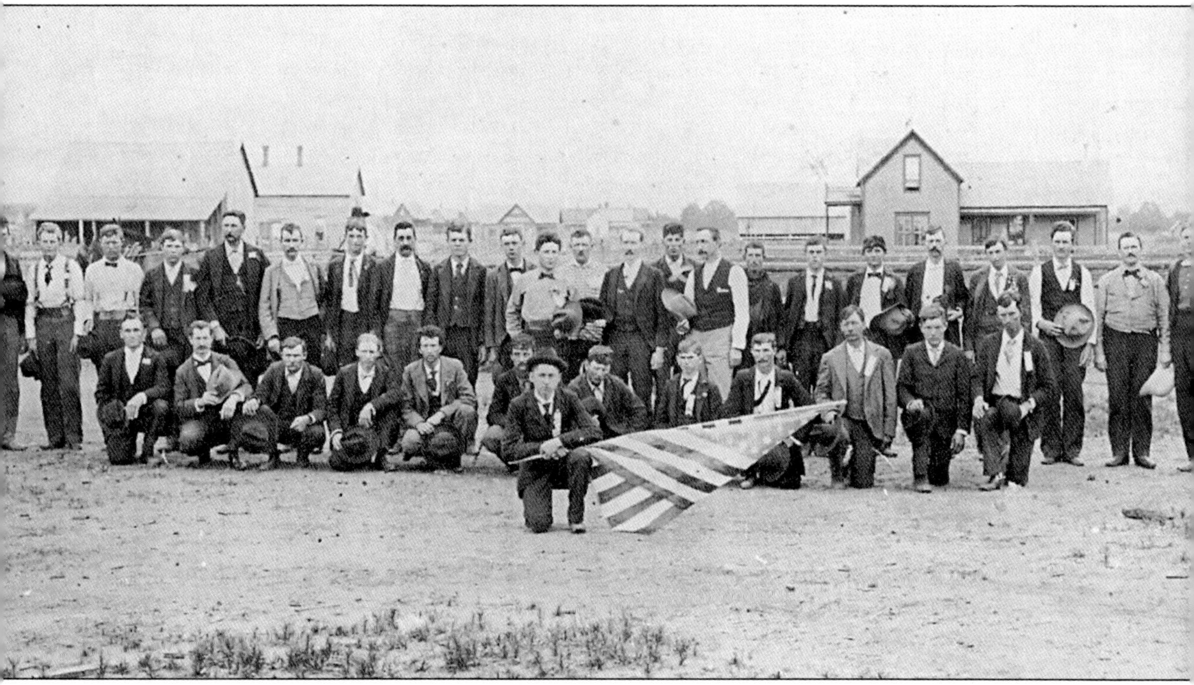

BOUND FOR SPANISH-AMERICAN WAR. This group of men is pictured in 1898 just east of the present-day site of the courthouse before marching off to the Spanish-American War. O.C. Nichols, editor of the *Durant Eagle* and a veteran, was selected as captain of the Durant company. Organizer W.L. Poole was a postmaster, mayor, and the first county register of deeds. (Courtesy of Marion Downs, David L. Crouch, and the *Durant Daily Democrat*.)

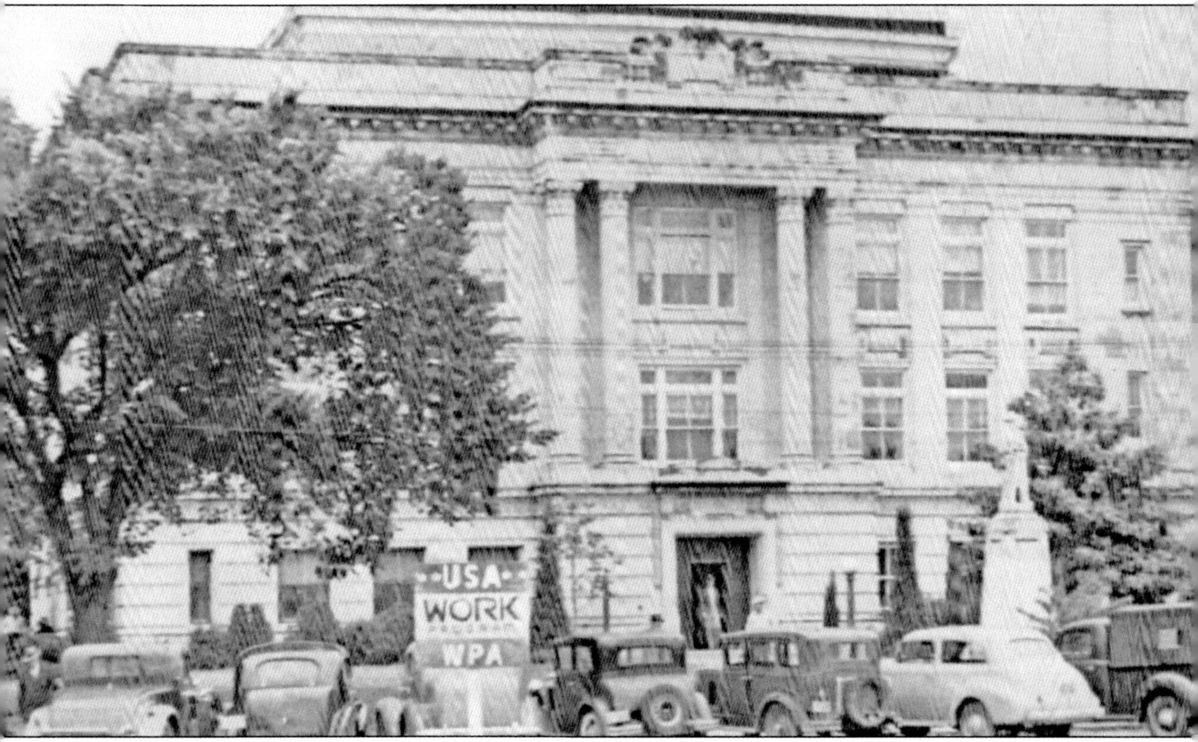

Bryan County Courthouse. This 1930s photograph shows a promotion for the Works Progress Administration. (Courtesy of David L. Crouch and the *Durant Daily Democrat*.)

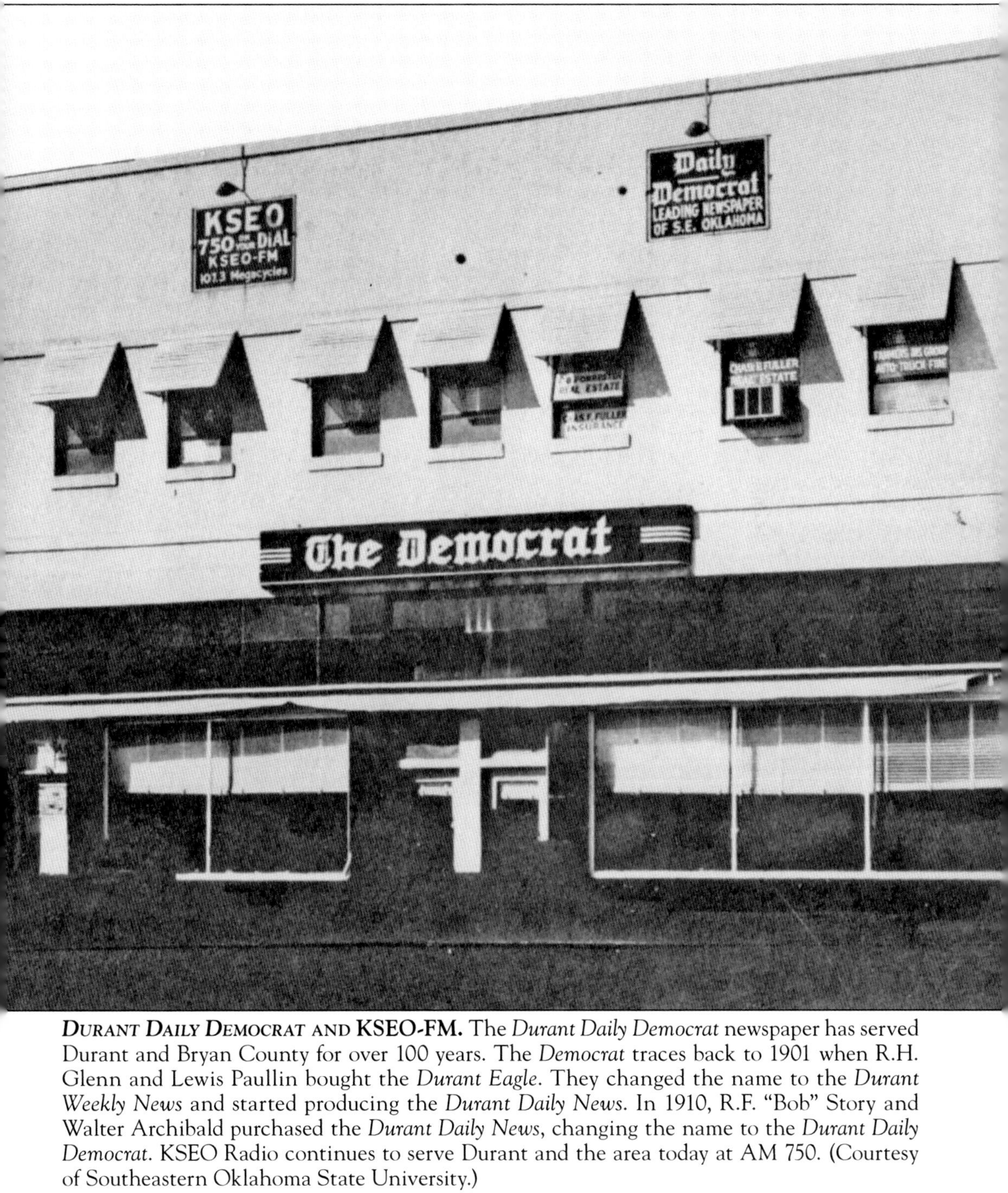

DURANT DAILY DEMOCRAT AND KSEO-FM. The *Durant Daily Democrat* newspaper has served Durant and Bryan County for over 100 years. The *Democrat* traces back to 1901 when R.H. Glenn and Lewis Paullin bought the *Durant Eagle*. They changed the name to the *Durant Weekly News* and started producing the *Durant Daily News*. In 1910, R.F. "Bob" Story and Walter Archibald purchased the *Durant Daily News*, changing the name to the *Durant Daily Democrat*. KSEO Radio continues to serve Durant and the area today at AM 750. (Courtesy of Southeastern Oklahoma State University.)

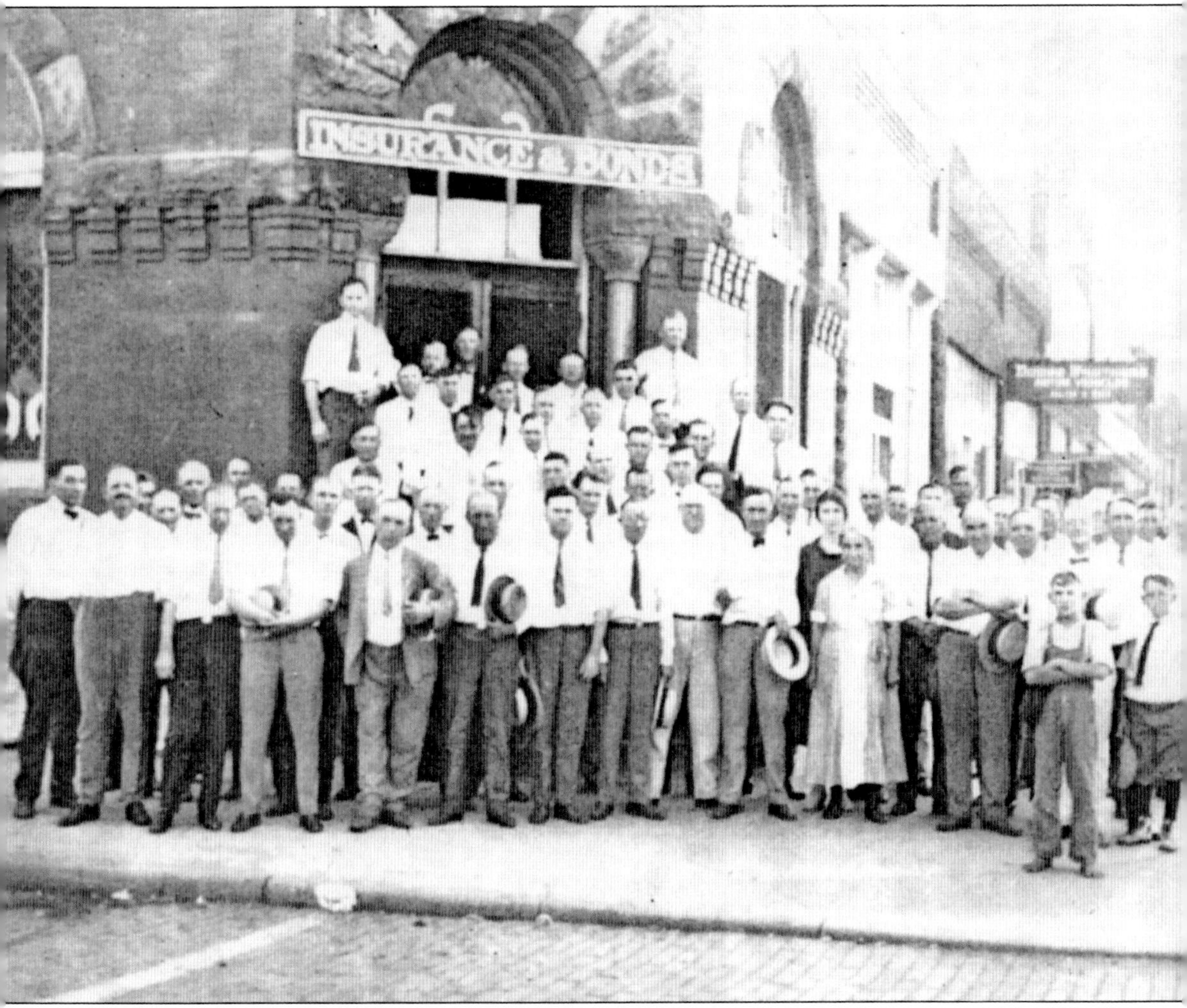

DURANT'S 1923 LEADING BUSINESSMEN. Among those pictured here are Amos Bass, Willard Reed, John Mason, C.C. Dunlap, Wainright Bridges, Howard Holmes, J.W. Downs, Jim Keirsey, John Willhoyt, C.C. Tompkins, Juluis Foote, Walter Archibald, Bob Story, Tuck and Lawton England, Judge A.H. Ferguson, W.E. Carpenter, Gene Matlock, Ed Clark, Galen McKinney, S.C. Boswell, Gordon Baxter, Paul Laird, John Leonard, Dr. Henry Bennet, ? Kolb, and ? Scott. (Courtesy of Albert Mason, David L. Crouch, and the *Durant Daily Democrat*).

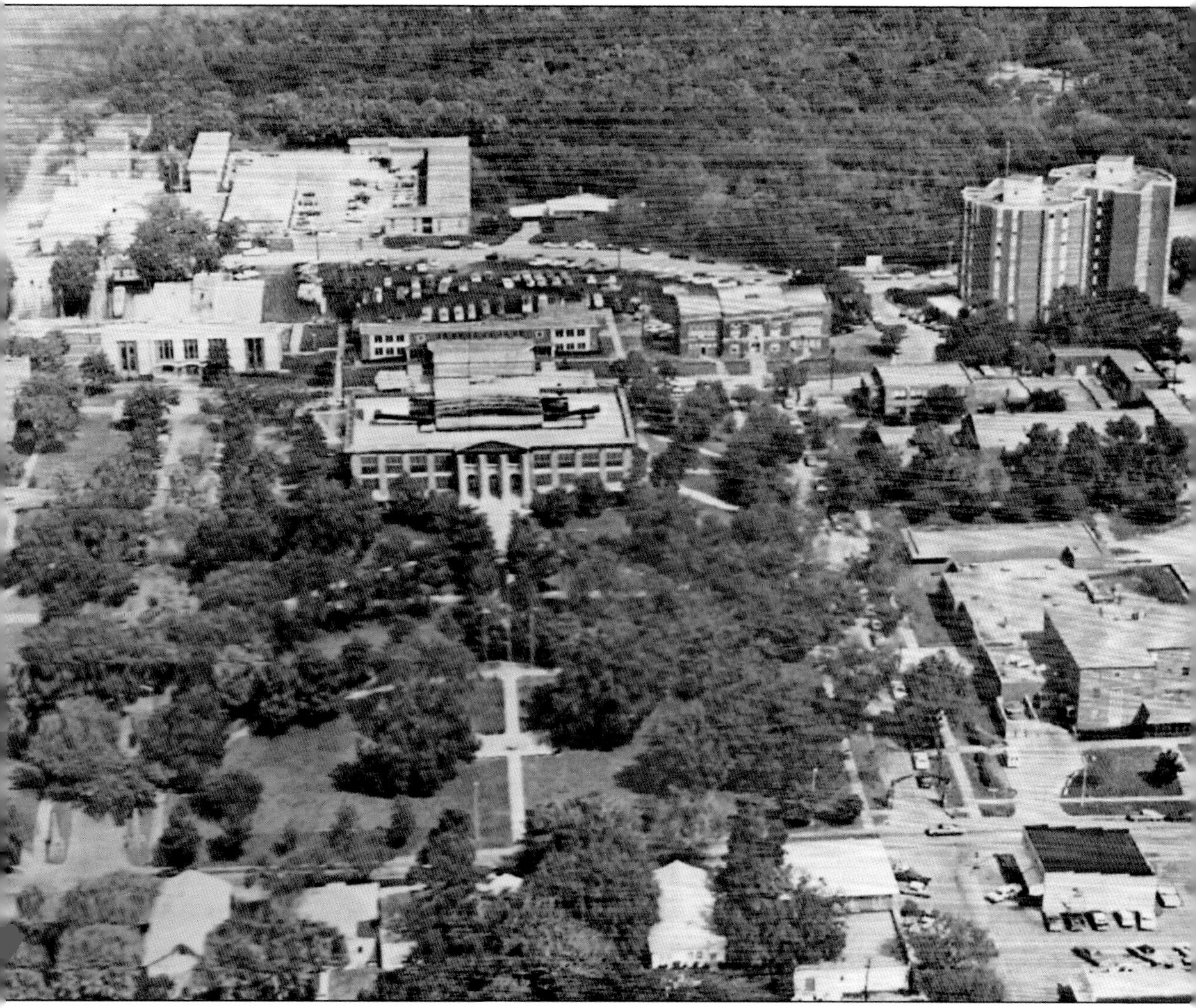

AERIAL VIEW OF SOUTHEASTERN STATE COLLEGE, 1974. This is Southeastern State College immersed among green space and the city of Durant. (Courtesy of Southeastern Oklahoma State University.)

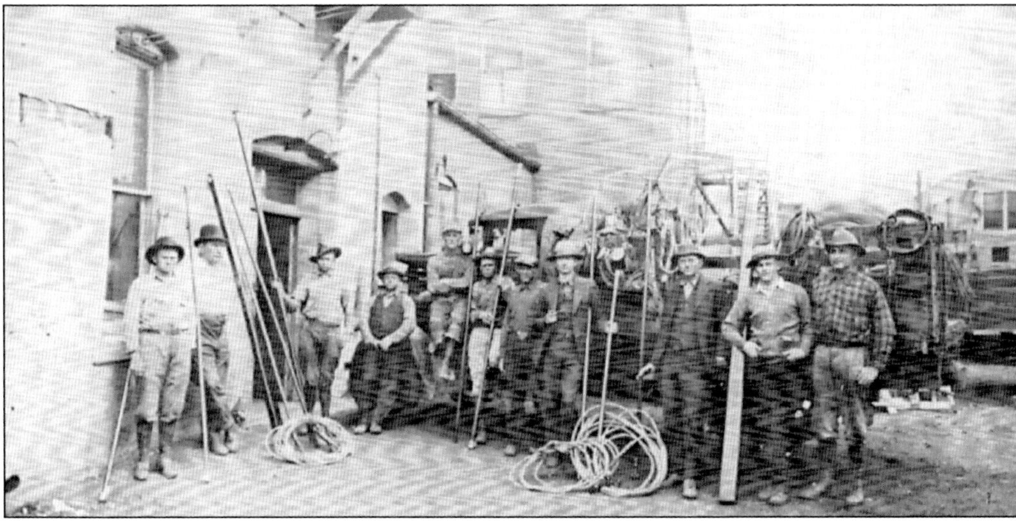

ICEHOUSE ON NORTH THIRD AVENUE. This icehouse was built shortly after 1900 and provided electricity as a by-product; most of the power was used to operate Durant's first streetlights. Included among the workers pictured here is E.T. Pope, standing third from the left. (Courtesy of David L. Crouch and the *Durant Daily Democrat*.)

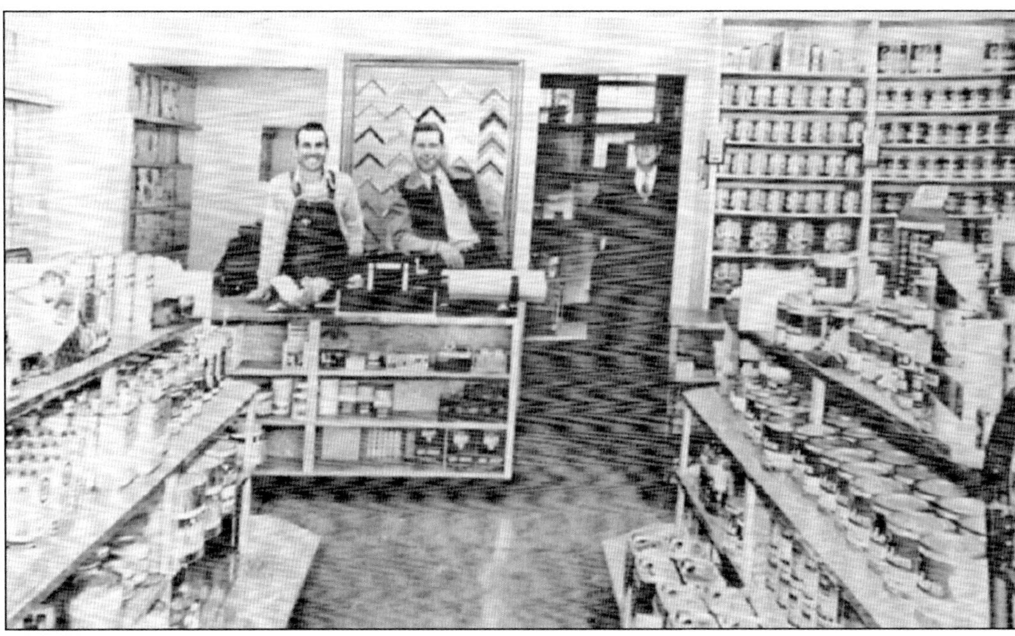

LEE & MARROW COMPANY. Wayne Morrow (left), Quinton Dunham (center) and an unidentified salesman are pictured at the store's grand opening on April 16, 1948, at 211 North Second Avenue. (Courtesy of David L. Crouch and the *Durant Daily Democrat*.)

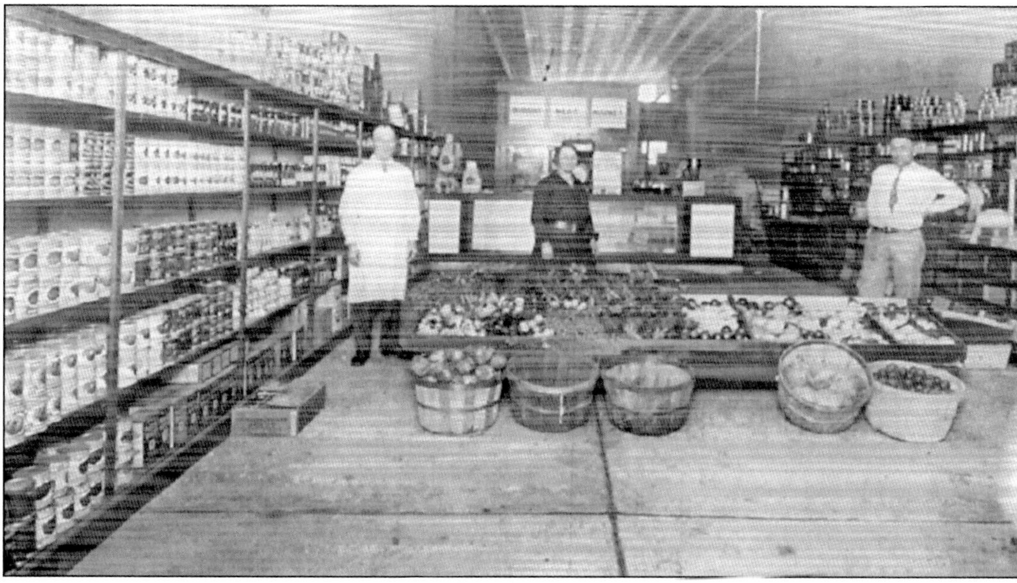

Keener's Durant Grocery & Market. Seen here are Durant Grocery & Market owners Carl N. and Rosa Keener with employee John Gravitt. At the time of this photograph, the store was located at 116 North Second Avenue; future locations of the business included 200 West Evergreen, 402 North First Avenue (under the name Keeners Food Store), 124 North Third Avenue (under the name Keeners' White House Grocery), and 130 West Main Street (under the name Keener Cash Grocery). (Courtesy of David L. Crouch and the *Durant Daily Democrat.*)

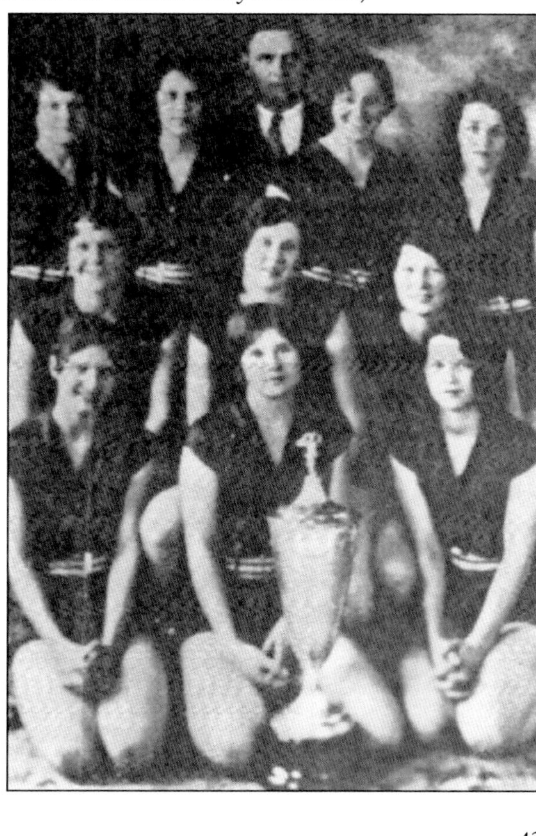

Oklahoma Presbyterian College Basketball Team. Coach S.F. Babb is pictured here with the 1930–1931 team. The players, shown with their trophy, include Maybee (guard), Faulk (guard), Fields (forward), Hamilton (forward), Harris (forward), Kays (guard), Lorance (forward), Northington (forward), Park (guard), Schaffer (forward and guard). (Courtesy of Bryan County Archives.)

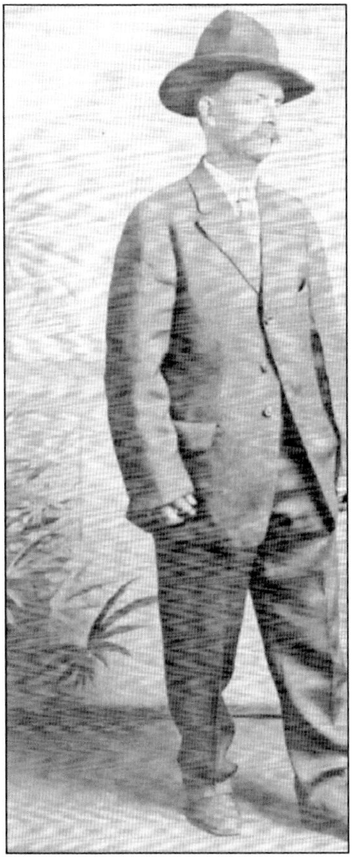

JOHN J. ADAMSON. Adamson was a shoemaker and owned a shop on Third Avenue in Durant. He made shoes and repaired holster belts for policemen and also did other leatherwork. Adamson fed cattle on a ranch located where the Durant Cemetery was later built. This photograph was taken in 1913. (Courtesy of David L. Crouch and the *Durant Daily Democrat.*)

O.L. KOLB'S LAUNDRY, DRY CLEANING, AND DYEING. This is opening day in the mid-1930s of a Durant business at 124 South Second Avenue. Those pictured include Key Kolb (far left) and Fred and Lulu Wilson. Kolb also operated Durant Steam Laundry. (Courtesy of David L. Crouch and the *Durant Daily Democrat.*)

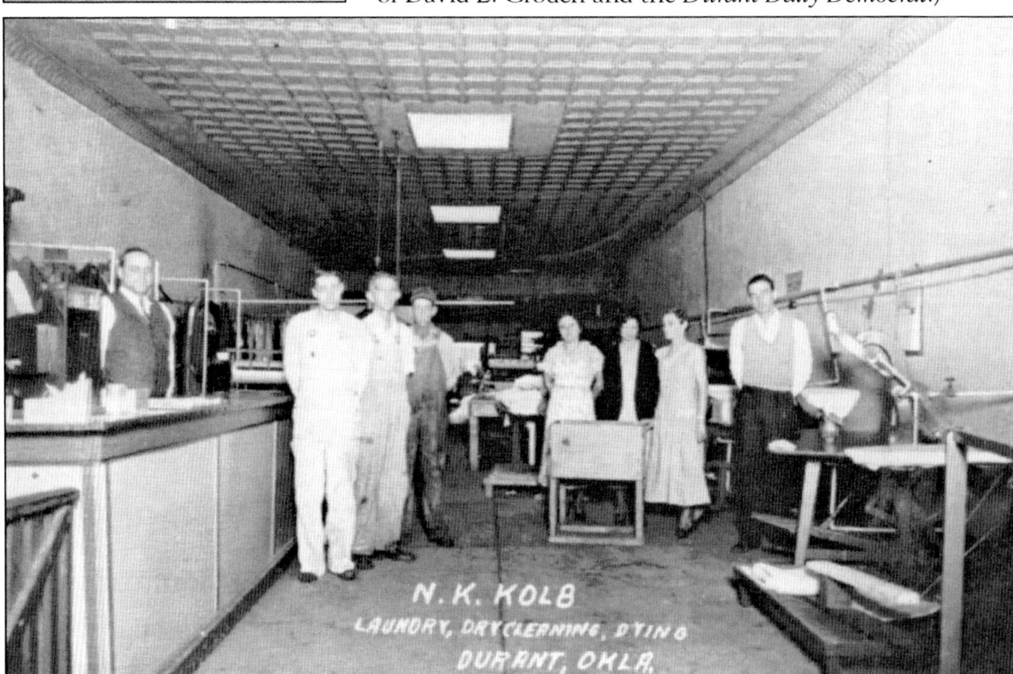

Two

Oklahoma Statehood

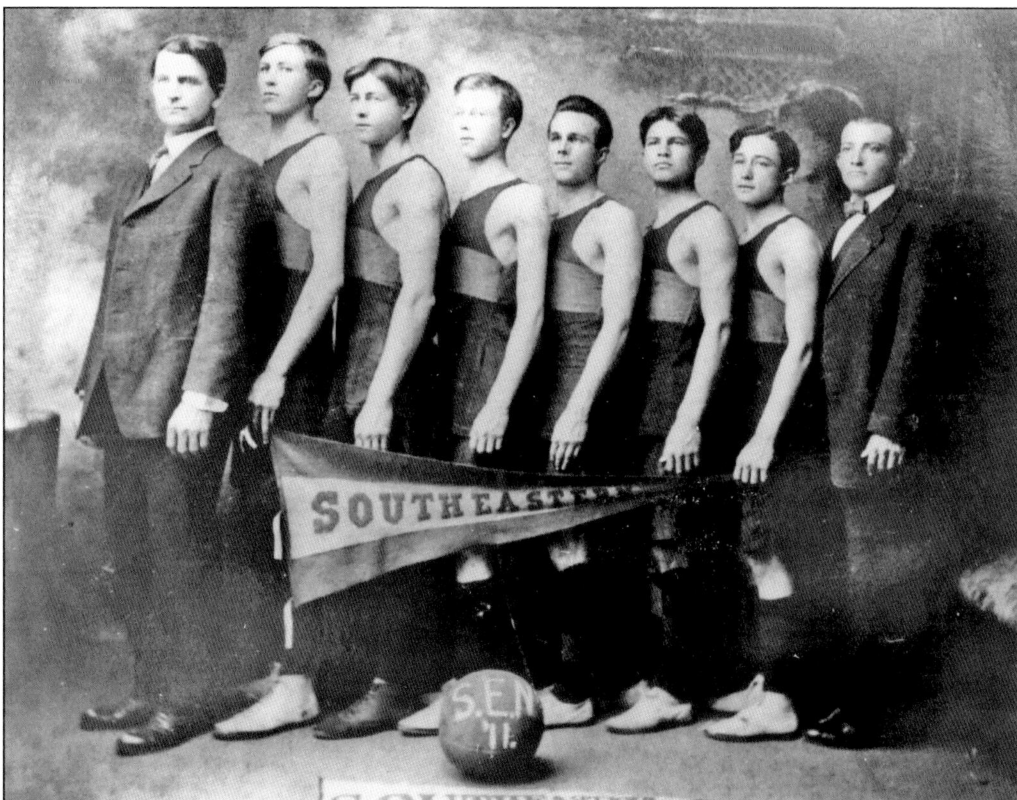

Southeastern Normal Basketball Team, 1911. On March 6, 1909, the second Oklahoma State Legislature designated Durant as the location for a normal school to serve 12 counties: Atoka, Bryan, Carter, Choctaw, Latimer, LeFlore, Love, Marshall, McCurtain, McIntosh, Pittsburg, and Pushmataha. Southeastern Oklahoma State University first opened on June 14, 1909, as Southeastern State Normal School. The early program of instruction consisted of four years of high school and freshman and sophomore years of college. (Courtesy of Southeastern Oklahoma State University.)

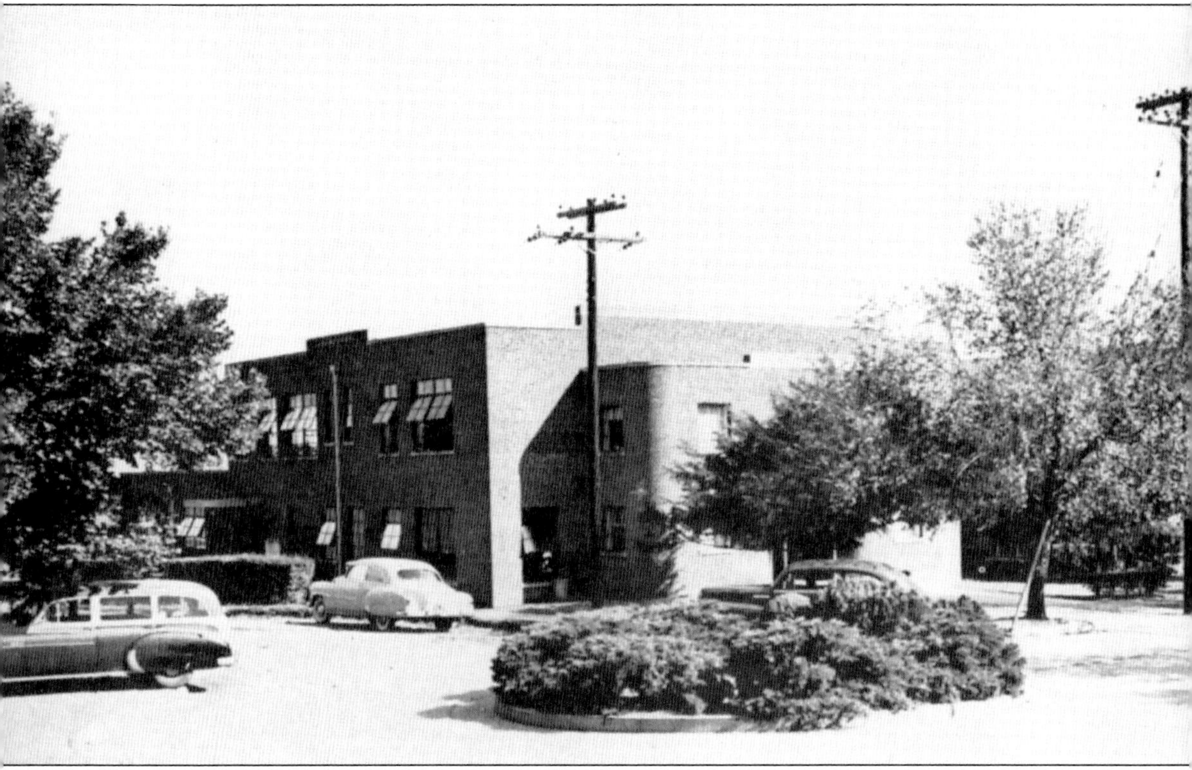

SOUTHEASTERN STATE COLLEGE. This is the Industrial Arts Building at Southeastern State College, photographed about 1955. (Courtesy of Southeastern Oklahoma State University.)

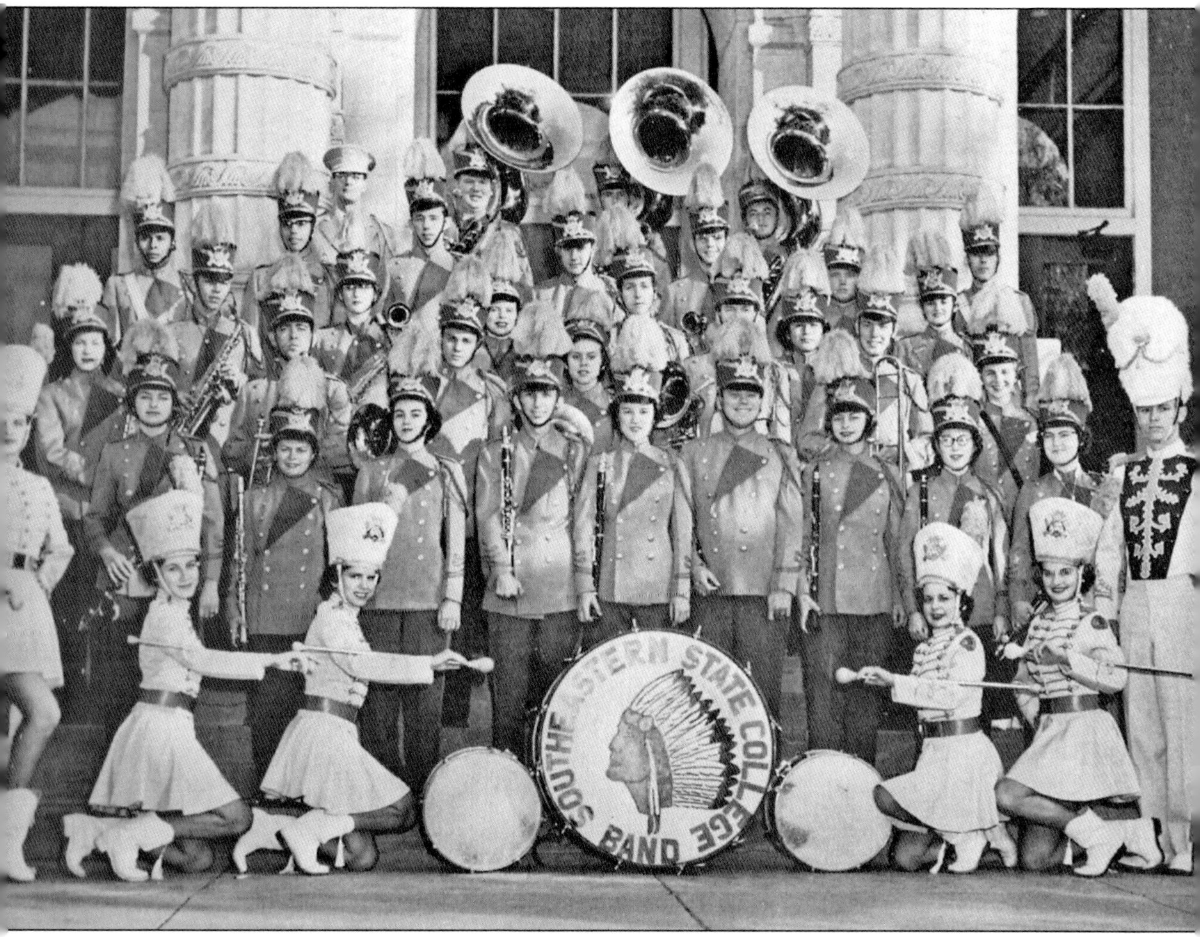

SOUTHEASTERN STATE COLLEGE BAND. This is the 1955 Southeastern College Band. The group functions as a marching band during the first semester and as a concert band during the second. (Courtesy of Southeastern Oklahoma State University.)

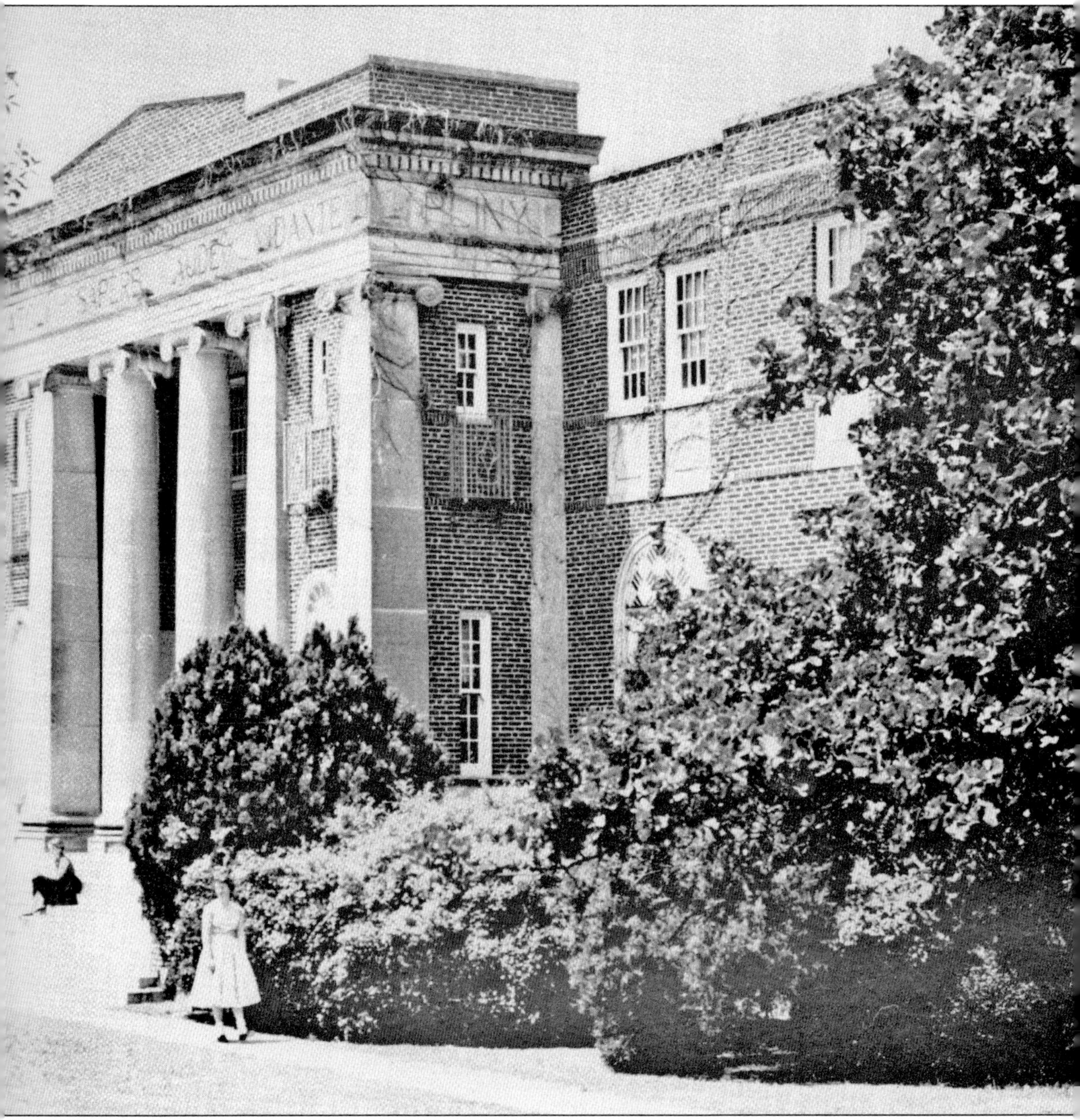

STC Henry G. Bennett Memorial Library. Pictured here is the Southeastern State Teachers College Library. Henry G. Bennett was the sixth president of what would become Southeastern Oklahoma State University, from 1919 to 1928. After his presidency at SOSU, Bennett was nominated as president at Oklahoma A&M College, where he served from 1928 to 1950. The library building was renamed the Henry G. Bennett Memorial Library in 1982 during homecoming festivities. (Author's collection.)

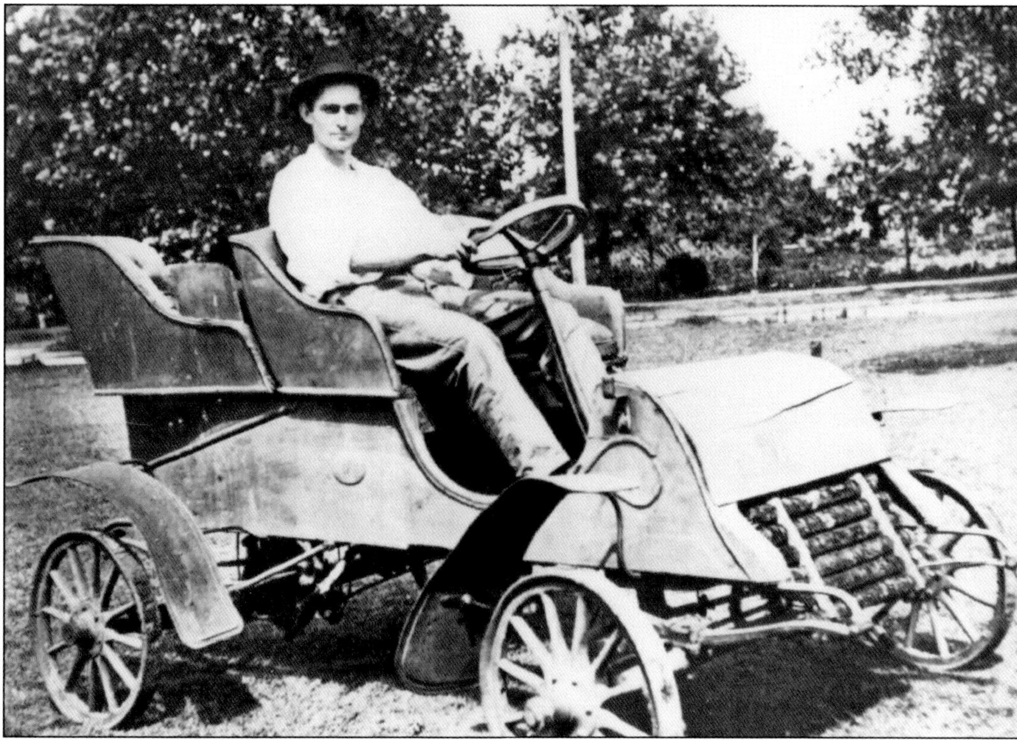

Cadillac in Durant. In 1907, this Cadillac—with one cylinder, chain drive, and solid, nonrubber tires—was one of the first automobiles in Durant. (Courtesy of Matt Swearengin.)

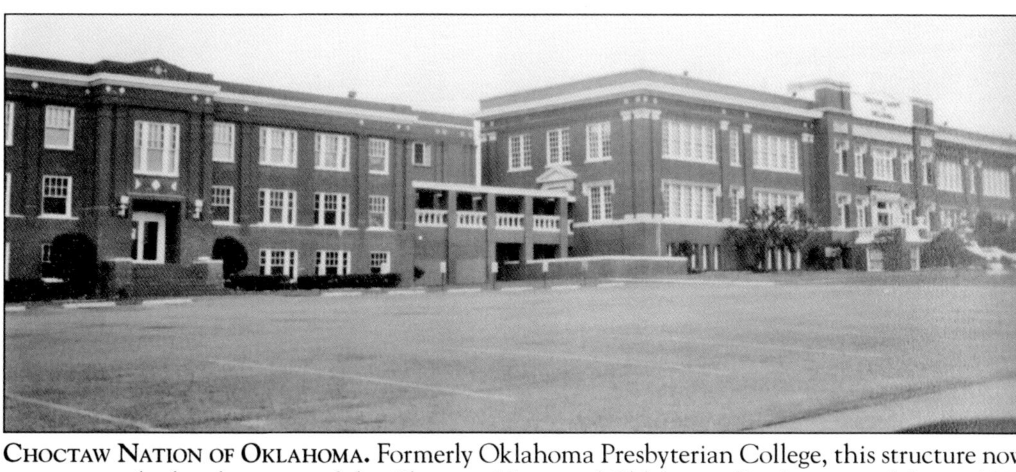

Choctaw Nation of Oklahoma. Formerly Oklahoma Presbyterian College, this structure now operates as the headquarters of the Choctaw Nation of Oklahoma. By the time of this c. 2006 photograph, the building had been extensively remodeled. (Author's collection.)

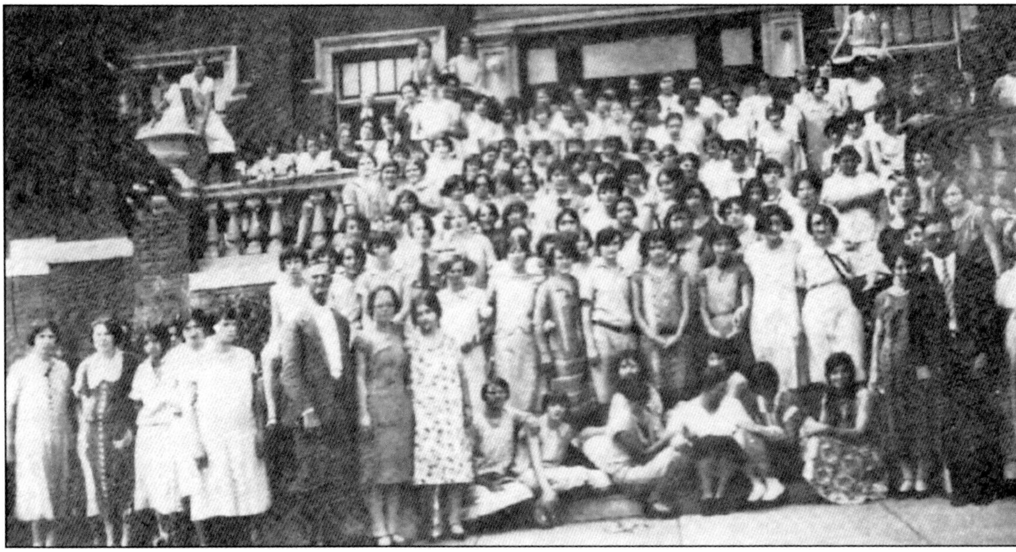

Oklahoma Presbyterian College. Oklahoma Presbyterian College (OPC) was an all-female school, financed by endowments from the church and by gifts. The two men in this 1926 photograph are Rev. Ebenezer Hotchkiss (left) and Rev. Roy Craig (right). Among the young ladies pictured are Erma L. Taylor (seated in the upper left, on the right) and Ann Semple (first row, far right). As part of treaty obligations, the government paid half of the expenses of Choctaw and Chickasaw students (about half of the student body). The building is now the headquarters of the Choctaw Nation of Oklahoma. (Courtesy of Bryan County Archives.)

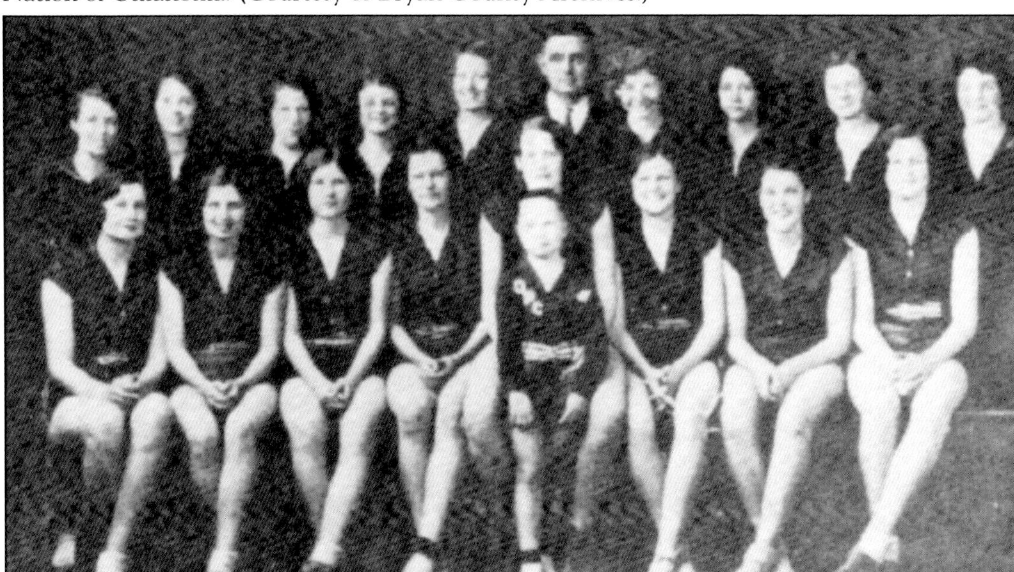

OPC Cardinals, National Champions, 1932. The Oklahoma Presbyterian College Cardinals won the women's basketball national tournament at Shreveport, Louisiana. The players are, from left to right, (first row) Lera Dunford, Toka Lee Fields, Juanita Park, Lucille Thurman, Hazel Vickers, Earnestine Lampson, Lahoma Lassiter, and Vera Dunford; (second row) Susie Lorance, Doll Harris, Gwen Hamilton, "Monk" Mitchell, Buena Harris, Coral Worley, Alice Hamilton, Allene West, and Leona Mitchell; coach S.F. Babb stands in the center rear, and mascot J.T. Colwick Jr. poses in front. (Courtesy of Bryan County Archives.)

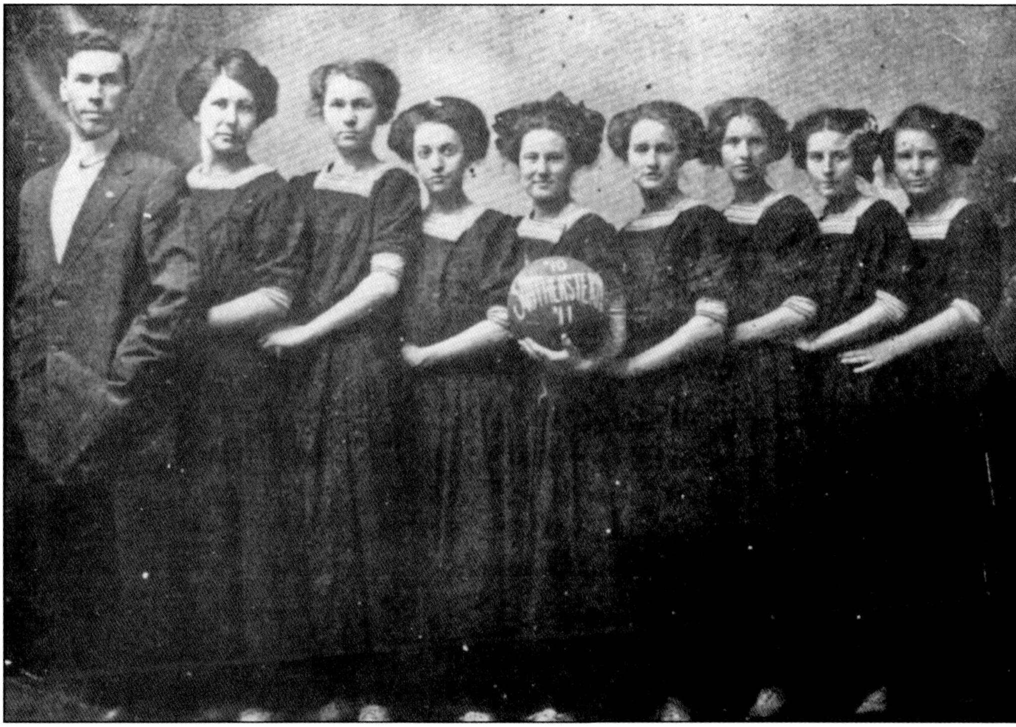

Southeastern Girls' Basketball Team. Pictured here is the 1910–1911 girls' basketball team of Southeastern State Normal School. (Courtesy of Southeastern Oklahoma State University.)

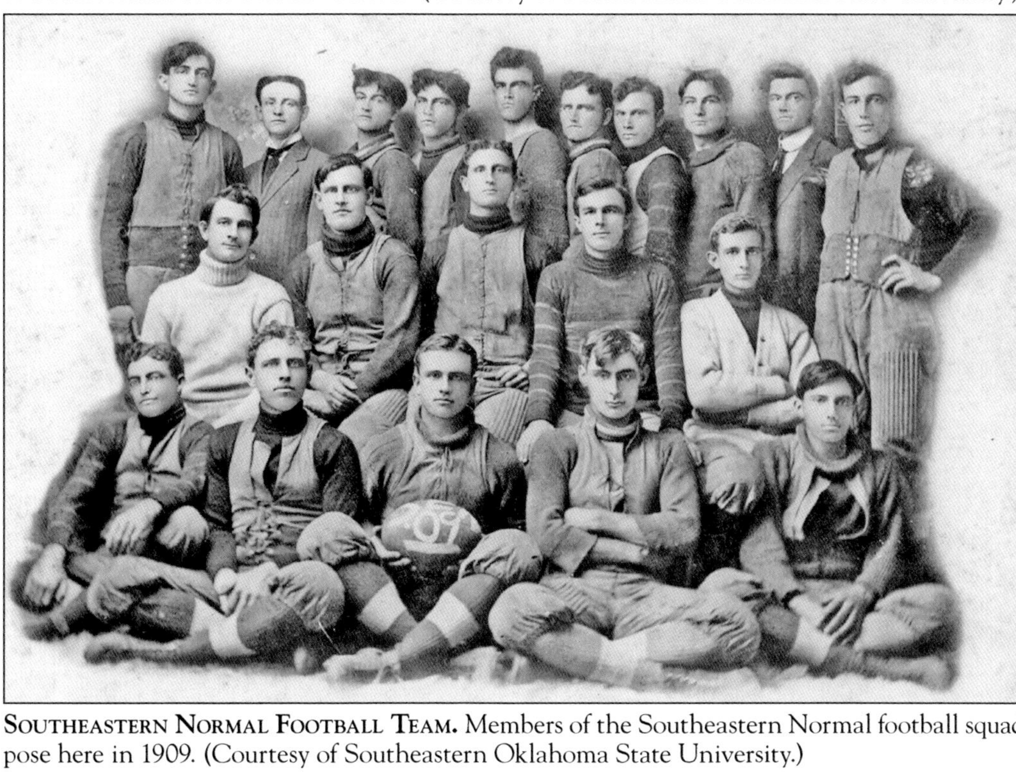

Southeastern Normal Football Team. Members of the Southeastern Normal football squad pose here in 1909. (Courtesy of Southeastern Oklahoma State University.)

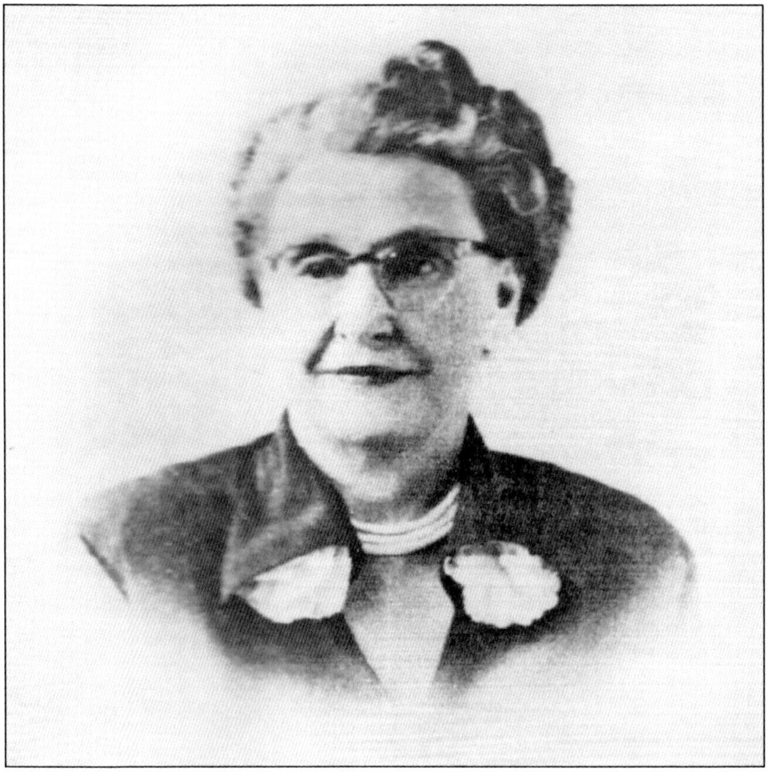

Clara White. Clara, honored as Woman of the Year in 1973, was a volunteer worker for the March of Dimes, as well as for polio-, heart-, and cancer-related health campaigns. She was a committee member instrumental in getting Market Square paved and in establishing Bryan Memorial Hospital in Durant. White was listed in *Who's Who of Business Women*. (Courtesy of Bryan County Archives.)

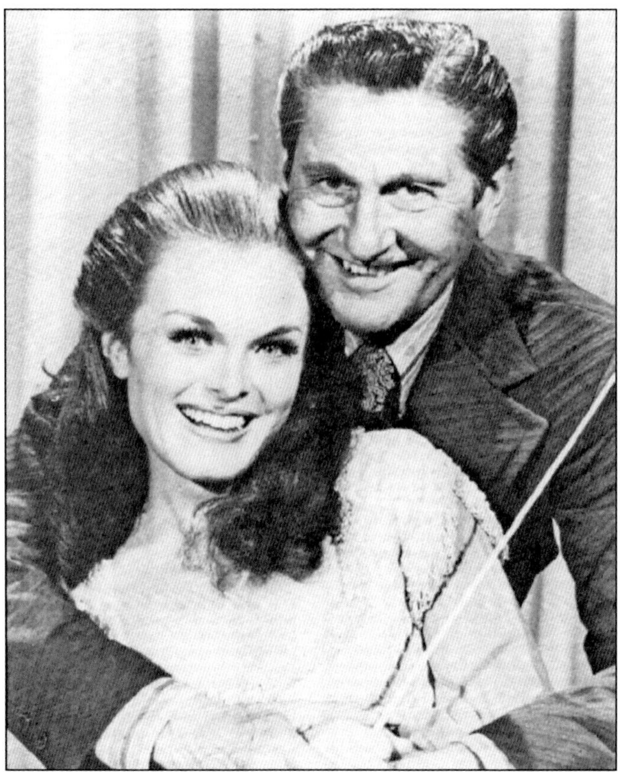

Gail Farrell and Lawrence Welk. Gail Farrell of Durant graduated from the University of Tulsa and was the school's representative in the Miss Oklahoma contest. In 1969, she moved to Los Angeles, California, where she performed weekly on *The Lawrence Welk Show* as an arranger and singer until Welk's retirement in 1982. (Courtesy of Bryan County Archives.)

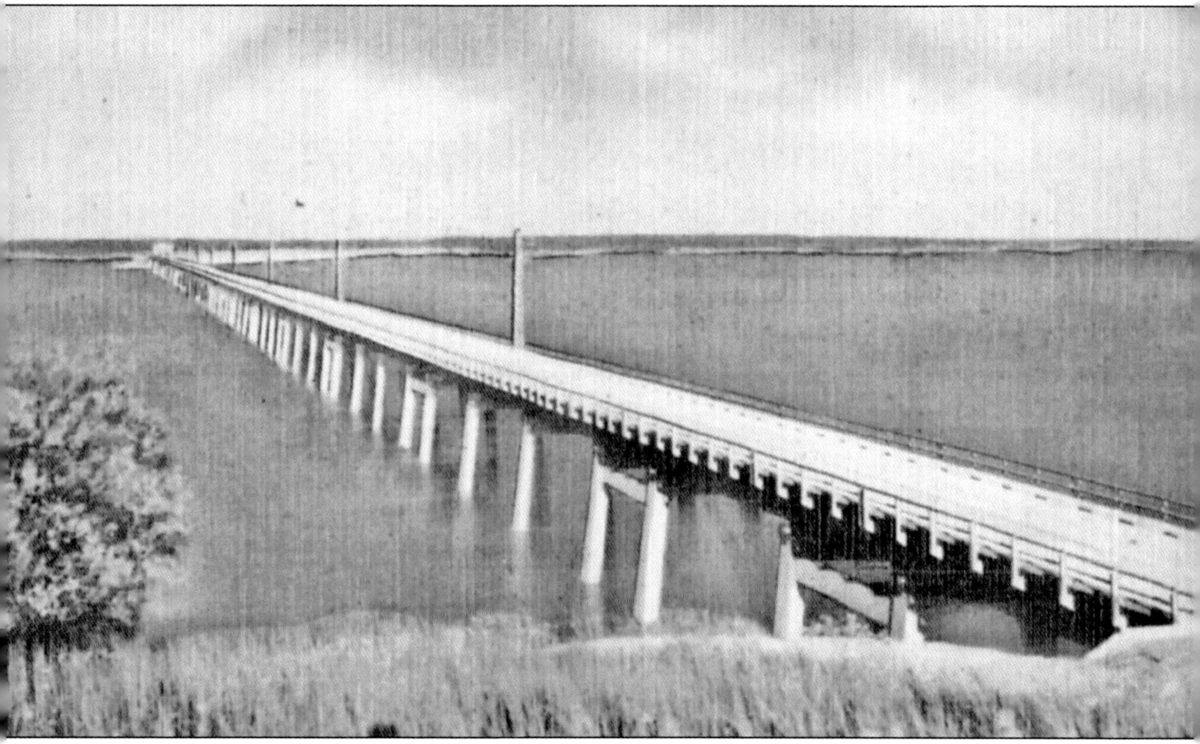

Franklin D. Roosevelt Memorial Bridge, Lake Texoma. Lake Texoma, Oklahoma's second-largest lake, is a great place for fishing (striped bass are very populous) and boating. Lake Texoma State Park is also located here, offering swimming, camping, picnic areas, wildlife viewing, and hiking. Roosevelt Bridge is the longest in Oklahoma, just short of one mile in length. The bridge, constructed in 1942, is on Highway 70 just west of Durant. (Author's collection.)

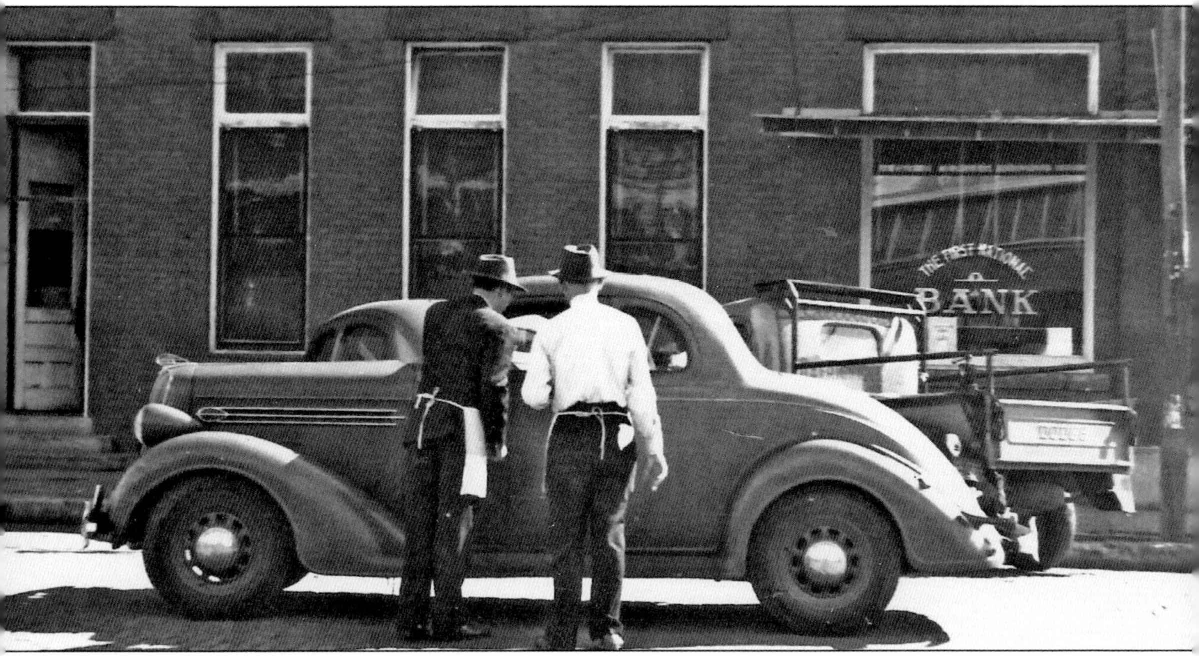

RECTOR SWEARENGIN AND MELVIN POOL, BEFORE 1940. Rector Swearengin (right) and Melvin Poole stand on North Third Avenue beside the old First National Bank. The men are collecting money for the Lions Club project to purchase a bus for the high school athletic department. (Courtesy of Matt Swearengin.)

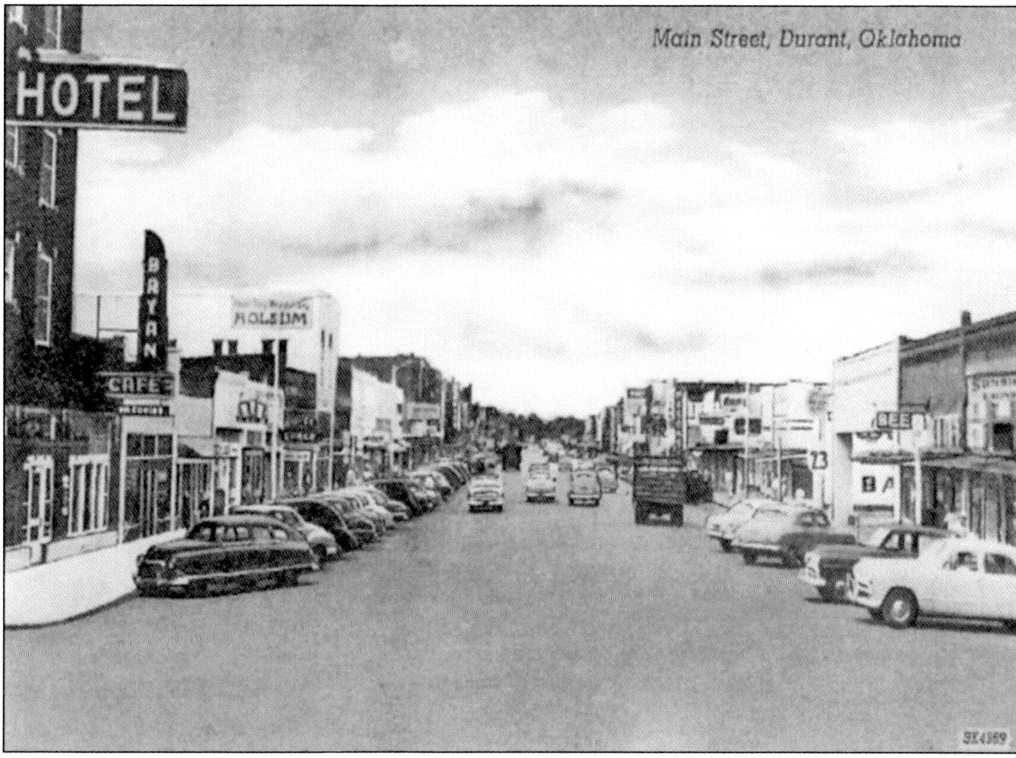

MAIN STREET. This postcard view shows Main Street looking especially busy, with little parking available. (Author's collection.)

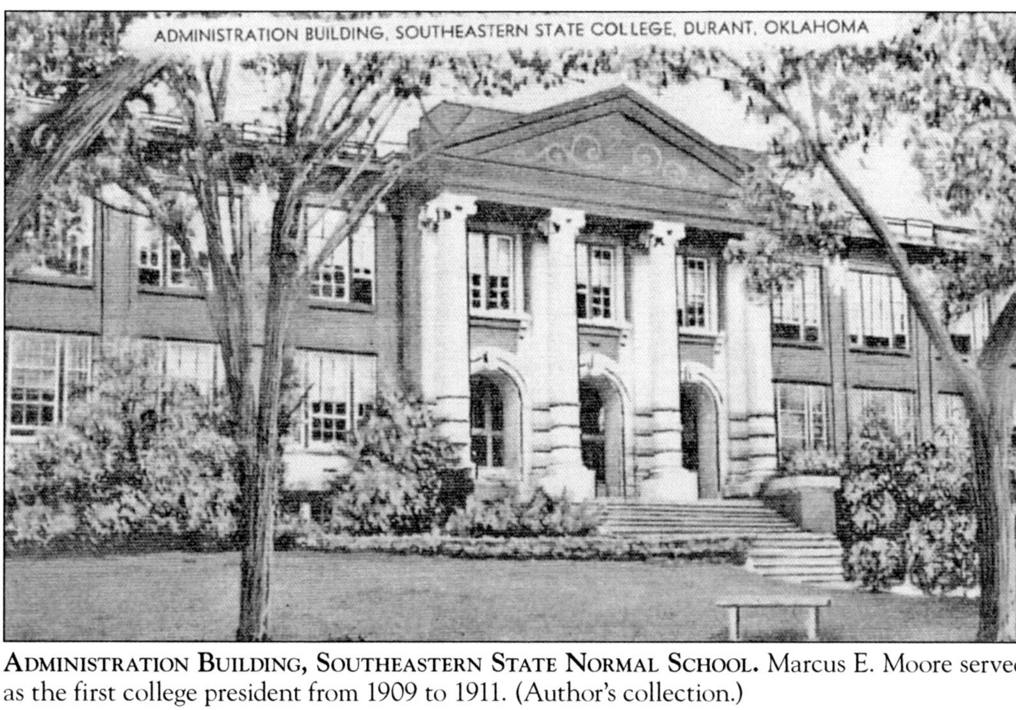

ADMINISTRATION BUILDING, SOUTHEASTERN STATE NORMAL SCHOOL. Marcus E. Moore served as the first college president from 1909 to 1911. (Author's collection.)

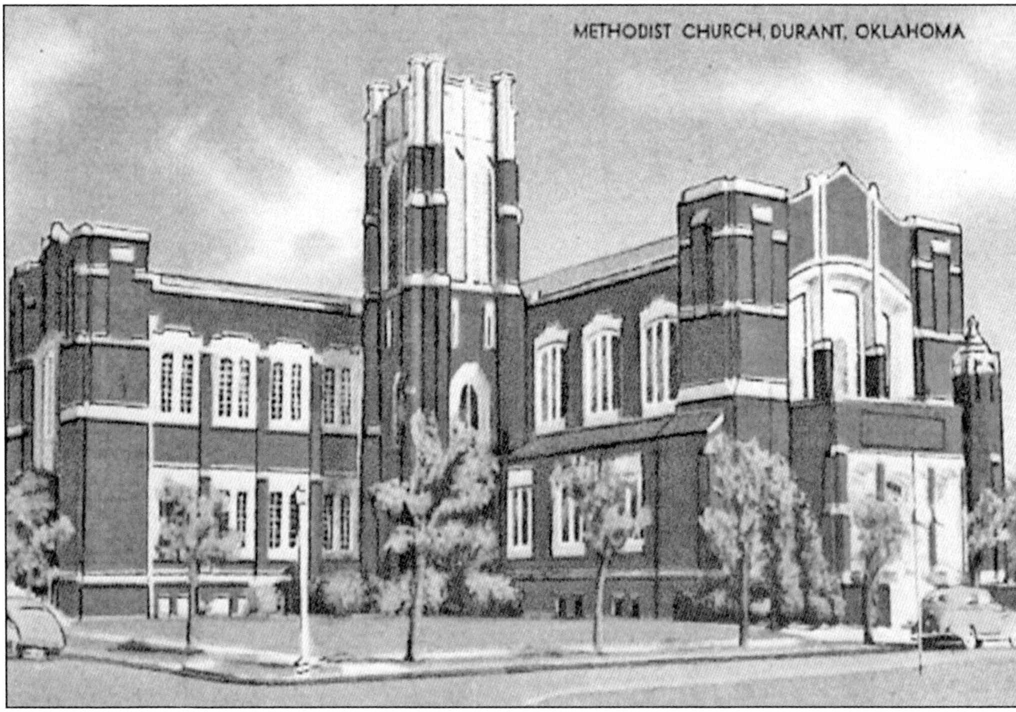

METHODIST CHURCH. A postcard depicts the Methodist Church in Durant. (Author's collection.)

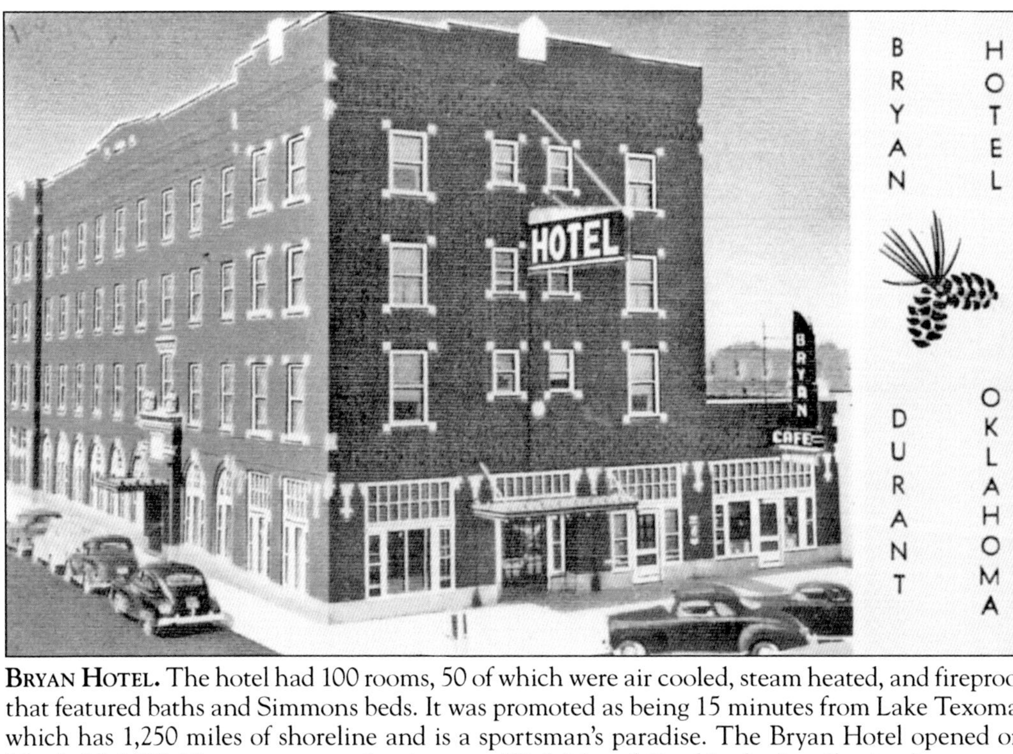

BRYAN HOTEL. The hotel had 100 rooms, 50 of which were air cooled, steam heated, and fireproof that featured baths and Simmons beds. It was promoted as being 15 minutes from Lake Texoma, which has 1,250 miles of shoreline and is a sportsman's paradise. The Bryan Hotel opened on March 25, 1929. The manager at the time was J.R. McLaughlin. (Author's collection.)

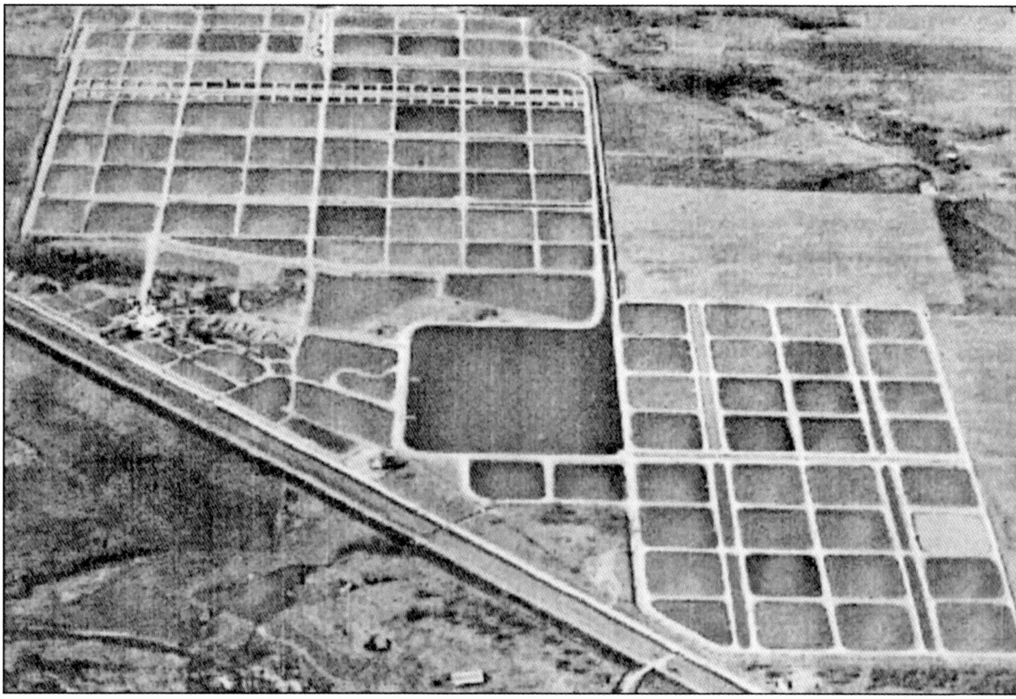

Durant State Fish Hatchery. The fish hatchery is located six miles north of Durant on Highway 69. Built in 1917 at Armstrong/Durant, this is one of four State Fish Hatcheries in Oklahoma. (Author's collection.)

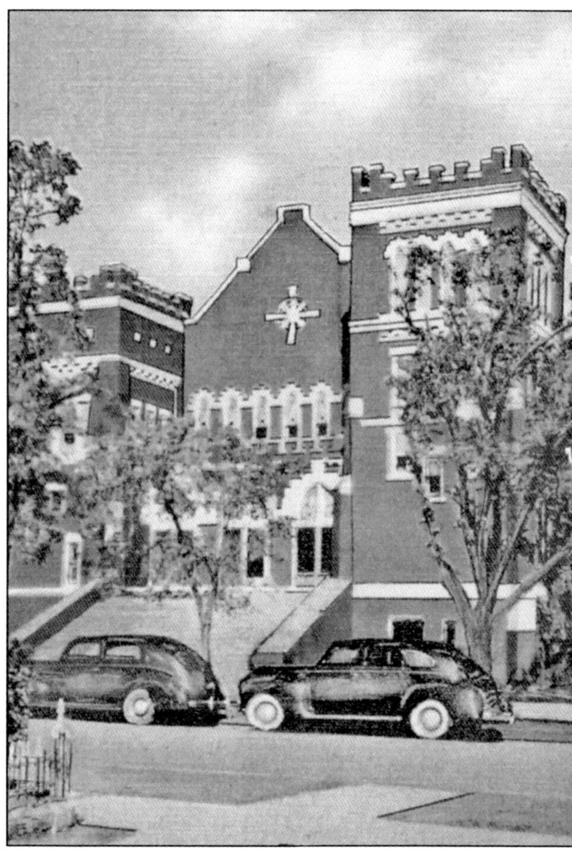

Presbyterian Church. This is the Presbyterian Church in Durant. (Author's collection.)

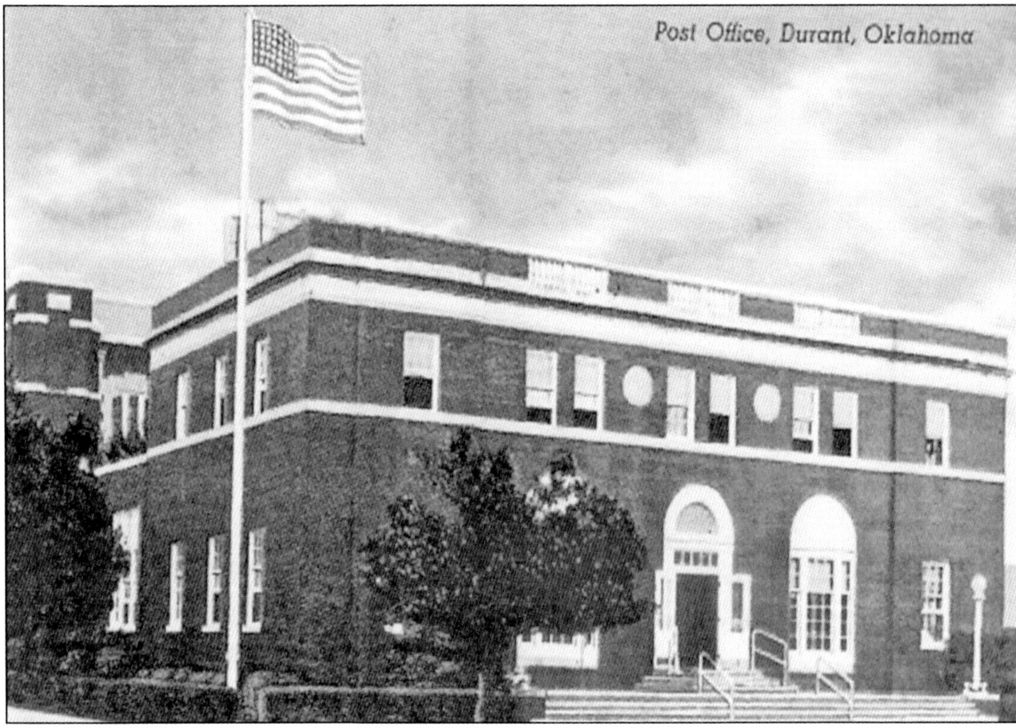

US Post Office. Durant's post office is pictured here. (Author's collection.)

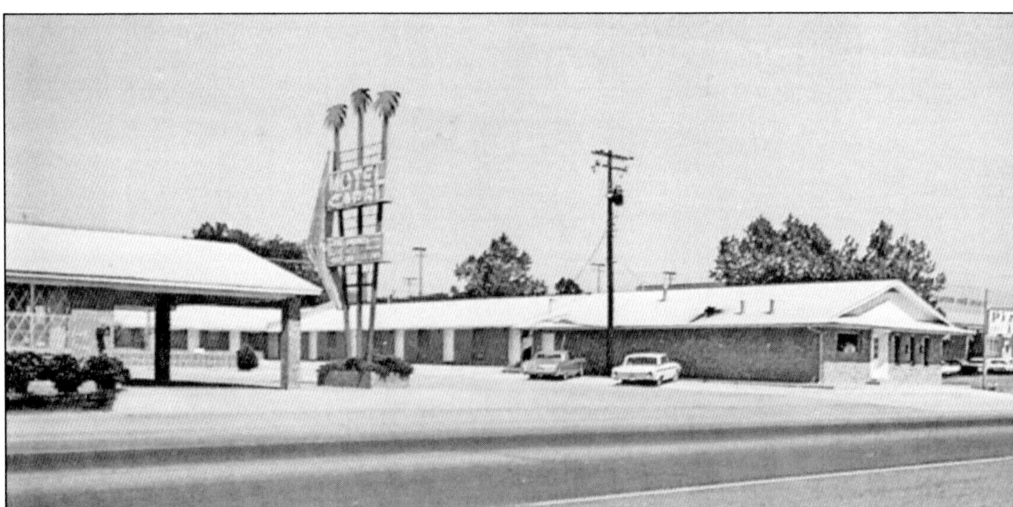

Motel Capri. The Capri Motel listed 37 units with wall-to-wall carpet, tile baths, air-conditioning, electric heating, a restaurant, and family rates. The owners were John and Tom Grider, and Bob and Betty Robbins were the managers. It was located at the junction of Highways 78 and 69 and 75 North in the heart of Texoma land. (Author's collection.)

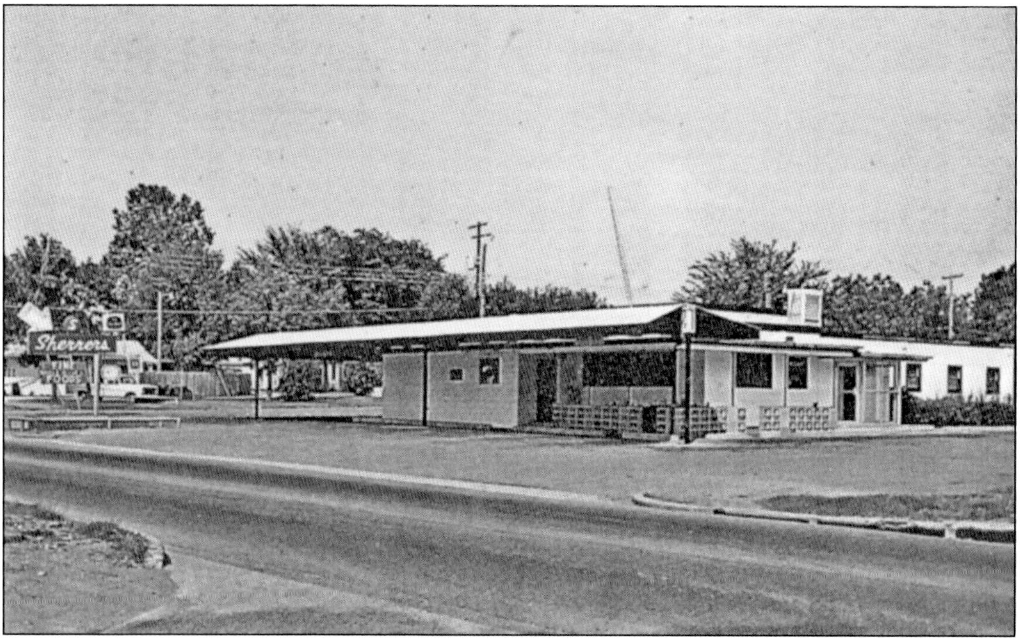

SHERRER'S FINE FOODS RESTAURANT. Owned and operated by Leon and Verta Sherrer, this restaurant boasts a large dining room, banquet facilities, and curb service; it is also newly redecorated. Fine food has been served at this location since 1948. (Author's collection.)

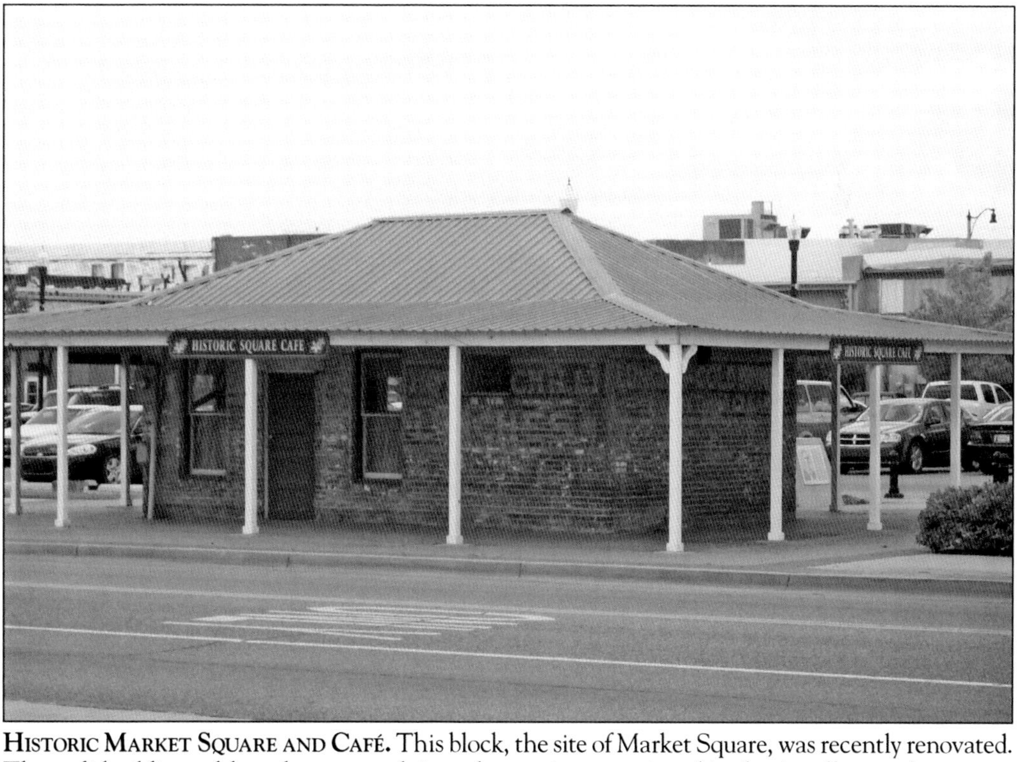

HISTORIC MARKET SQUARE AND CAFÉ. This block, the site of Market Square, was recently renovated. The café building, although preserved, is no longer in operation. (Author's collection.)

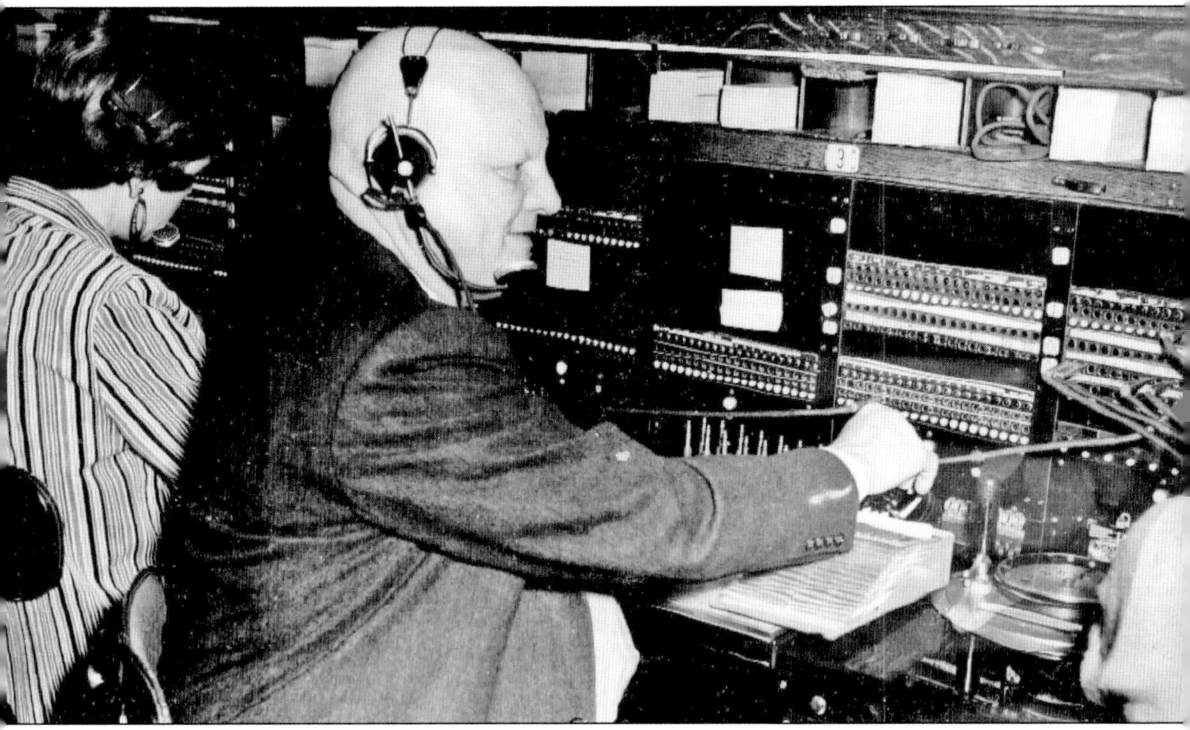

Southwestern Bell Telephone Company in Durant. Following World War II, Southwestern Bell Telephone Company installed a new switchboard that enabled operators to dial long-distance numbers for customers. Rector Swearengin, president of the Durant Chamber of Commerce, is pictured here putting through the first calls. He dialed a New York City number that played a recorded prayer and pep talk for the depressed and downhearted. (Courtesy of Matt Swearengin.)

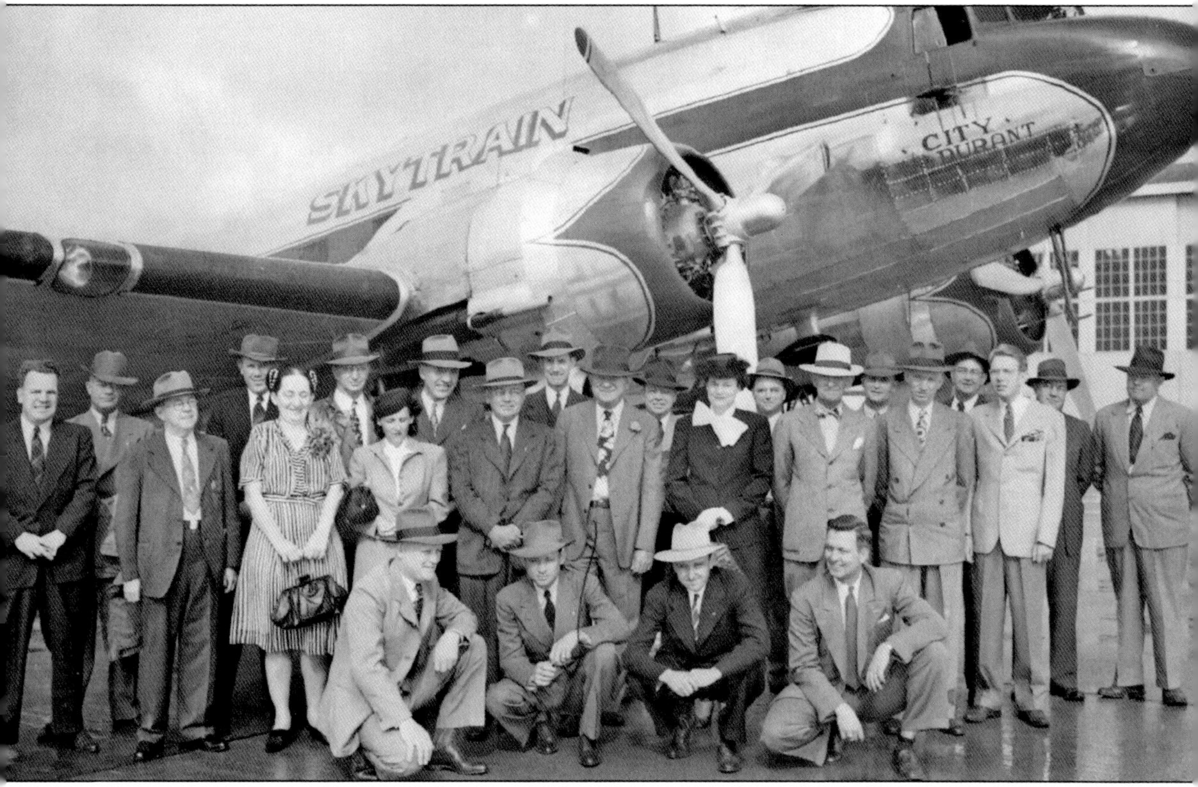

DC-3 Air Freight Transport. This image, dated April 4, 1946, captures a booster trip. Skytrain Air Express was owned by Ed McGee and Roy Paul, and the business was later moved to Tulsa. Pictured are, from left to right, (first row) Rector Swearengin, Garland Harper, Kay Bass, and Ed McGee; (second row) Roy David, C. Rowland, Anna Pappas, Mrs. Loy Fry, Allen Hill, S.W. McGee, Mrs. Frank Dyer, Frank Dyer, Miller Davidge, and Geo. Pendleton Jr.; (third row) David Bates, Jack Foote, Miller Pitts, P.L. Moore, O.W. Davison, Art Holmes, Roy Hamilton, R.W. Fleak, R.W. Reeves, Bennett Story, and Geo. Pendleton Sr. (Courtesy of Matt Swearengin.)

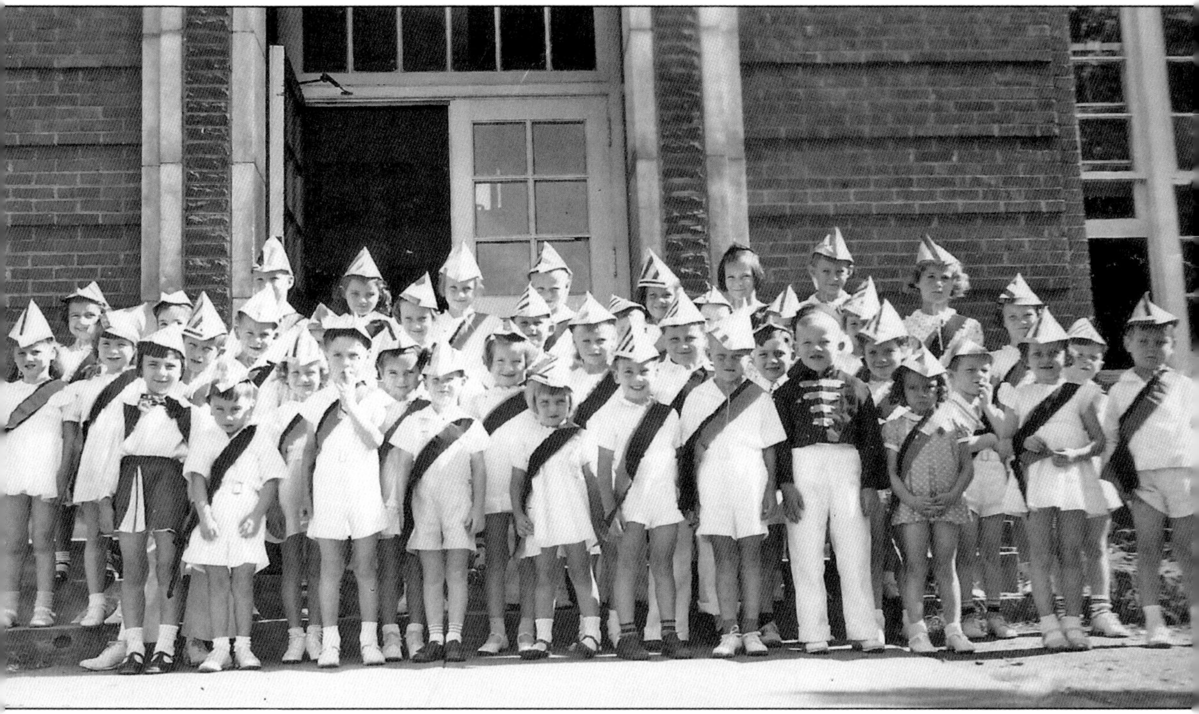

RHYTHM TRAINING BAND AND RUSSELL TRAINING SCHOOL. This group of kindergarten students from Russell Training School put on a program for the college assembly around the Fourth of July in 1940. Their teacher was Marion Severance, and among the students, Bob Swearengin was leader of the band (he had to turn around and bow when the audience clapped at the end of each number). Other students included Jerry Jo Mitchell, Gail Malahy, Bob and David Paul, Madge Fort, ? Stewart, Buddy Morris, Marylin Miller, Caroline Lee, Carol Morris, Patricia ? , Ann Arfstrom, and Bunky Clark. (Courtesy of Matt Swearengin.)

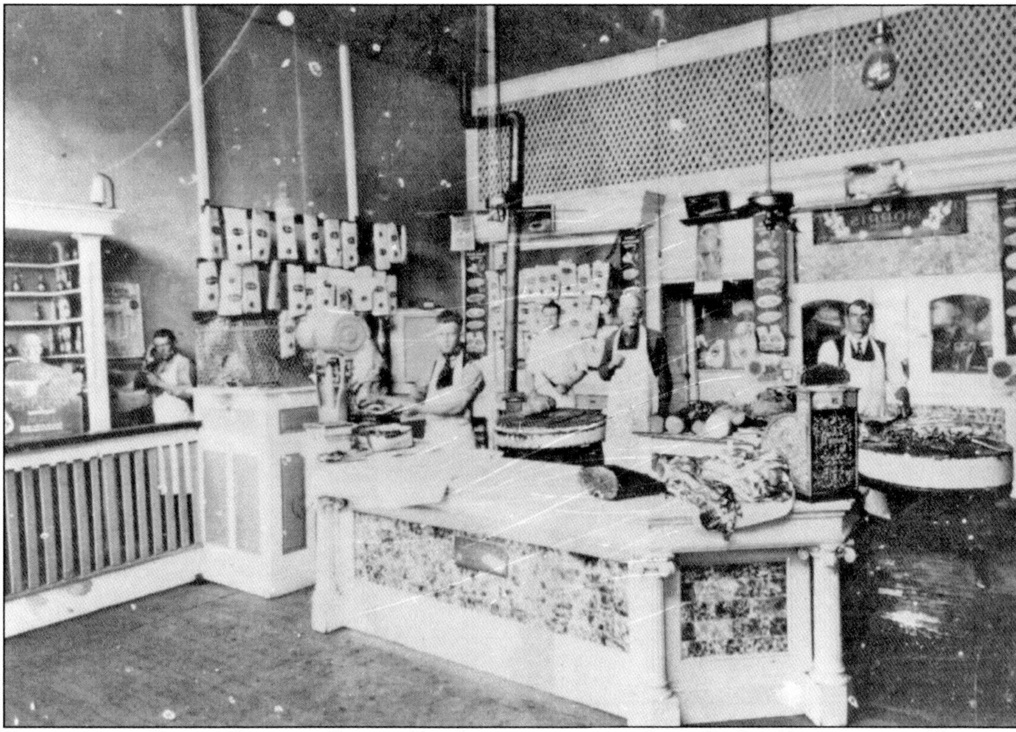

BUSINESSMEN INSIDE DURANT STORE. Employees are pictured inside this Durant store. (Courtesy of the *Durant Daily Democrat*.)

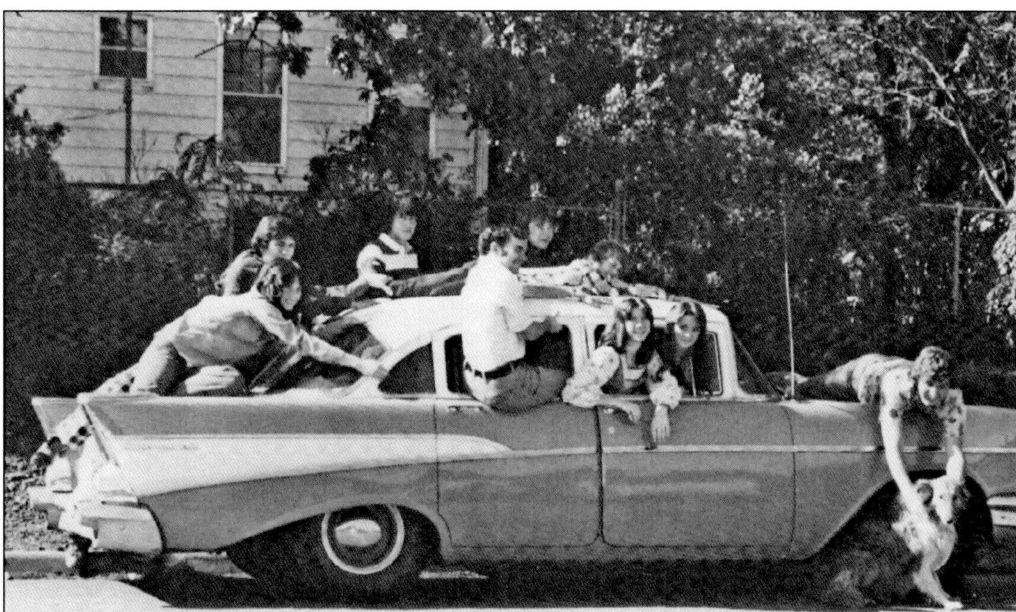

LIONS ROAR NEWSPAPER STAFF, MID-1970S. *Lions Roar* was the Durant High School newspaper. The staff included, from left to right, Lisa McMurry, Howard Williams, Tony Phillips, David Maze, David Pyrum, Robert Floyd, Sharon Castleberry, Sonya Morriss, and Mark Morrison. (Courtesy of the *Durant High School Lion*.)

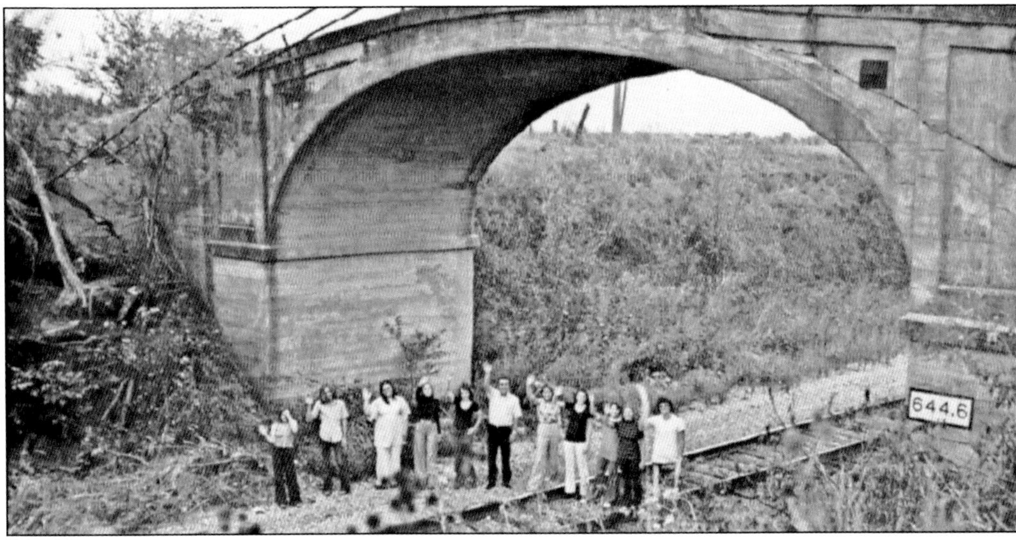

SOUTHEASTERN STUDENTS AT BRIDGE, MID-1970S. Pictured here are, from left to right, Sandy Wells, Cliff Ross, Kathy Grego, Ginny Decker, Lela Lyons, Ken Nichols, Sally Pennington, Candy Herron, Jill McPheron, Debby Nabors, and Rick Grubbs. (Courtesy of Southeastern Oklahoma State University.)

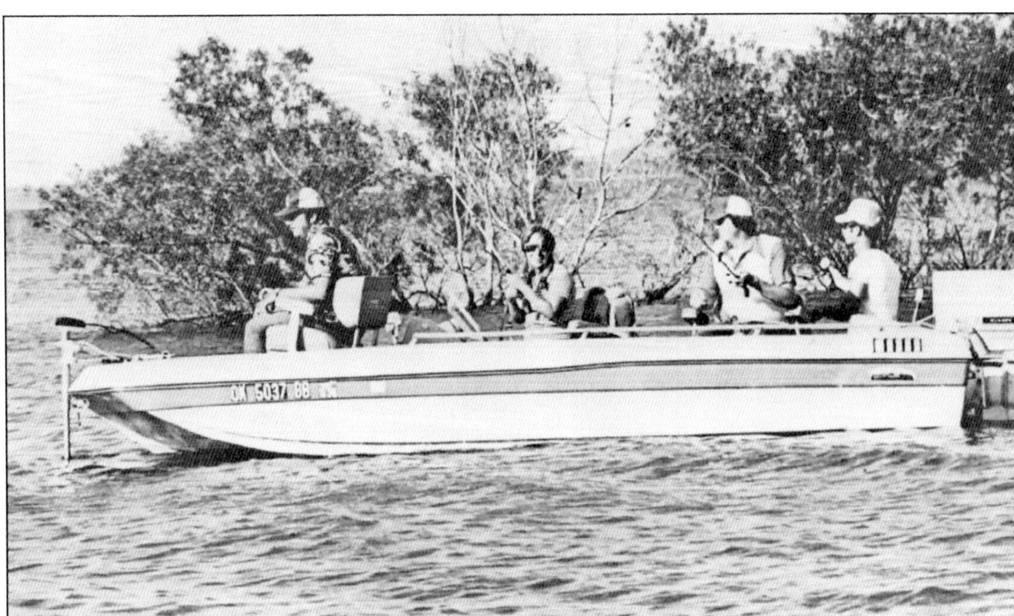

FISHING ON LAKE TEXOMA. Texoma offers premier striped bass fishing, which these four individuals seem to be enjoying. (Courtesy of Southeastern Oklahoma State University.)

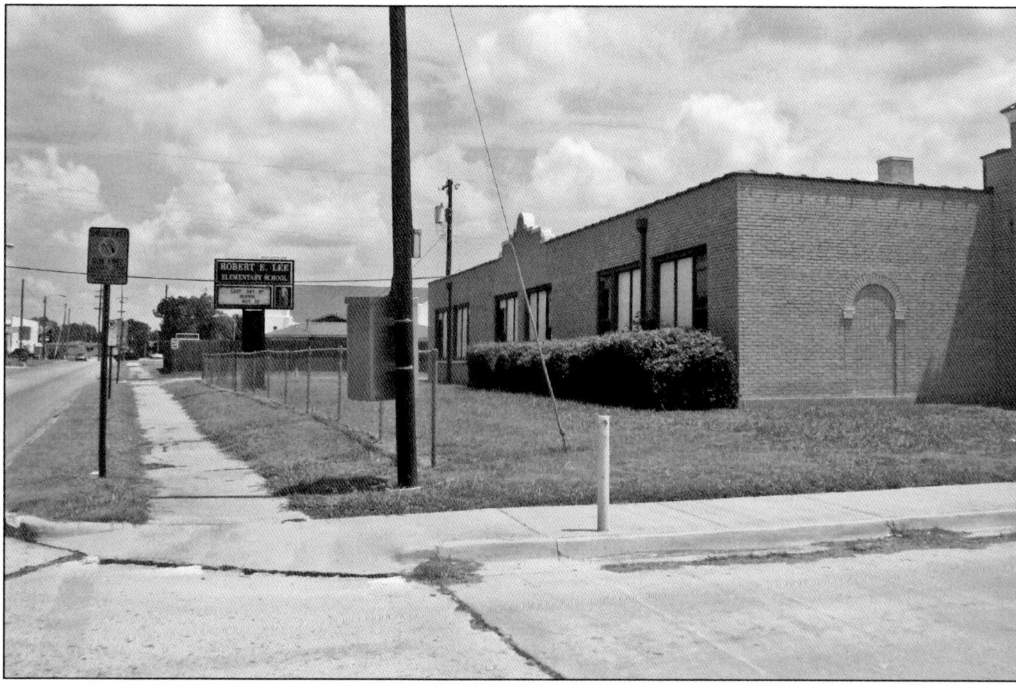

ROBERT E. LEE ELEMENTARY SCHOOL. This is Robert E. Lee Elementary School, located at 824 West Louisiana Street in Durant. (Author's collection.)

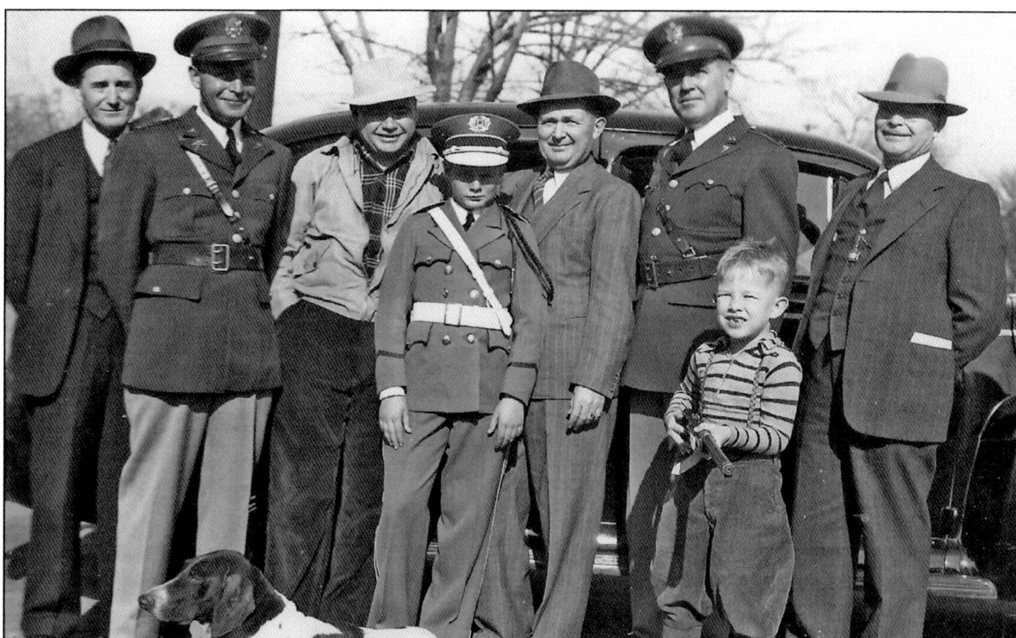

NATIONAL GUARD ACTIVATION. Pictured are, from left to right, Charlie Hodges, Ted Houk, Ted Shoemate, Billy Bob Houk, Willie Hall, Edward Williams, ? Houk, and Bob Swearengin; Queenie the dog can also be seen. This January 1941 photograph was taken in front of Houk's house. The 45th Division of the National Guard had been activated in September 1940. (Courtesy of Matt Swearengin.)

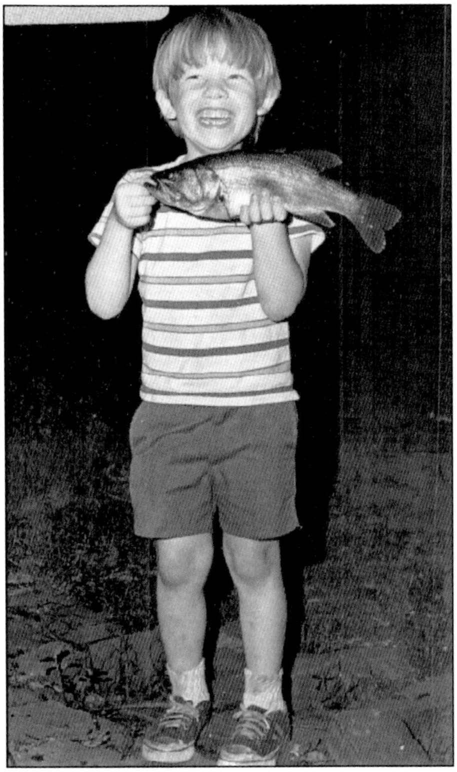

Matt Swearengin. Matt displays his prize bass in 1974. Today, he is the managing editor of the *Durant Daily Democrat*. (Courtesy of Matt Swearengin.)

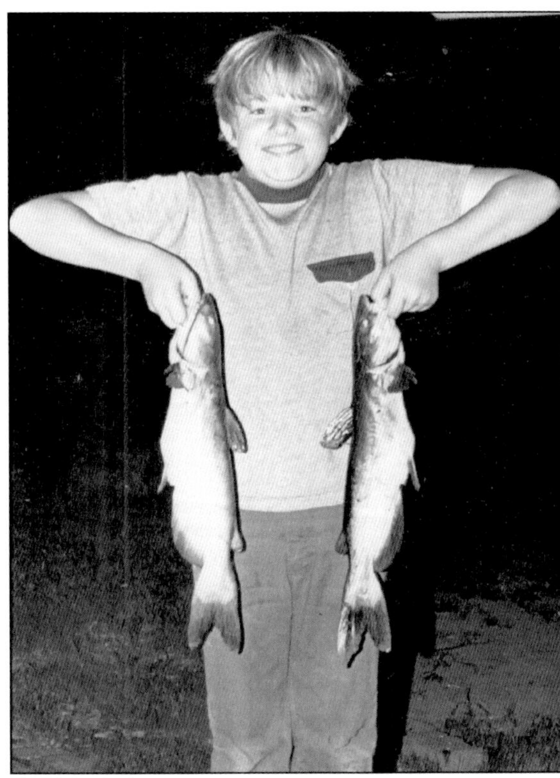

Mark Swearengin. Mark is holding two catfish in this 1974 photograph. (Courtesy of Matt Swearengin.)

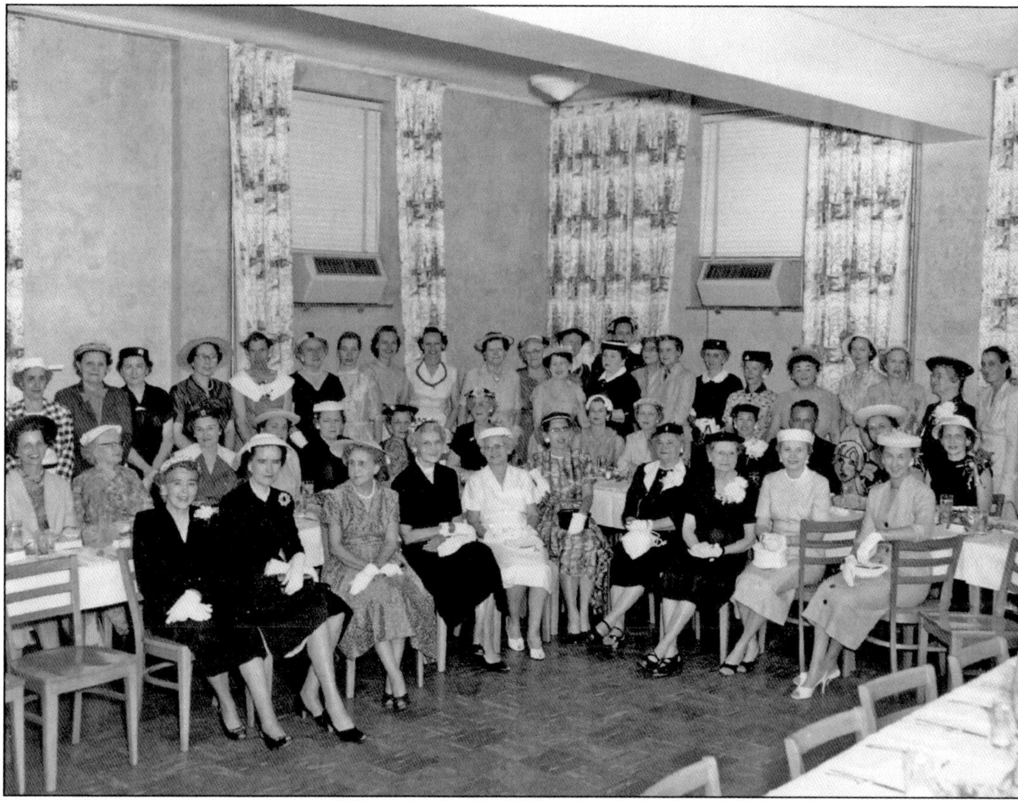

Fortnightly Club and Guests. Members and guests of the Fortnightly Club, a women's club, have gathered for this photograph in May 1956. (Courtesy of Matt Swearengin.)

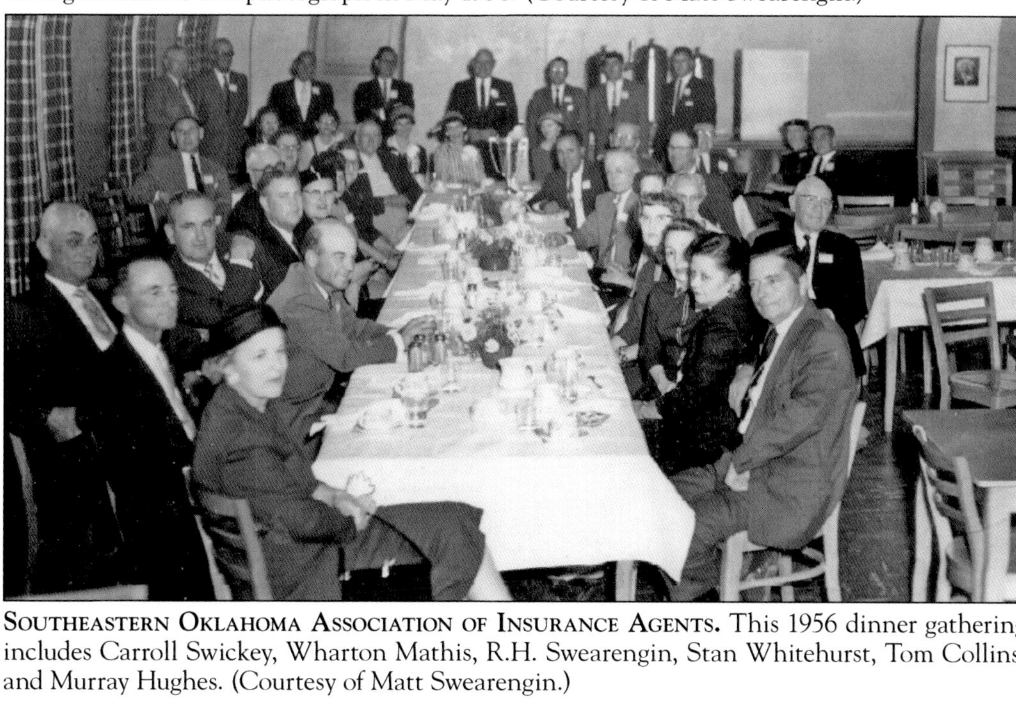

Southeastern Oklahoma Association of Insurance Agents. This 1956 dinner gathering includes Carroll Swickey, Wharton Mathis, R.H. Swearengin, Stan Whitehurst, Tom Collins, and Murray Hughes. (Courtesy of Matt Swearengin.)

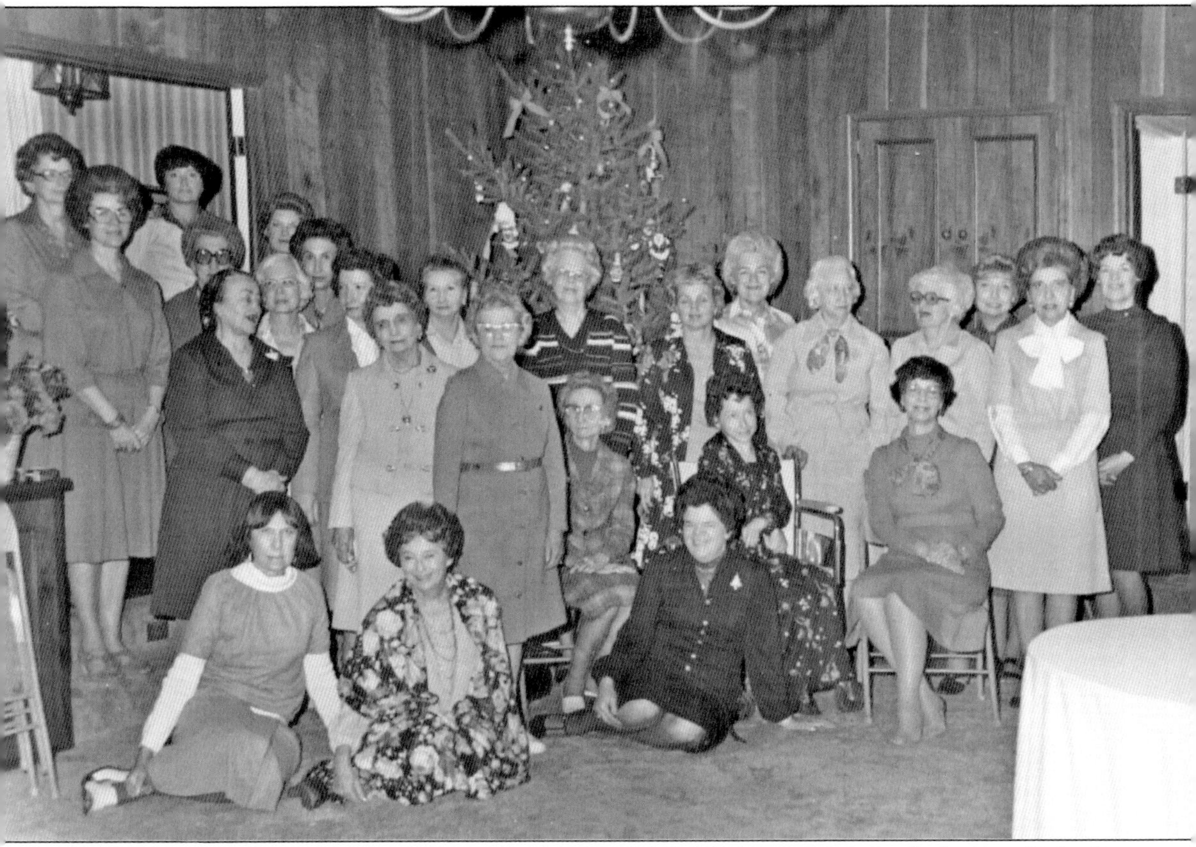

FORTNIGHTLY CLUB, DECEMBER 15, 1977. The club held this meeting at the home of Mrs. Joe Barker. Pictured from left to right are, (on the floor) Mrs. Fred Vorhies, Mrs. W.K. Young, and Mrs. T.G. Potter; (seated in chairs) Mrs. Floy P. Gates, Mrs. Joe Clay, and Doris H. Andrews; (standing, first row) Mrs. S.O. Pool, Mrs. John MacDonald, and Mrs. Bennett Story; (standing, second row) Mrs. Carl McCoy, Mrs. Charles Villines, Paula Platter, Mrs. A.E. Shearer, Mrs. Ben Gunter, Mrs. Ronald Ridgway (directly behind Mrs. Gunter), Mrs. George Morrow, Mrs. Bob Peterson, Mrs. Bob Davis, Mrs. E.C. Stribling, Mrs. Gordon Wright, Mrs. Ed Boynton, Flavia Swearengin, Mrs. George Carter, Emily Hill, Mrs. Arthur Alexander, and Mrs. Joe Barker. Absent are Mrs. Denton Anderson, Minnie Baker, Mrs. W.R. Bradford, Mrs. O.W. Brady, Mrs. John Carrington, Mrs. H.A. Hewett, Mrs. W.D. Manahan, Mrs. John A. Phillips, and Mrs. Herb Clark. (Courtesy of Matt Swearengin.)

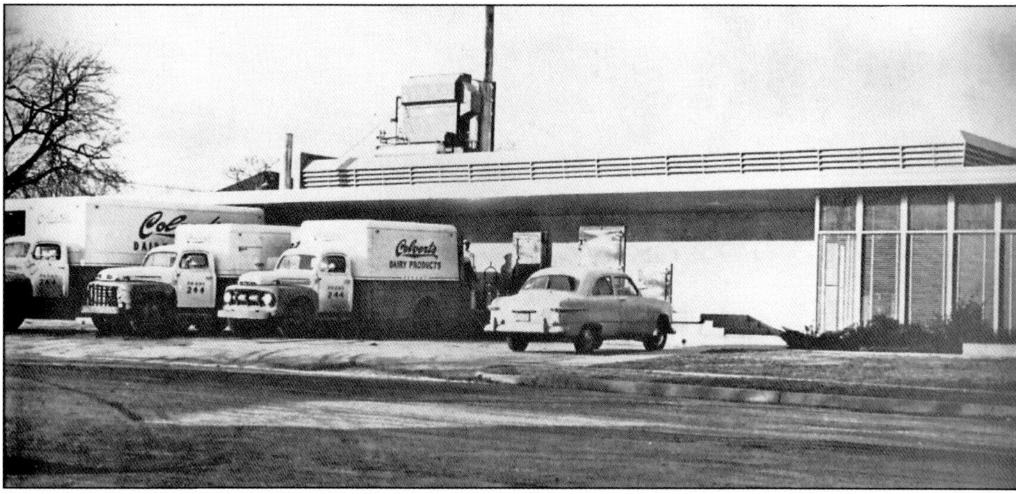

Colverts Dairy Products. This photograph was taken about 1958 as a promotion for Colverts and their fine ice cream, milk, and dairy products. (Courtesy of Southeastern Oklahoma State University.)

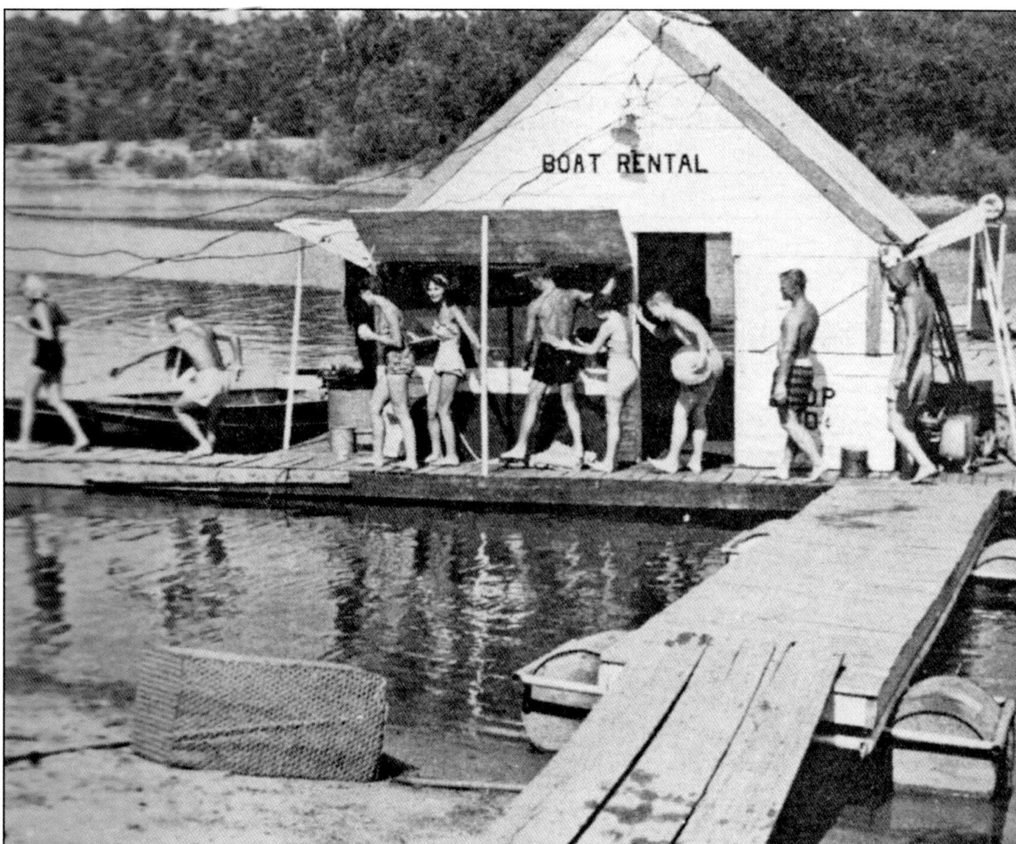

Boat Rental Dock. Young men and women are enjoying recreation time on the water at the boat rental dock. (Courtesy of Southeastern Oklahoma State University.)

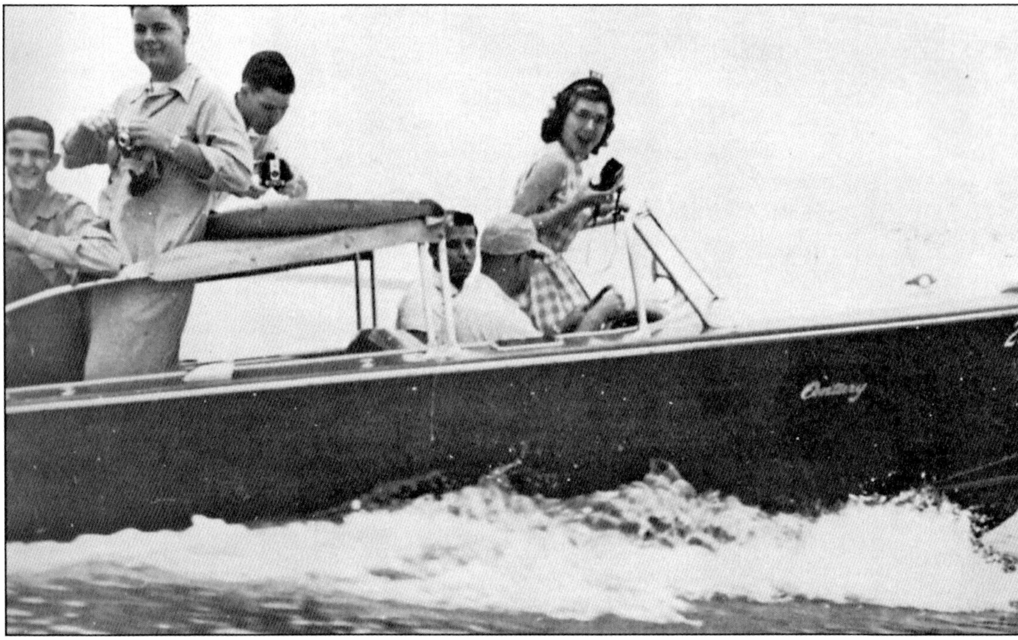

SOUTHEASTERN STUDENTS BOATING. These students are pictured enjoying a boat ride on the lake around 1955. (Courtesy of Southeastern Oklahoma State University.)

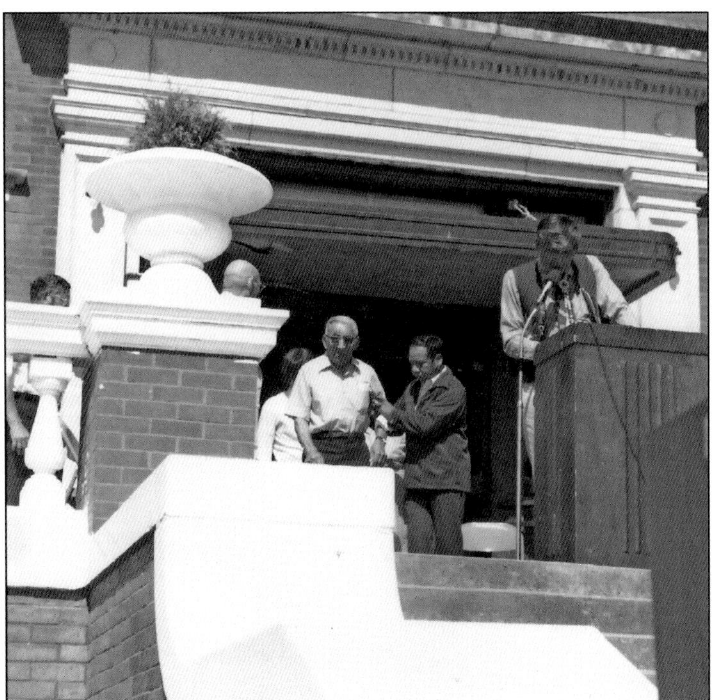

CHIEF GARDNER AT CHOCTAW NATION FOR OKLAHOMA DEDICATION. Choctaw chief Clark David Gardner addresses attendees on August 17, 1976, at the Oklahoma Presbyterian College. The title of ownership for the site was transferred to the tribe, which began a major renovation project. The location evolved into one of the finest tribal headquarters in the United States. Rector Swearengin, who served as the master of ceremonies for the event, is visible to the right of the large white flower vase. (Courtesy of Matt Swearengin.)

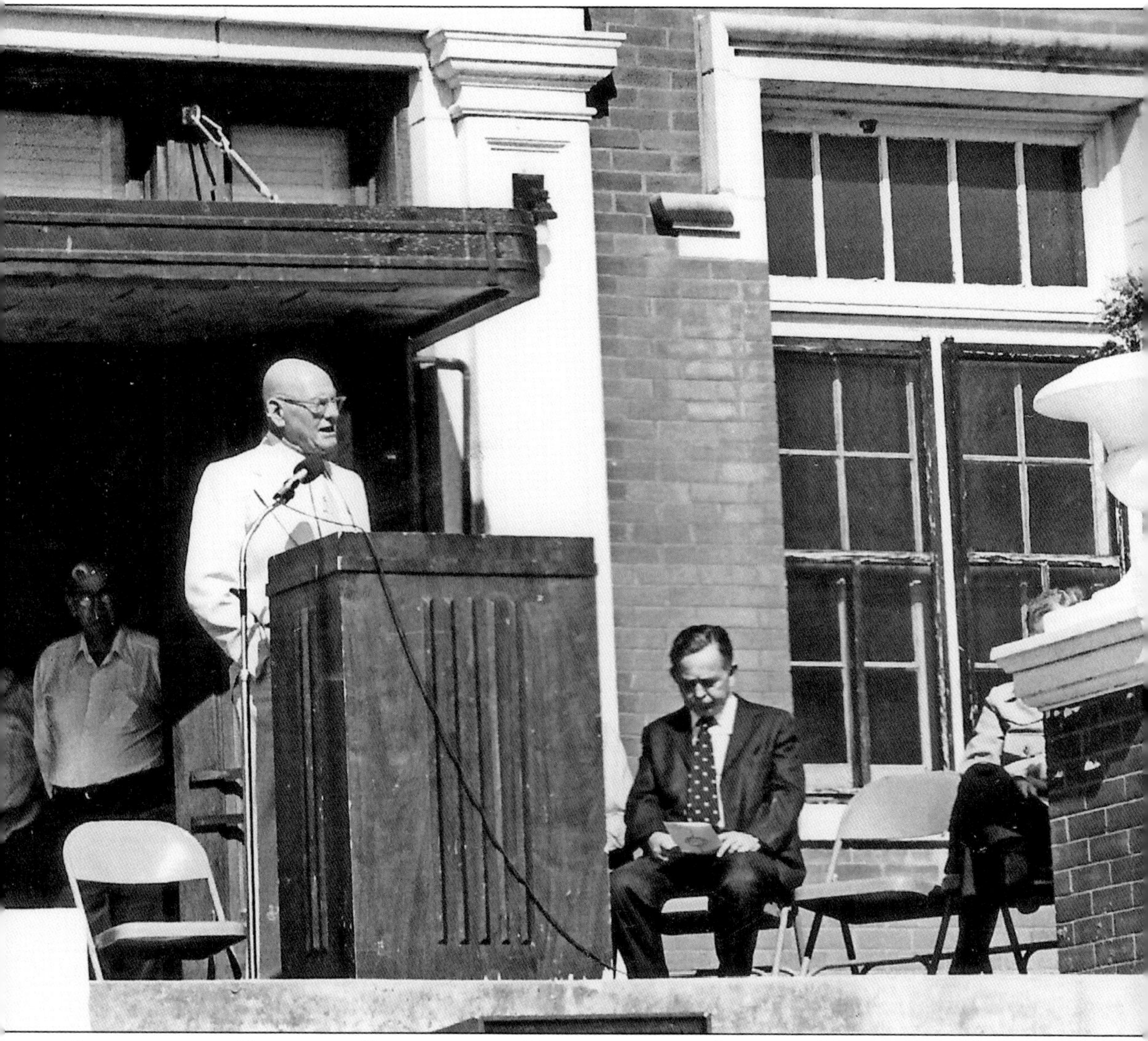

Dedication of Oklahoma Presbyterian College to the Choctaw Nation. A dedication was held for the Choctaw Nation of Oklahoma as they received the OPC building on August 17, 1976. Rector Swearengin is the master of ceremonies; Carl Albert, Chas. Ward, Choctaw chief David Gardner, and the author also attended the event. (Courtesy of Matt Swearengin.)

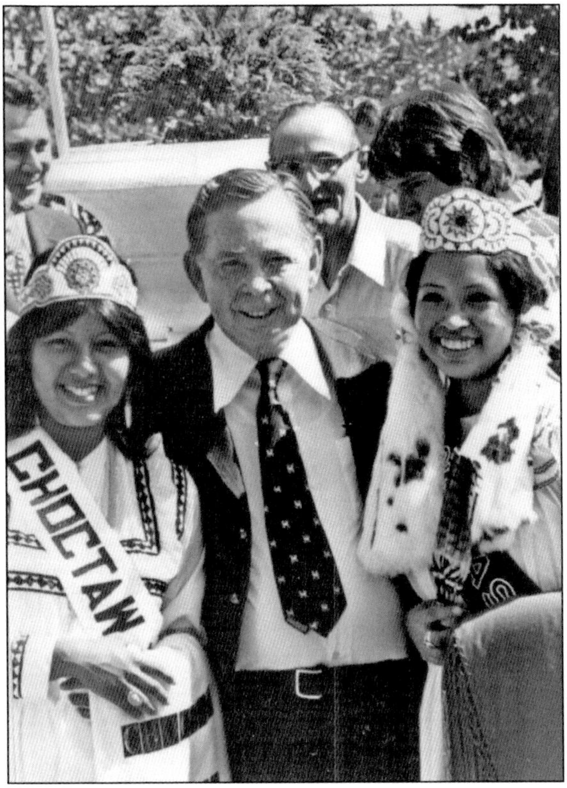

US CONGRESSMAN AND US SPEAKER OF THE HOUSE, CARL ALBERT. Congressman and Speaker of the House Carl Albert is shown here with two Choctaw princesses; Jerry Steakley is standing behind him. They are attending the dedication of the Oklahoma Presbyterian College building to the Choctaw Nation on August 17, 1976. (Courtesy of Matt Swearengin.)

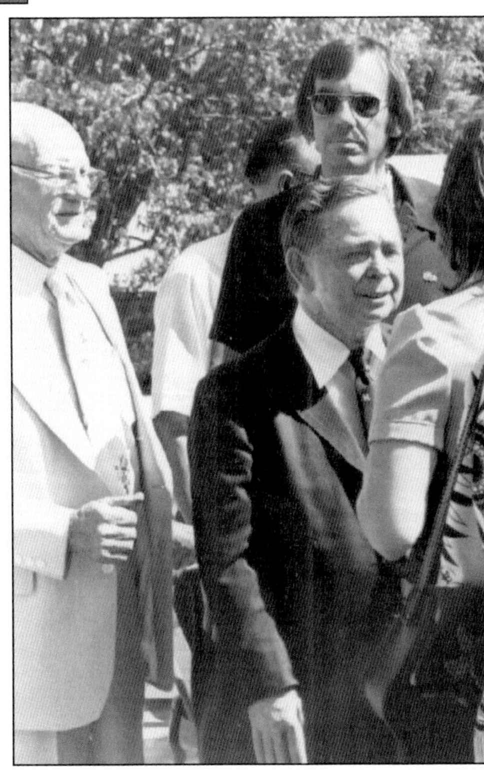

RECTOR SWEARENGIN (LEFT) AND CONGRESSMAN CARL ALBERT. This is another image from the 1976 Choctaw Nation dedication. (Courtesy of Matt Swearengin.)

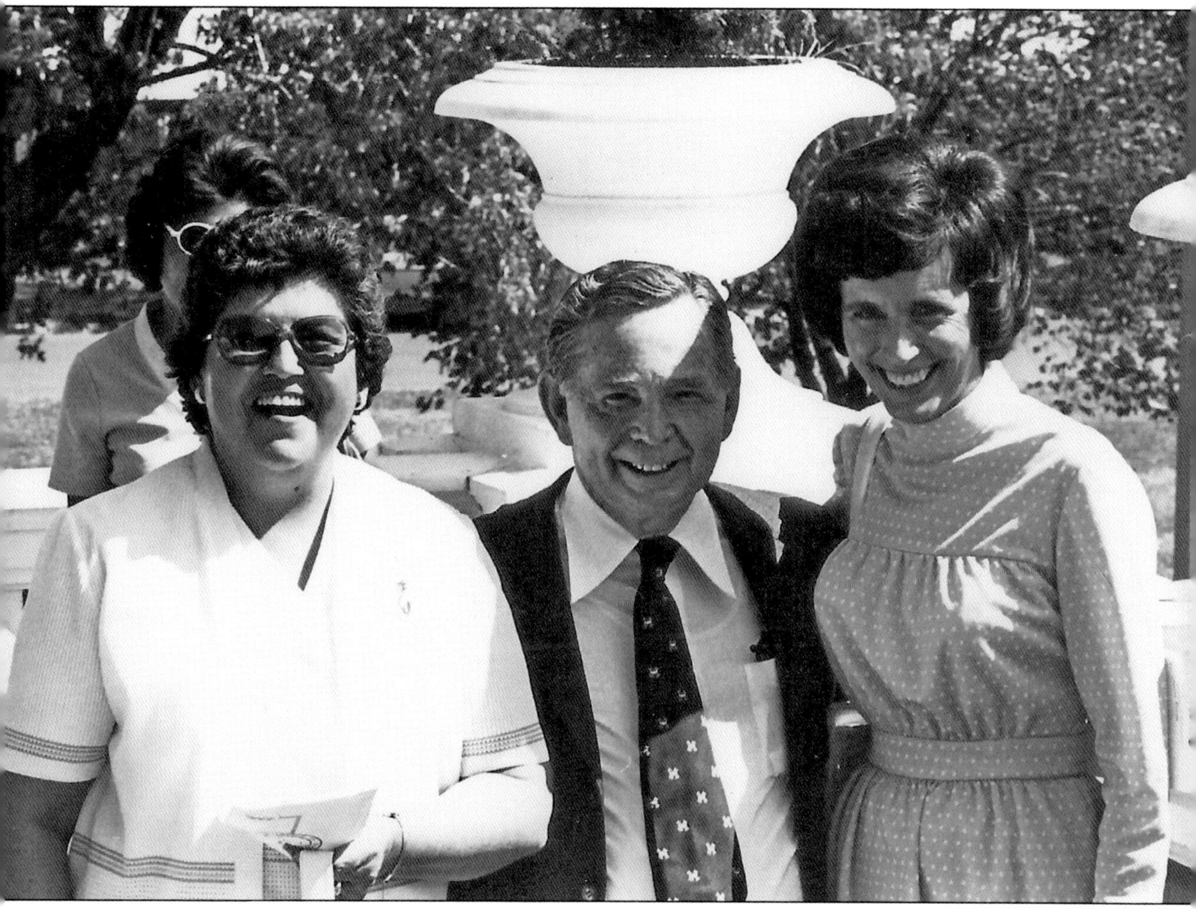

Carl Albert and Friends. This photograph was also taken at the Choctaw Nation dedication of the OPC building in 1976. (Courtesy of Matt Swearengin.)

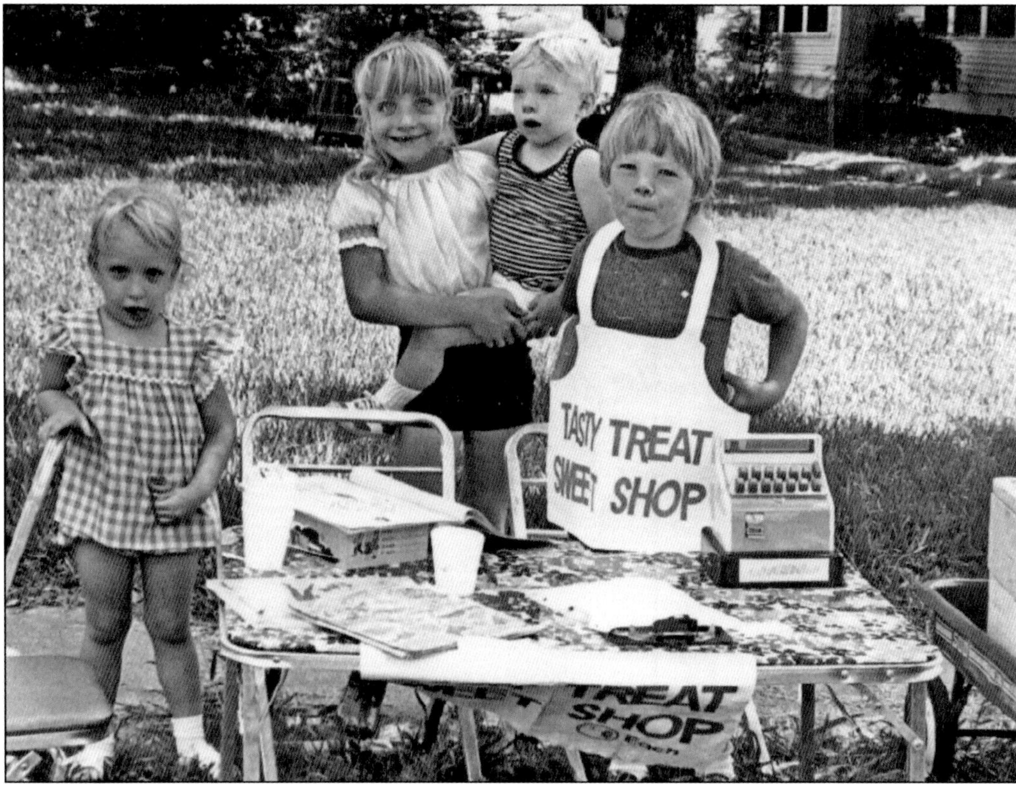

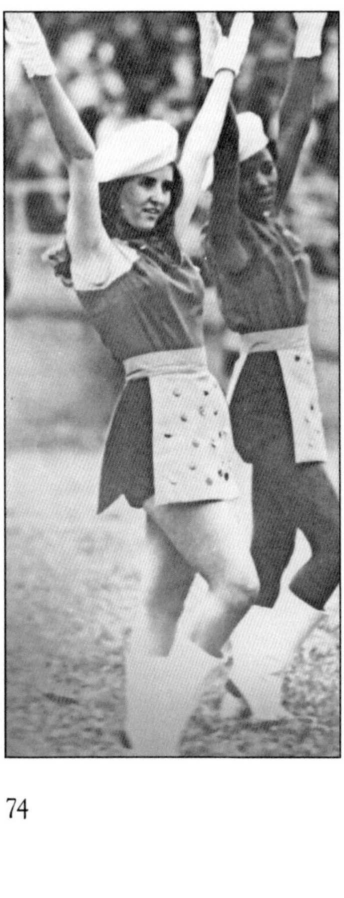

Tasty Treats Sweet Shop with Matthew Swearengin and Friends. This photograph of the Tasty Treat Sweet Shop was taken in Durant in the summer of 1974. Pictured with Matt Swearengin (wearing the apron) are possibly Tracy Bond and Brian Bond. (Courtesy of Matt Swearengin.)

Southeastern State College Drill Team, around 1969. Pictured are Kathi Stansel (left) and Clommer Ellis taking part in homecoming activities. (Courtesy of Southeastern Oklahoma State University.)

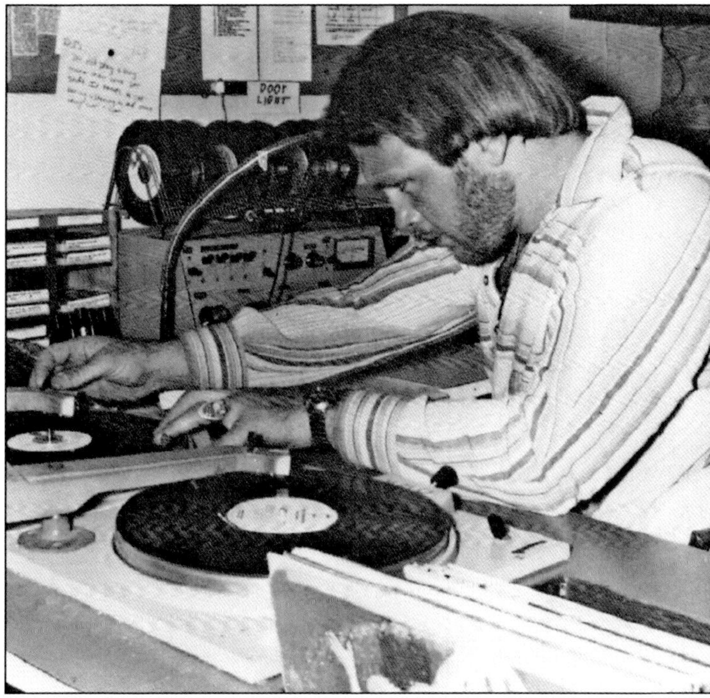

Disc Jockey. A college DJ spins the vinyl for radio listeners. (Courtesy of Southeastern Oklahoma State University.)

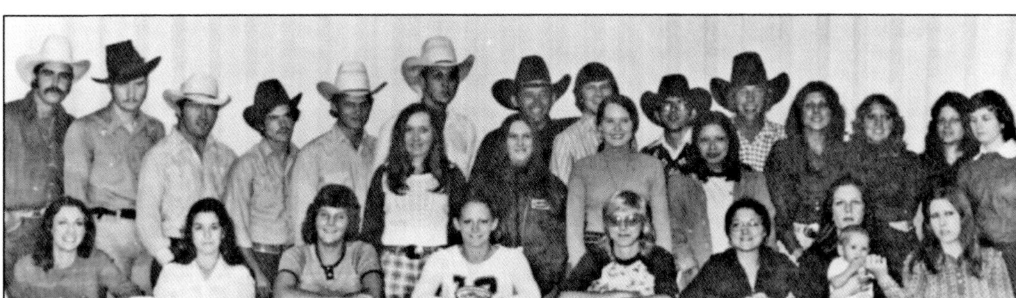

Southeastern Rodeo Club. This is the 1975 Rodeo Club. Pictured among the group are Decca Carter, Mary Nell Ballard, Beth Crump, Reba McEntire (future country music star, first row center), Toni Echelle, Mary McCoy, Vennessa ? , Jean ? , Sandy Underwood, Janet Rose, Pat Baken, John ? , Vernon Brock, Ron Bishop, Sherman Southerd, Shorty ? , Bob Shillings, Phil Whisenhunt, Ron Smith, Wayne Cassidy, Linda Cassidy, Lois ? , and Charmel Blount. (Courtesy of Southeastern Oklahoma State University.)

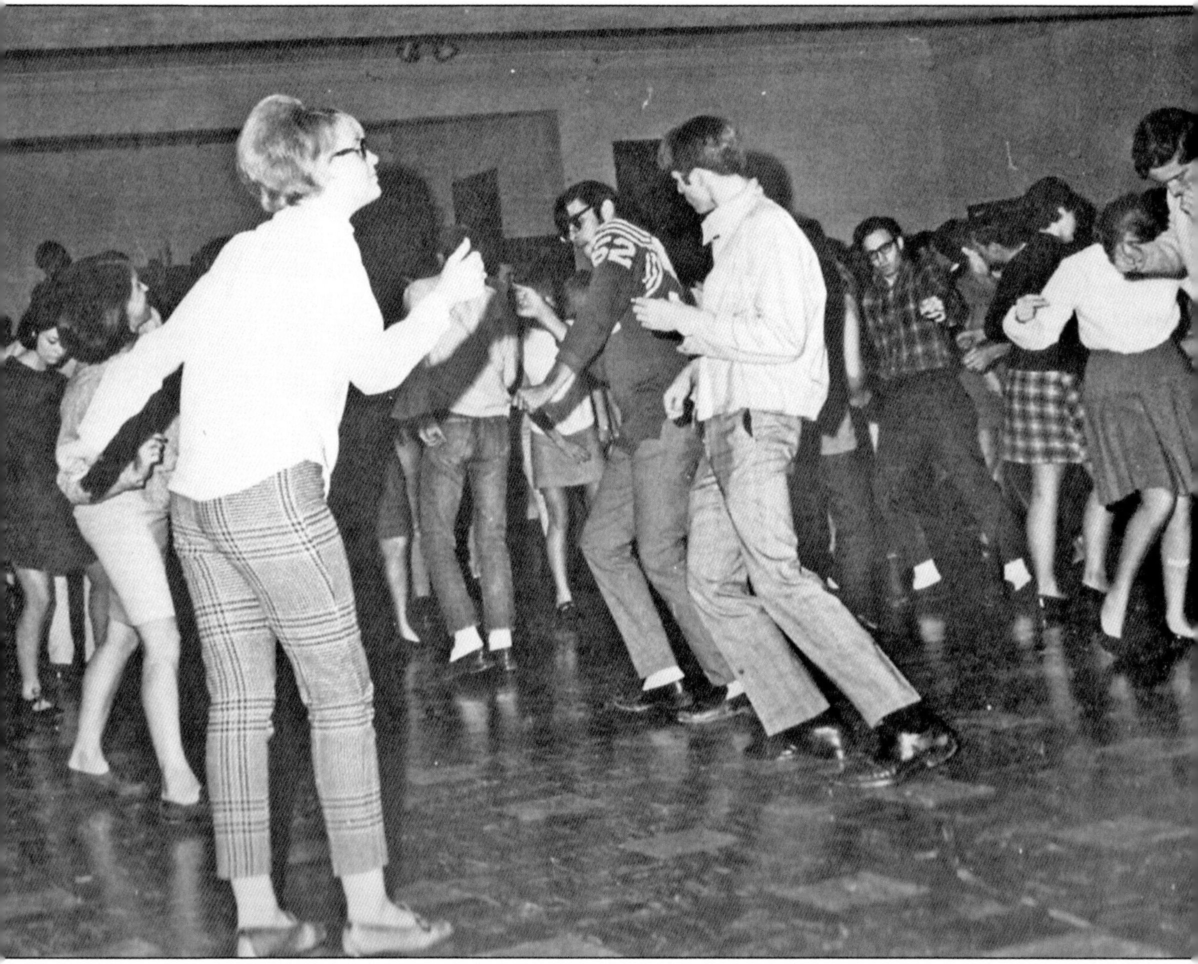

Southeastern State College. The disc-jockey student organization sponsored weekly music, including the dance pictured here. One of the bands, the Excentrics, was from Ardmore, Oklahoma. (Courtesy of Southeastern Oklahoma State University.)

Three

New Business, Culture, and Education

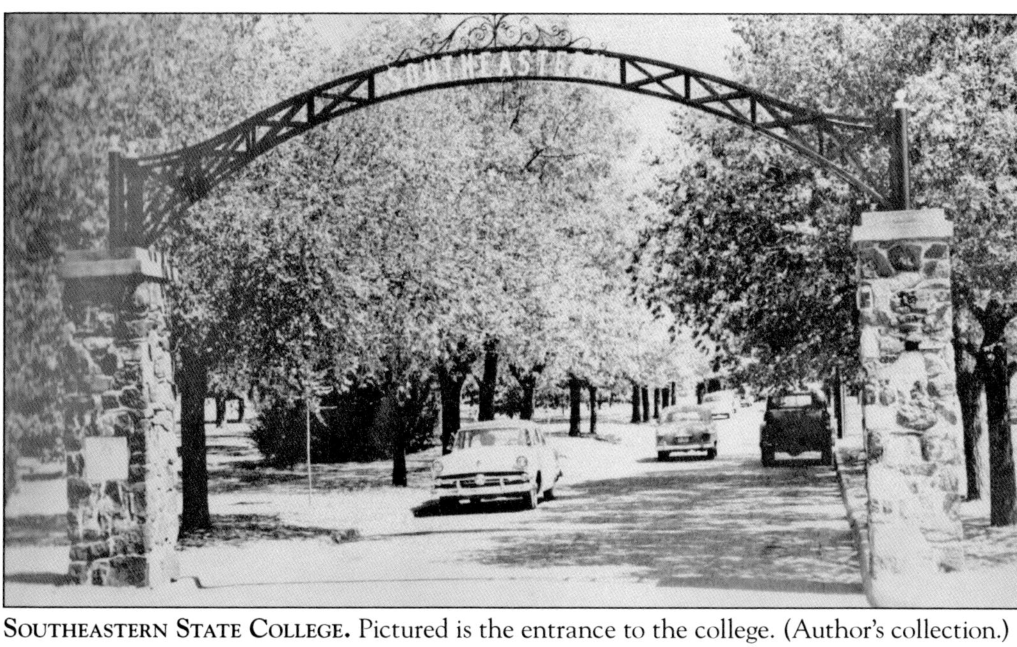

Southeastern State College. Pictured is the entrance to the college. (Author's collection.)

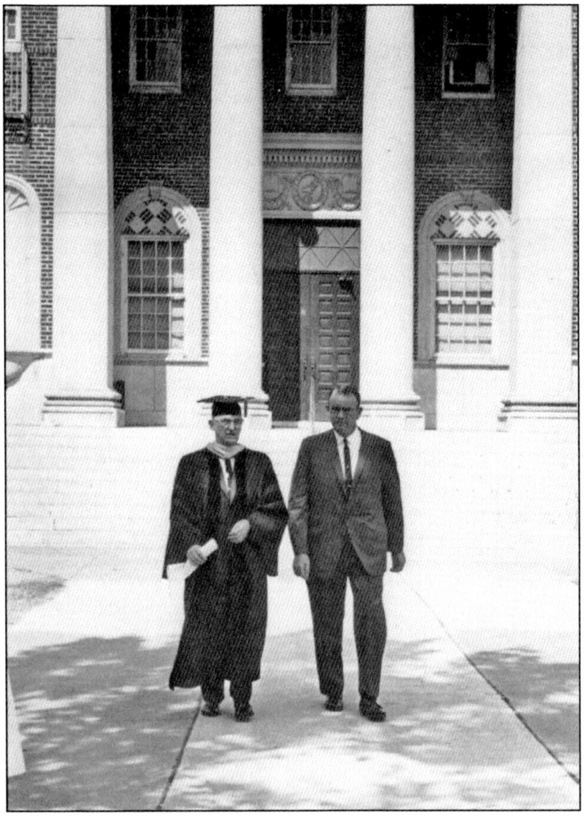

Dr. Allen Shearer and Oklahoma Governor Henry Bellmon. Dr. Shearer (left), the 13th president of Southeastern State College, walks down the steps of the library with Oklahoma governor Henry Bellmon in the 1960s. (Courtesy of Southeastern Oklahoma State University.)

Aerial View of Southeastern State College. This is Southeastern State College as seen from above. (Courtesy of Southeastern Oklahoma State University.)

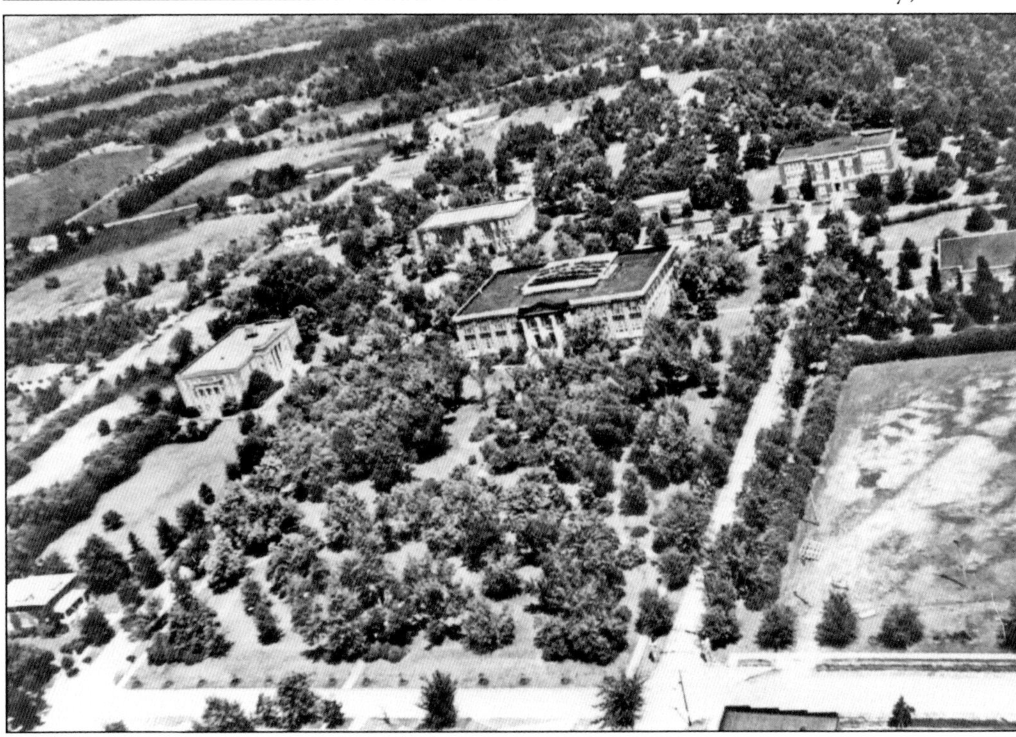

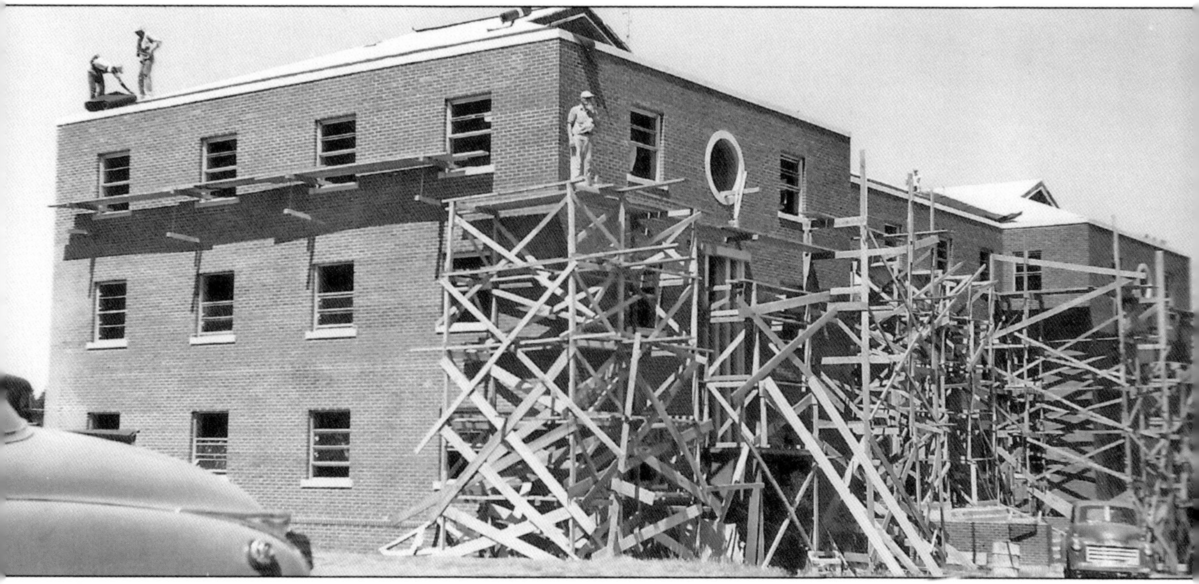

SHEARER HALL UNDER CONSTRUCTION. Shearer Hall is under construction in this 1955 photograph. This Southeastern State College dormitory was torn down sometime in the 2000s, and a new dorm by the same name was dedicated in 2006. (Courtesy of Matt Swearengin.)

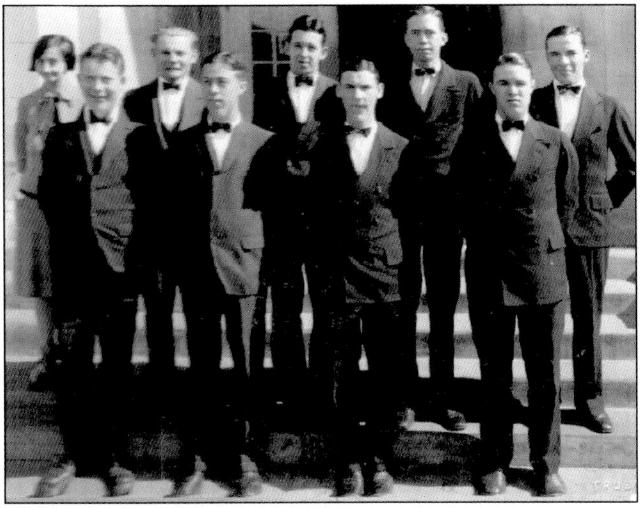

DURANT HIGH SCHOOL DOUBLE QUARTETTE, 1927–1928. Pictured here are, from left to right, (first row) Sam Sullivan, Pat Wade, Jack Pratt, and Frank Fuller; (second row) Hazel Bartheld (teacher), Rector Swearengin, Otis Donoho, Fred Lowry Jr., and B.C. Newberry. The group sang all over Oklahoma on goodwill tours and won first place in state contests. Rector Swearengin was a bass in quartettes and glee clubs during high school and college. (Courtesy of Matt Swearengin.)

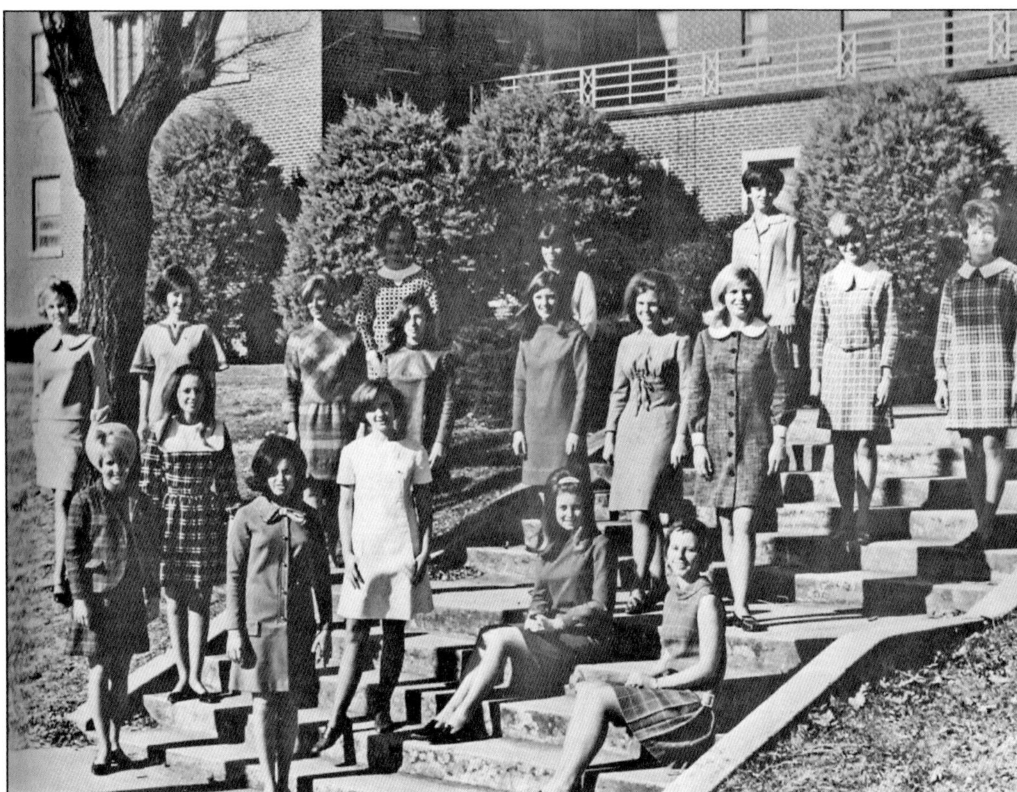

SOUTHEASTERN STATE COLLEGE, SIGMA KAPPA, LATE 1960S. This campus sorority performed community service projects. Members Linda Hayes, Cheryl Kilpatrick, Judy McNabb, and Joan Wilson were named to *Who's Who Among Students.* (Courtesy of Southeastern Oklahoma State University.)

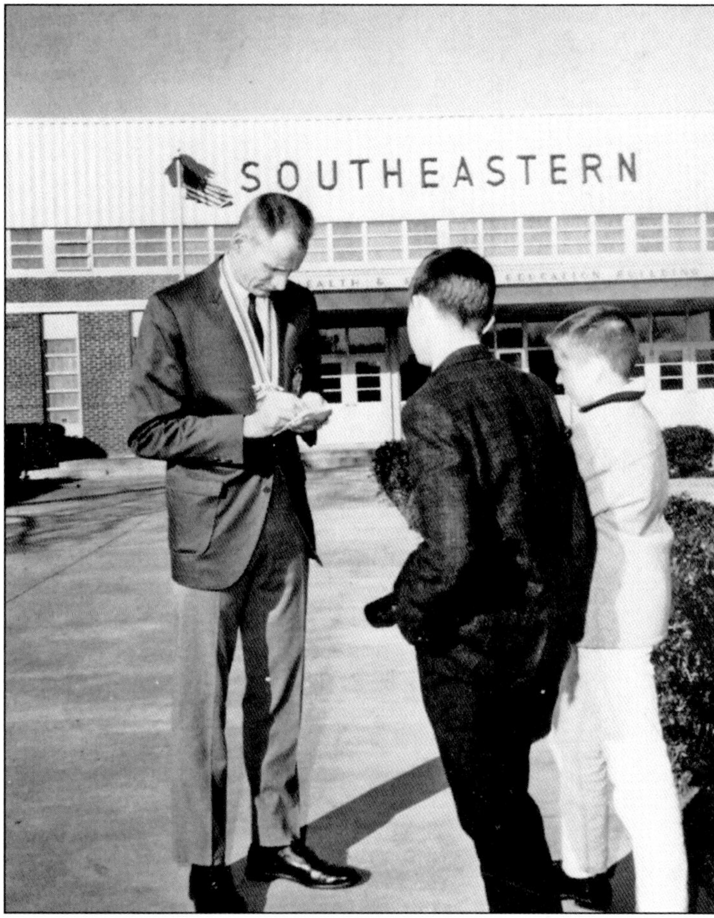

JERRY SHIPP, OLYMPIC ATHLETE. Basketball player Jerry Shipp, who won an Olympic gold medal, returned to the Southeastern State College campus in the mid-1960s. Here he is seen signing autographs for two admiring youngsters. Shipp is a 1959 graduate of the school. (Courtesy of Southeastern Oklahoma State University.)

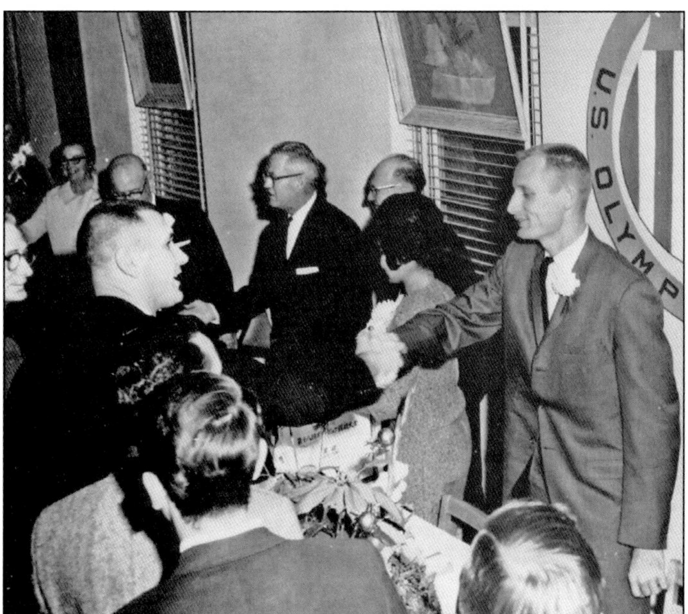

OLYMPIAN JERRY SHIPP AT SOUTHEASTERN. Here, Shipp is greeted at a banquet held in his honor. Jerry was from neighboring Blue, Oklahoma, and starred on the Savage basketball teams from1954 to 1959 under legendary coach Bloomer Sullivan. Shipp graduated from the college in 1959 and is a member of several halls of fame, including those of the National Association of Intercollegiate Athletics (NAIA), the Jim Thorpe Association, and Southeastern Oklahoma State University. (Courtesy of Southeastern Oklahoma State University.)

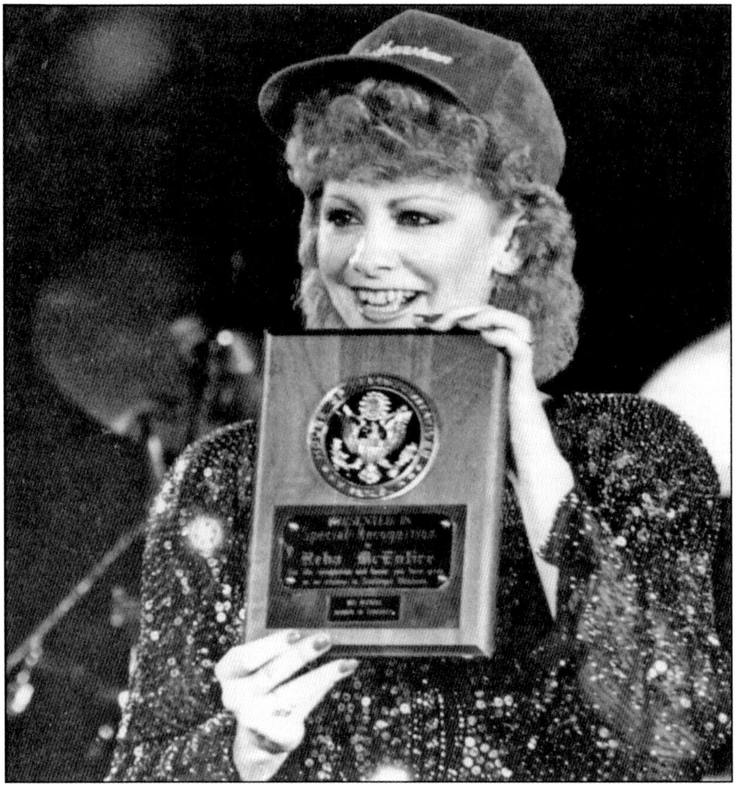

Reba McEntire. Country music superstar Reba McEntire attended Southeastern Oklahoma State University. She was born in McAlester, Oklahoma, and grew up on the family ranch in tiny Chockie in Atoka County. McEntire graduated from Kiowa High School in 1973 and earned a bachelor's degree in elementary education, with a minor in music, from Southeastern in 1976 (while working family land at nearby Caddo). The university honored her with its Distinguished Alumni Award in 1985. (Courtesy of Southeastern Oklahoma State University.)

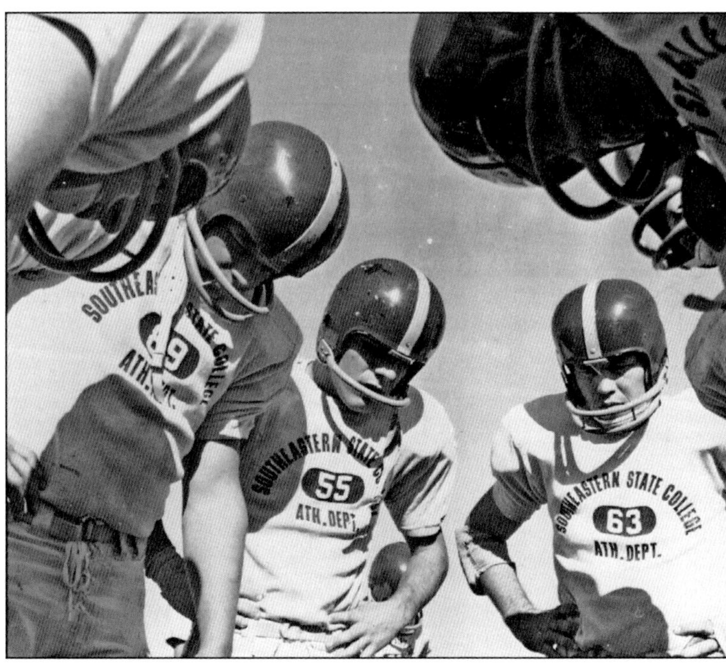

Southeastern State College Football Team. Pictured here is the Southeastern State College football team in a huddle. (Courtesy of Southeastern Oklahoma State University.)

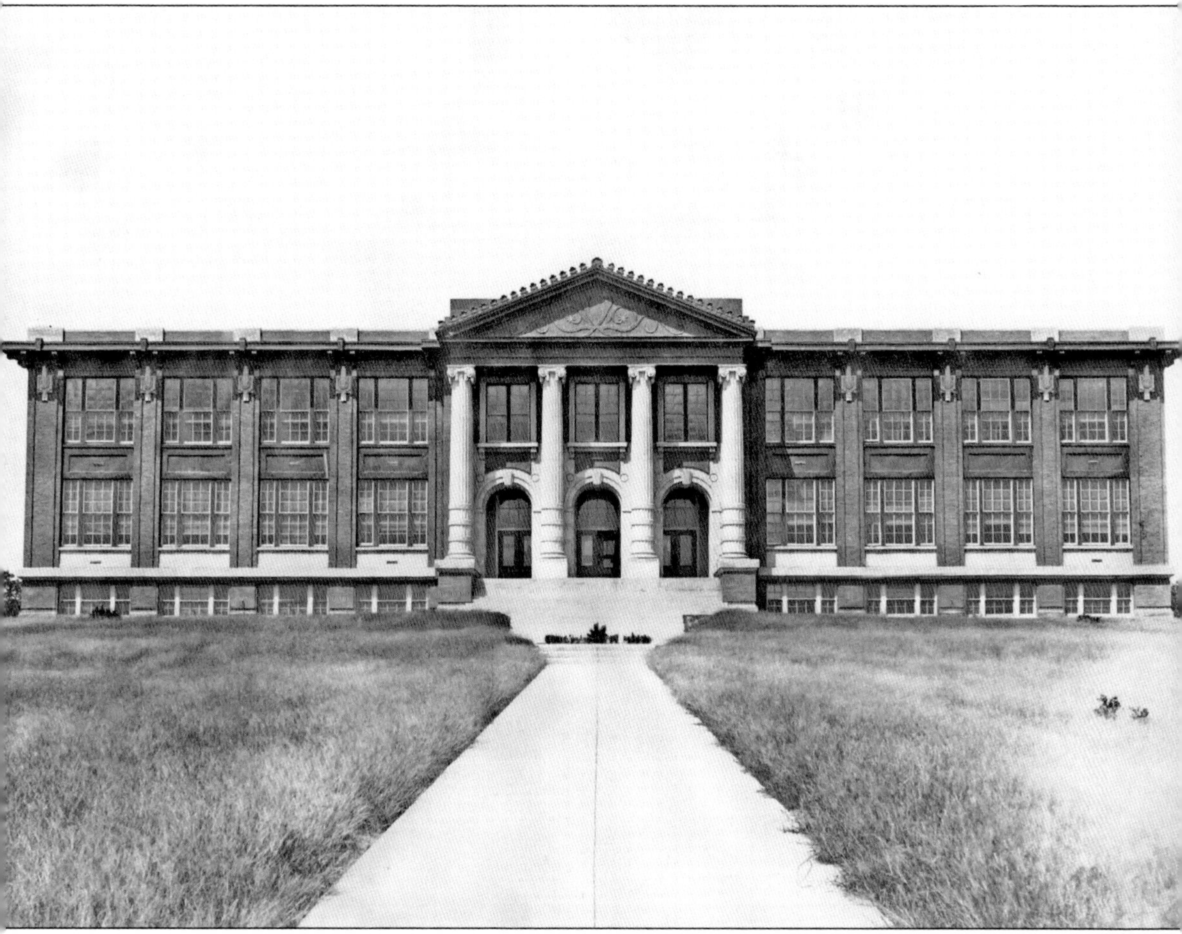

Normal School Building. The building opened in 1911 and housed administrative offices, classrooms, an auditorium, and a gymnasium. It is known today as Morrison Hall (after Dr. W.B. Morrison, a former school president and history professor) and houses faculty offices, the teacher education program, classrooms, and Montgomery Auditorium. (Courtesy of Southeastern Oklahoma State University.)

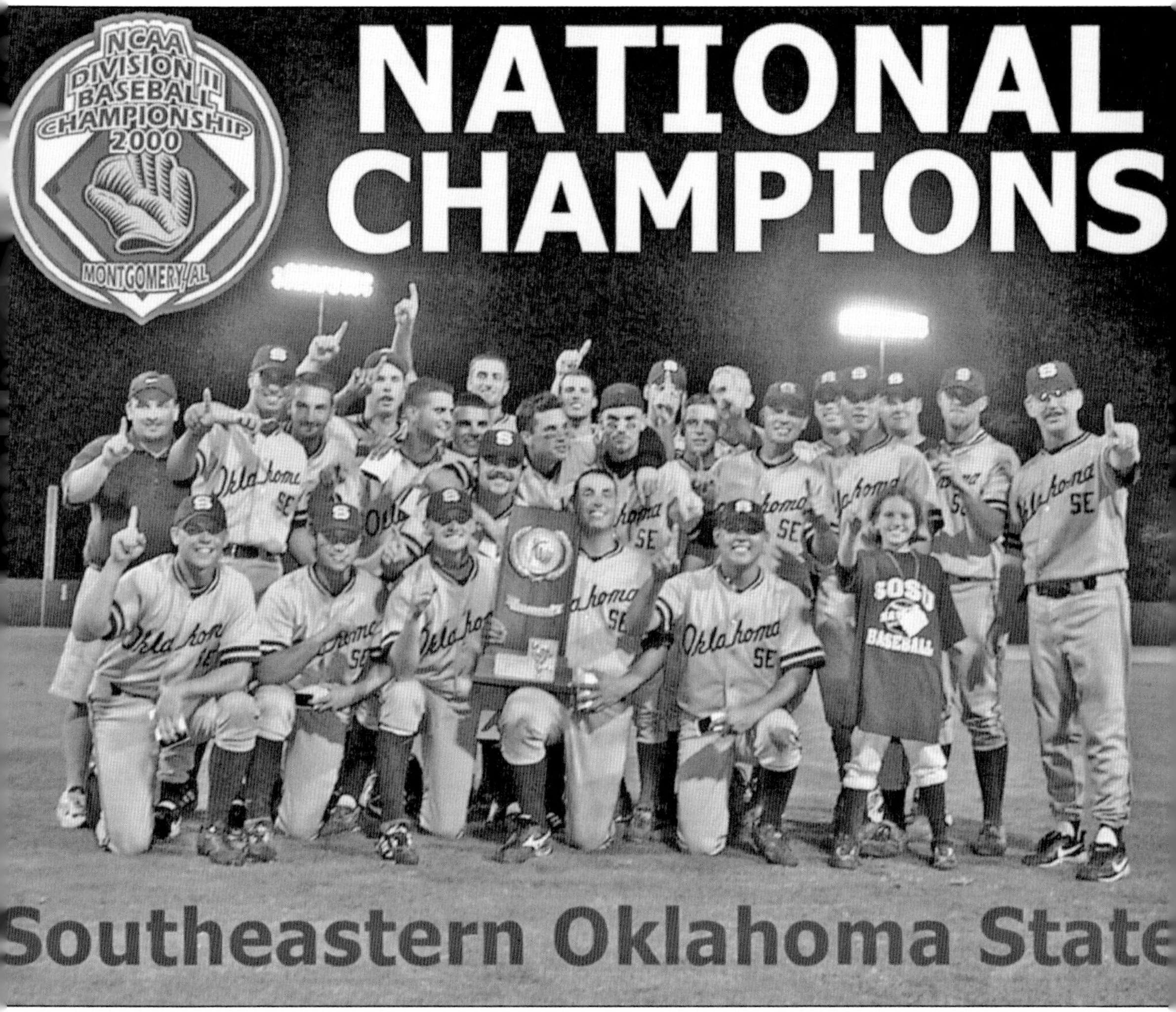

NATIONAL CHAMPIONS. On June 3, 2000, the Southeastern Oklahoma State University baseball team won its first national championship. Coach Mike Metheny's connection with SOSU has spanned more than 40 years from his beginnings as a player to his involvement as a graduate assistant, assistant coach, and eventually head coach. He was named the 2000 National Coach of the Year at the American Baseball Coaches Convention. Metheny's teams made seven trips to the NAIA World Series, earning three runner-up finishes. They have also claimed 15 conference championships, and Metheny is a nine-time Conference Coach of the Year and seven-time Regional Coach of the Year. (Courtesy of Southeastern Oklahoma State University.)

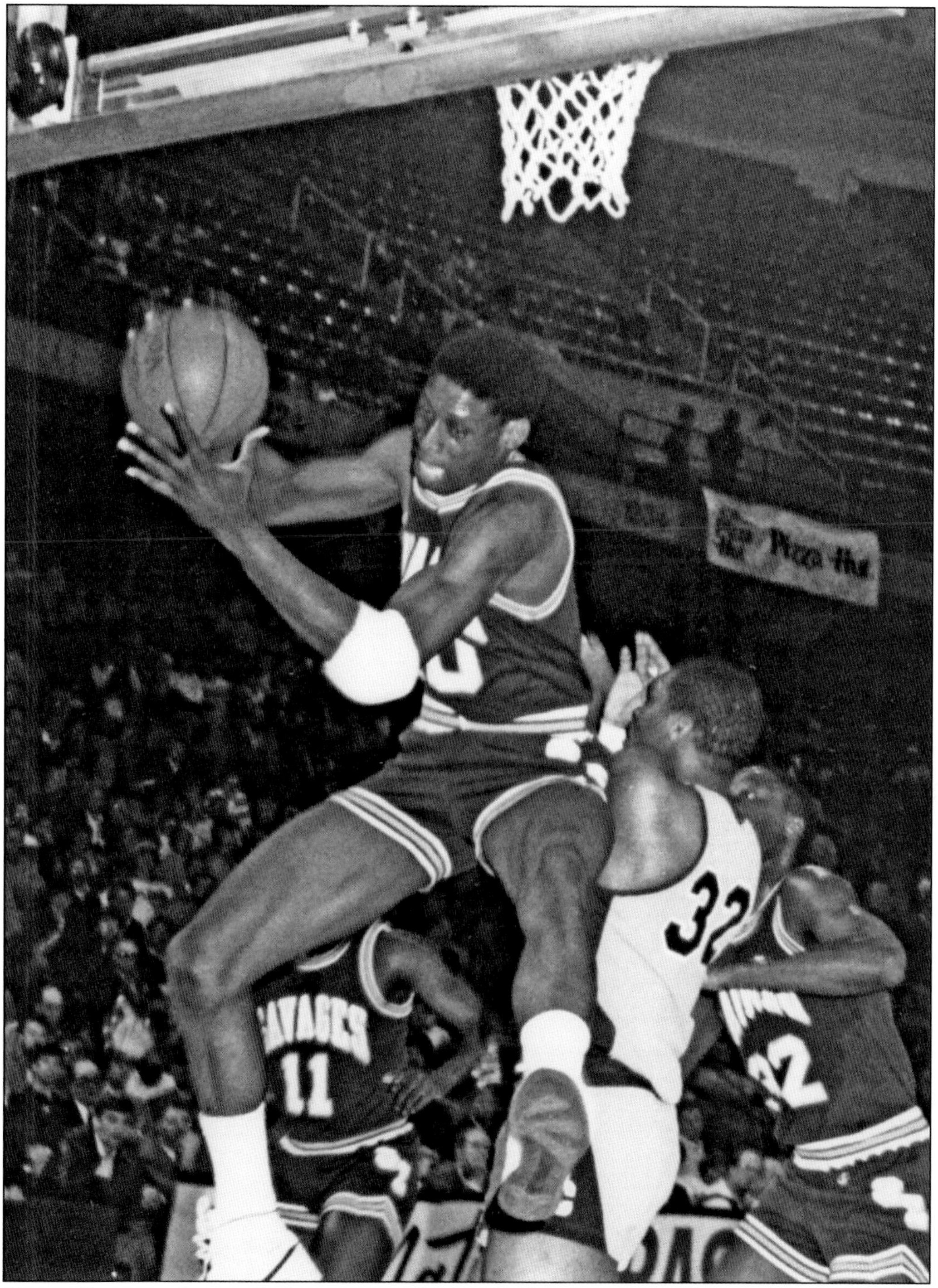

Dennis Rodman. Dennis Rodman, originally from Dallas, Texas, attended South Oak Cliff High School. He was named Oklahoma Intercollegiate Conference Most Valuable Player in 1984, 1985, and 1986. (Courtesy of Southeastern Oklahoma State University Intercollegiate Athletics.)

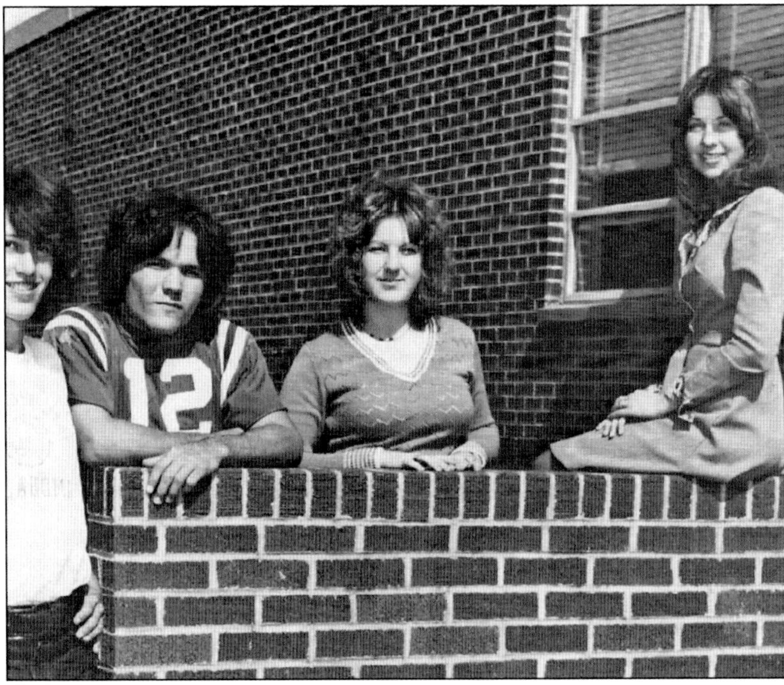

Durant High School Seniors, 1976. Pictured here are the senior class officers: vice president Tony Phillips, president Mitch McGar, secretary-treasurer Judy Fite, and reporter Sheri Cleveland. (Courtesy of the *Durant High School Lion*.)

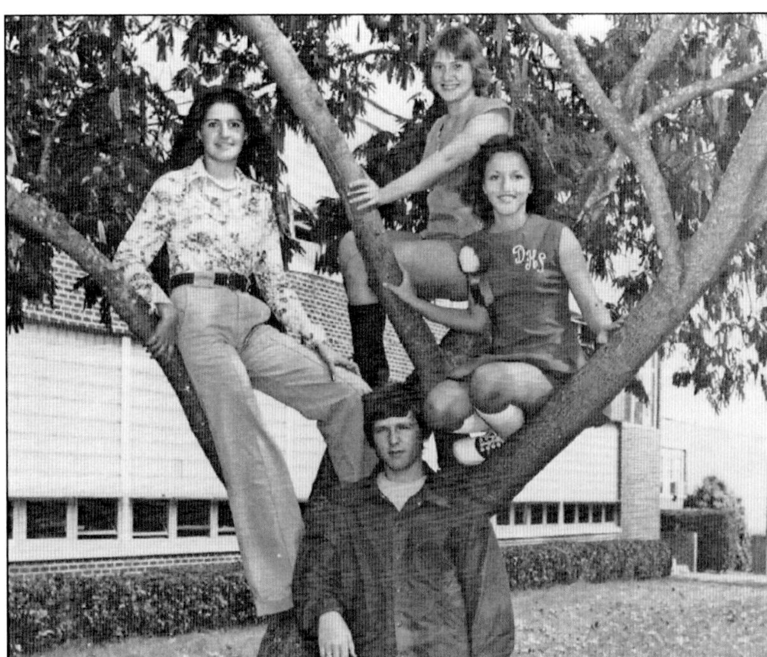

Durant High School Sophomore Officers, 1976. The sophomore class officers pictured here are president Traci Walker, vice president Sandy Tucker, secretary-treasurer Mark Villines, and reporter Laura Falls. (Courtesy of the *Durant High School Lion*.)

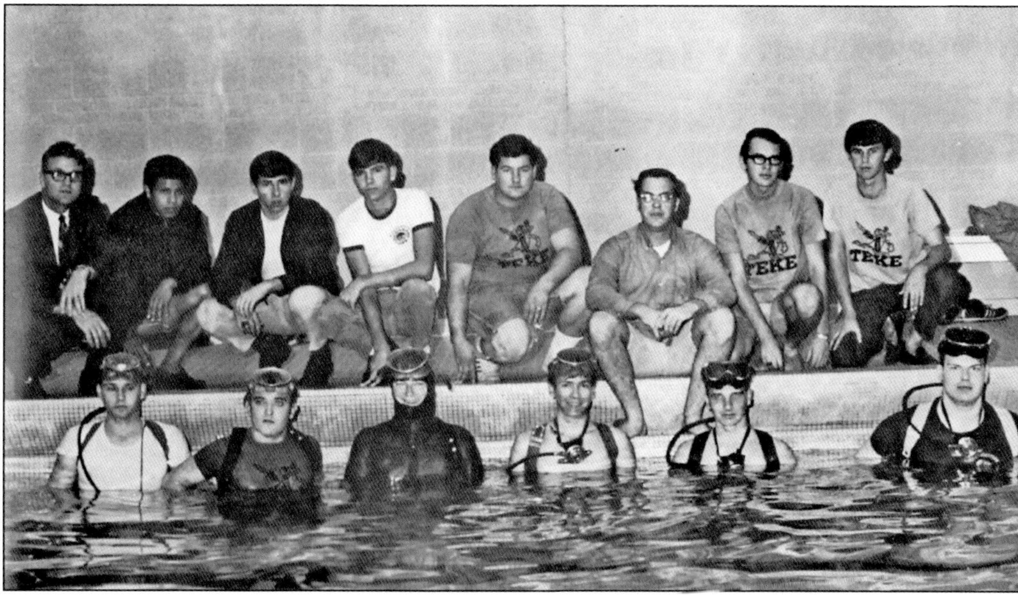

SOUTHEASTERN'S KNIGHTS OF NEPTUNE SCUBA DIVING TEAM, 1969. Pictured here are, from left to right, (first row, in water) Arthur May, Bill Burgoyne, Gene Fair, Mike Love, Everett Bailey, and Kurt Engleman; (second row) Charles Andrews (sponsor), Barnabas Grayson, Mike Newell, Joel Bray, Mike Sellers, Vic Schultz, Larry Krsak, and Fred Booth. (Courtesy of Southeastern Oklahoma State University.)

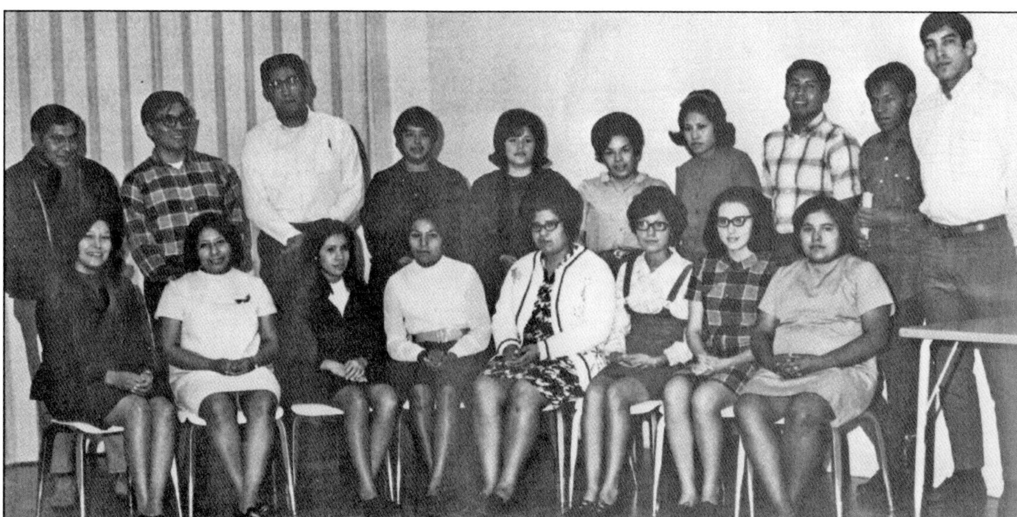

SOUTHEASTERN'S TRIBES COUNCIL GROUP, 1969. Members of this American Indian student organization included, from left to right, (first row) Delores Twohatchet, Patty Fisher, Margaret No-fire, JoAnn Wade, Delores Frazier, Alexis Wabnum, Rita Van Cleave, and Sammy Wade; (second row) Billy Horse, Ronald Twohatchet, Arnold Bayhylle, Shirley DaVault, Joyce England, Sue Anderson, Sue Williams, Wayne Ward, Abe Frazier, and Steve Barse. (Courtesy of Southeastern Oklahoma State University.)

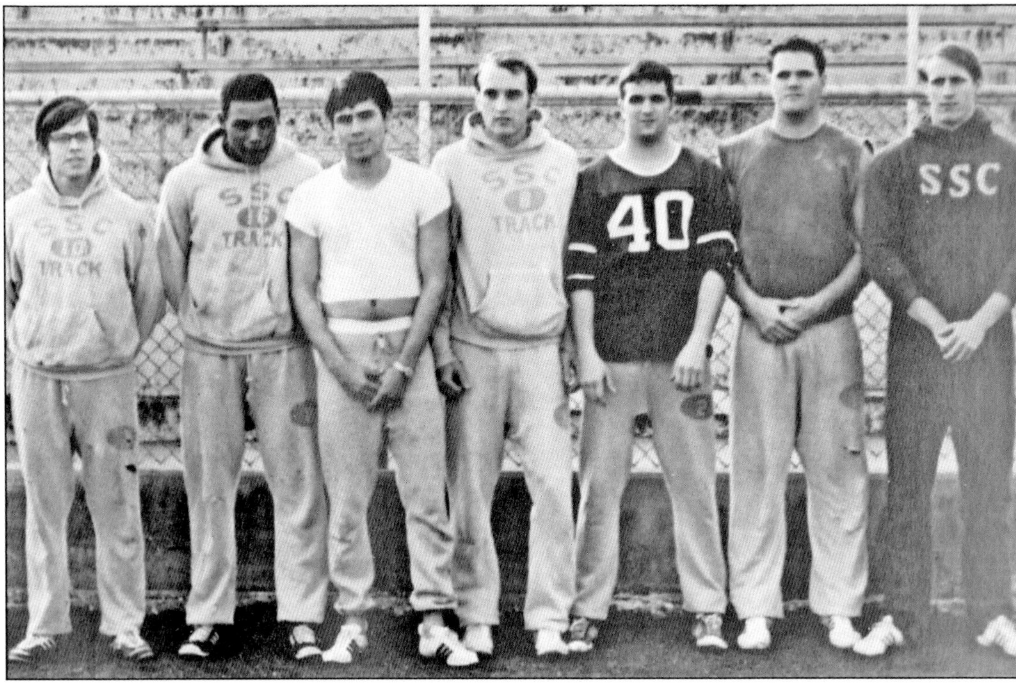

SOUTHEASTERN STATE COLLEGE TRACK, AROUND 1969. These members of the track team are, from left to right, Mike Vanway, Clarence Hudson, Barney Ingram, David Ramsey, Buddy Powell, Ross Powell, and Tommy Strode. (Courtesy of Southeastern Oklahoma State University.)

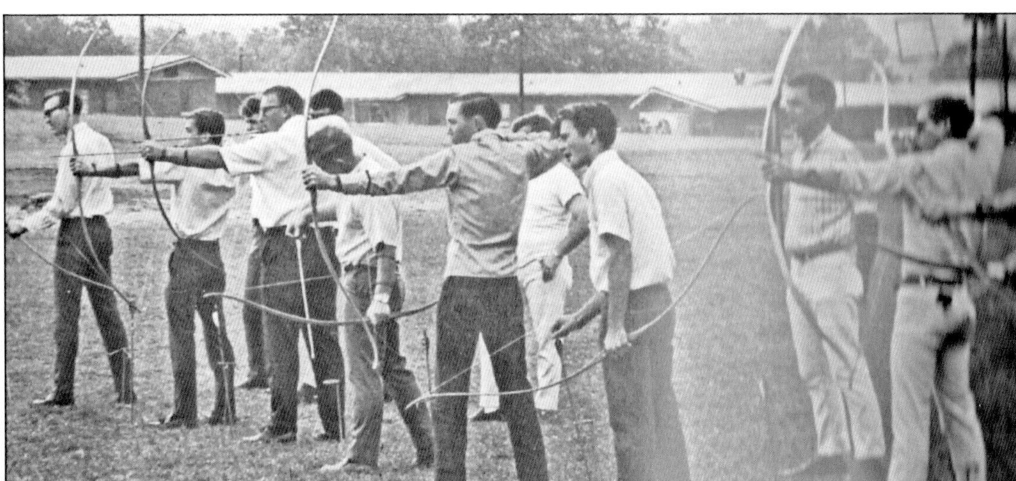

SENIORS AT SOUTHEASTERN. A 1969 archery team, which drew many participants, competes on the field of competition. (Courtesy of Southeastern Oklahoma State University.)

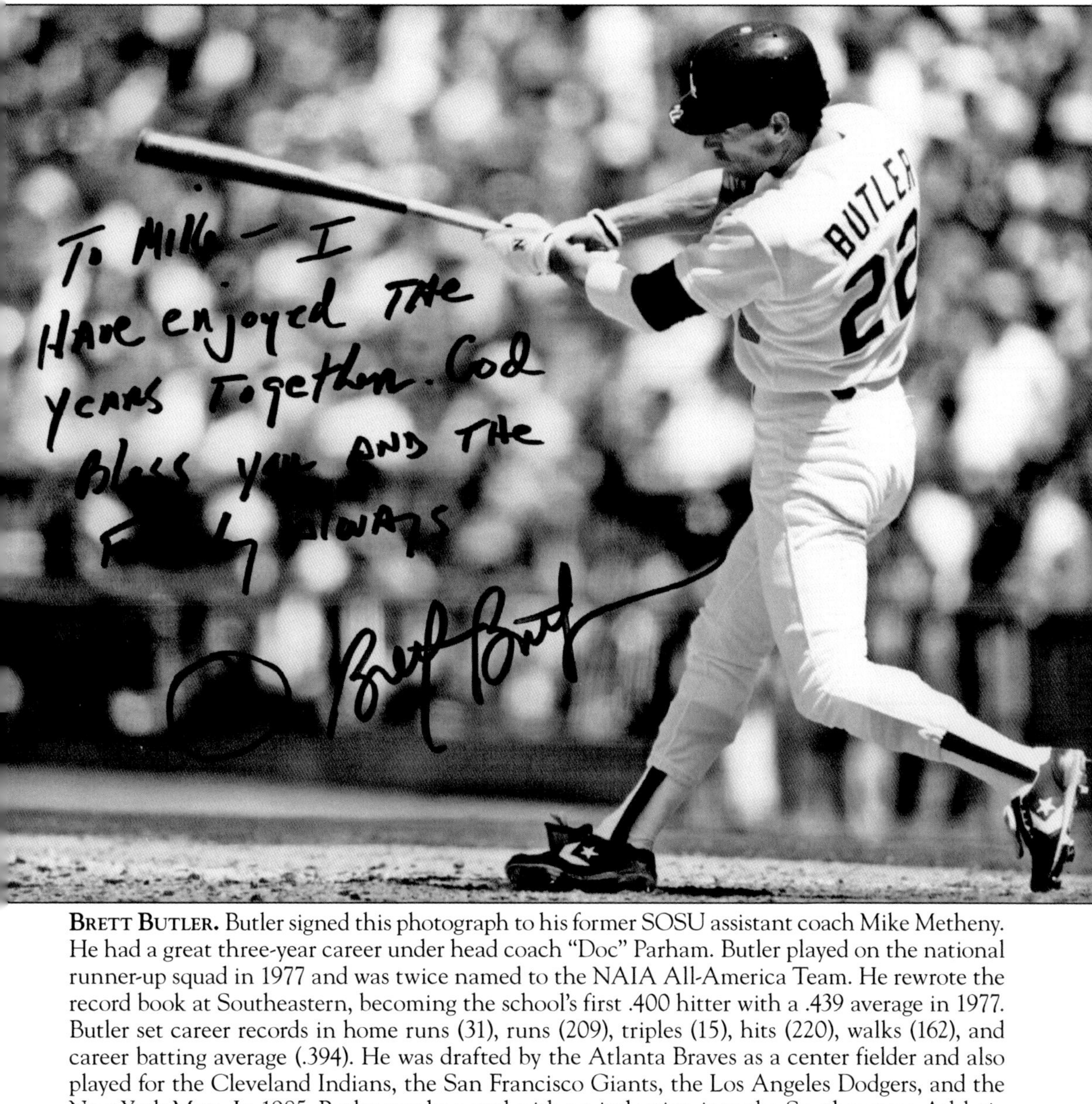

Brett Butler. Butler signed this photograph to his former SOSU assistant coach Mike Metheny. He had a great three-year career under head coach "Doc" Parham. Butler played on the national runner-up squad in 1977 and was twice named to the NAIA All-America Team. He rewrote the record book at Southeastern, becoming the school's first .400 hitter with a .439 average in 1977. Butler set career records in home runs (31), runs (209), triples (15), hits (220), walks (162), and career batting average (.394). He was drafted by the Atlanta Braves as a center fielder and also played for the Cleveland Indians, the San Francisco Giants, the Los Angeles Dodgers, and the New York Mets. In 1985, Butler was honored with an induction into the Southeastern Athletic Hall of Fame. (Courtesy of SOSU and Mike Metheny.)

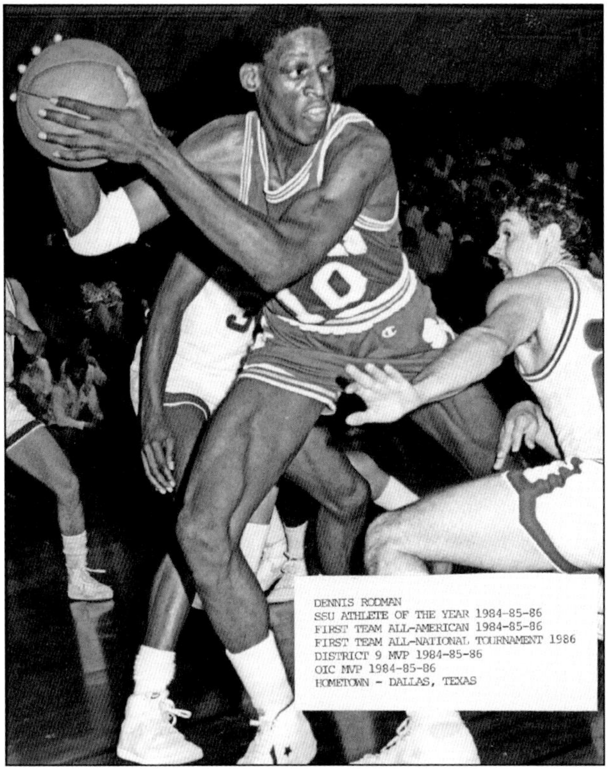

DENNIS RODMAN. Rodman attended Southeastern, where he distinguished himself as Athlete of the Year (1984–1986), 1st Team All-American (1984–1986), 1st Team All-National Tournament (1986), District 9 MVP (1984–1986), and Oklahoma Intercollegiate Conference MVP 1984–1986. (Courtesy of Southeastern Oklahoma State.)

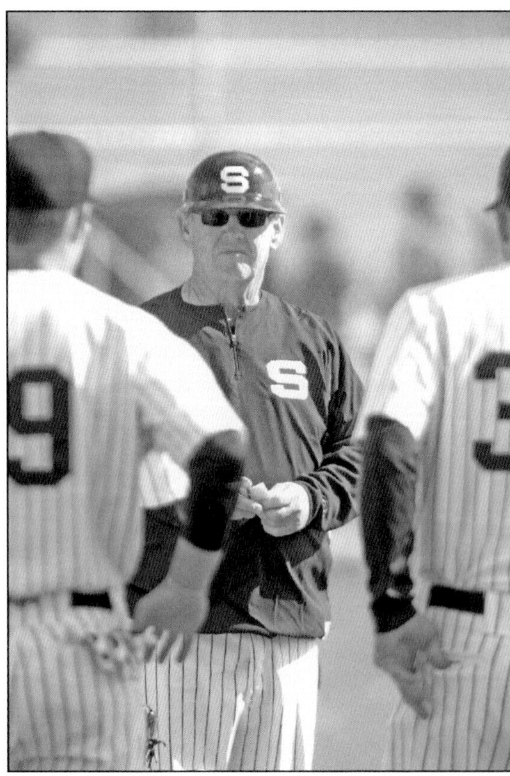

MIKE METHENY. Mike Metheny is one of eight Division II coaches to ever reach the 1,000-win plateau (and one of just three that are still active). He is second on the active-coaches list in victories at the Division II level and fifth all-time. Metheny guided the Southeastern baseball program through its successful transition from NAIA to NCAA Division II, and in just the second season at that level he led his squad to the NCAA Division II World Series. While a member of the NAIA, his teams made seven trips to the NAIA World Series and earned three runner-up finishes. (Courtesy of Southeastern Oklahoma State University Intercollegiate Athletics.)

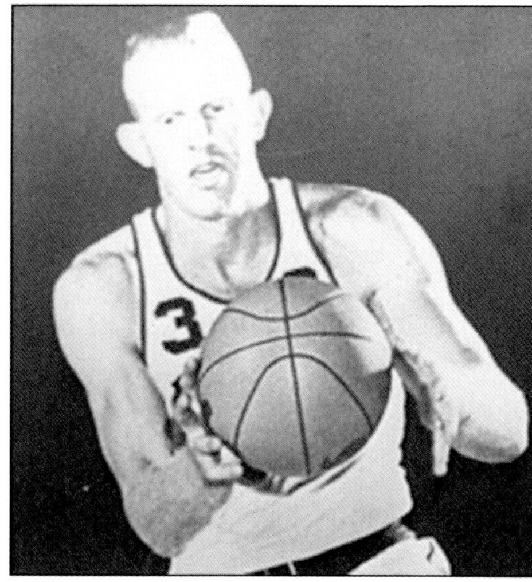

James Spivey. Jim Spivey led Southeastern to four straight trips to the NAIA National Tournament (1954–1957). In 1955 and 1957, Southeastern reached the finals, and Spivey was named the Most Valuable Player. He was on the NAIA All-Time Basketball Team for the period of 1952 to 1970 and was named to the Oklahoma Collegiate Conference All-Star Team three times. He set scoring records and, in 1957, was named to the Chuck Taylor and AP Small College All-American Teams. Spivey, who played with the Phillips 66 Team of the National Industrial Basketball League, was also inducted to the Helms Foundation Hall of Fame (in 1962) and to the Southeastern Athletic Hall of Fame (in 1978). (Courtesy of *Durant Daily Democrat*.)

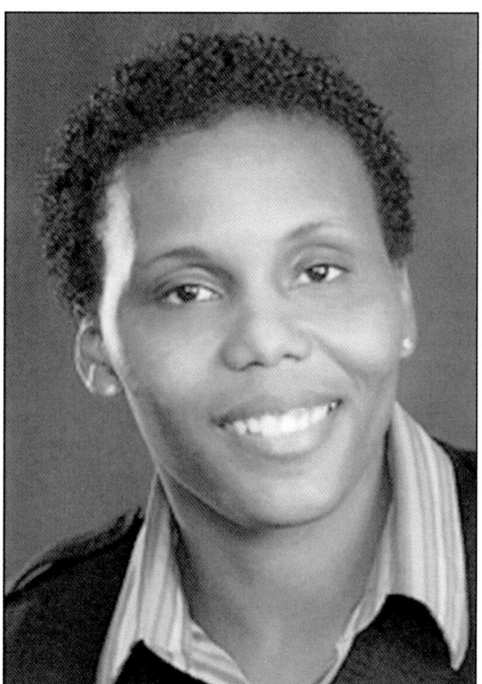

Crystal Robinson. A native of Atoka, Oklahoma, Crystal Robinson was a standout basketball player for Southeastern. She was NAIA All-American in 1994, 1995, and 1996, and Player of the Year in 1996. She played two years in the American Basketball League before joining the WNBA New York Liberty in 1999. She led her team to four WNBA Finals appearances in the six seasons she spent with the Liberty. In 2011, she was inducted into the Oklahoma Sports Hall of Fame. She became head women's basketball coach at Murray State College in Tishomingo, Oklahoma. (Courtesy of Crystal Robinson.)

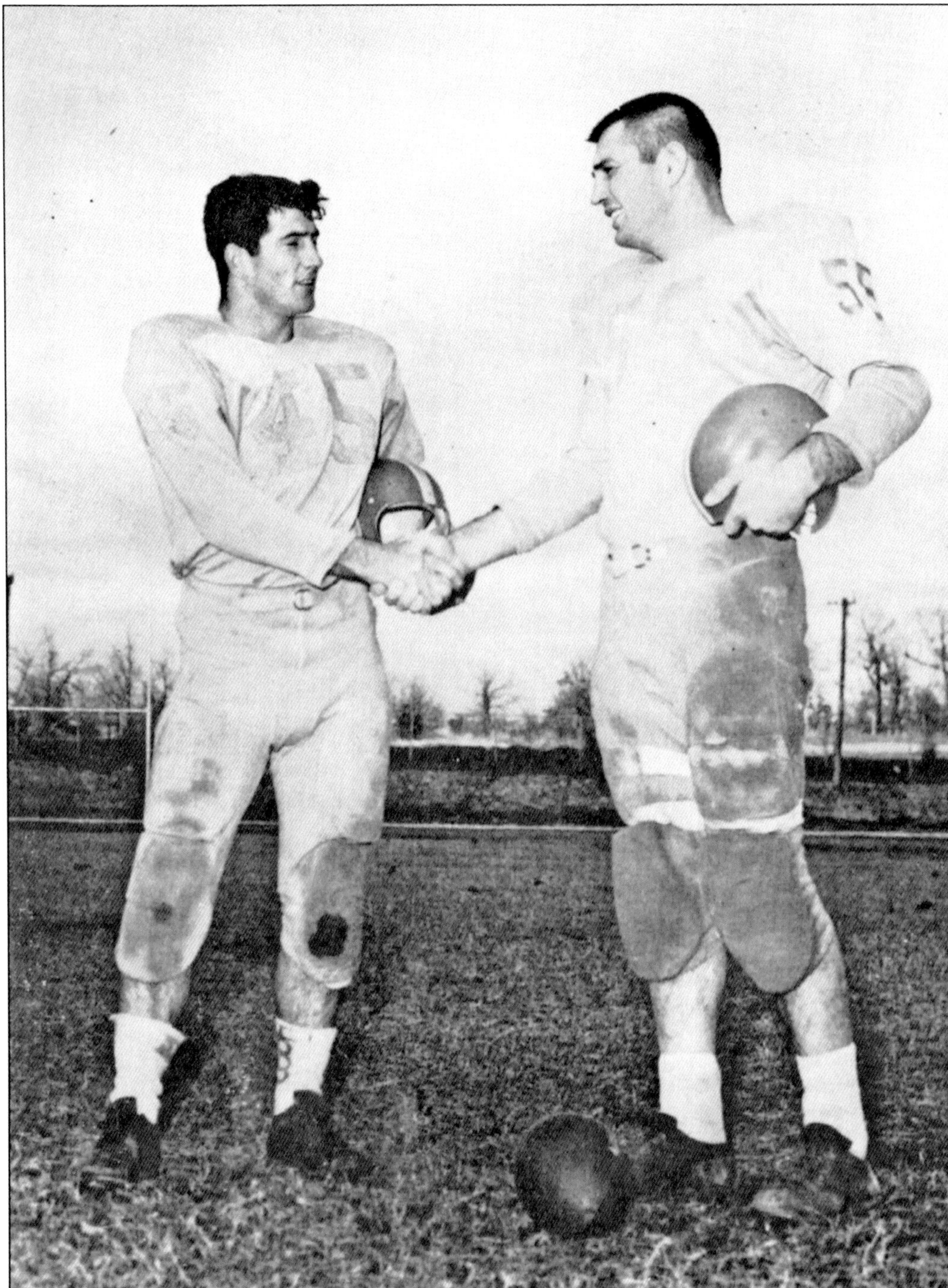

SOUTHEASTERN FOOTBALL PLAYERS. Pictured are co-captains Blackie Bracken and Marty Bacon from the 1958 Savages team. (Courtesy of Southeastern Oklahoma State University.)

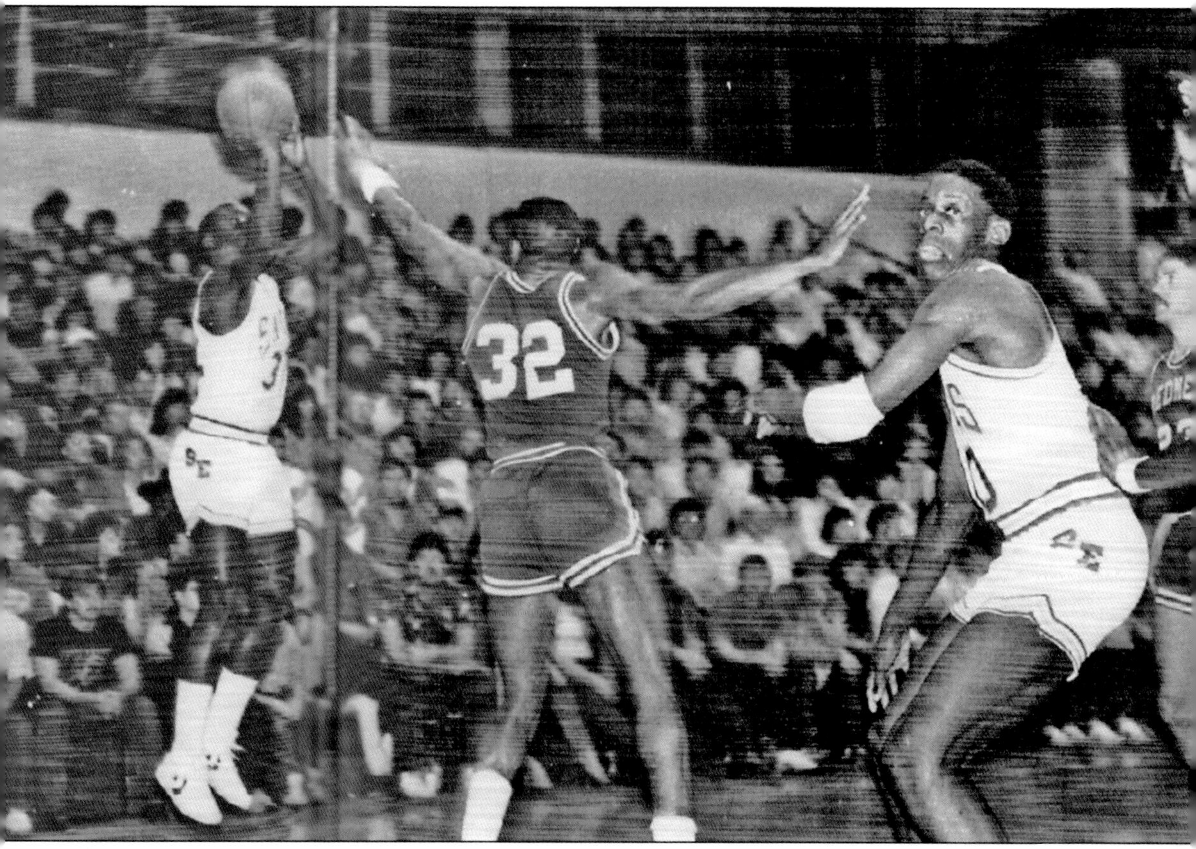

DENNIS "WORM" RODMAN OF SOSU. All-American Rodman led Southeastern Oklahoma State University basketball teams and thrilled fans during his years at the school. In this image, Carl Davis is shooting the ball, and Rodman is looking towards the camera. Rodman was a three-time NAIA All-American and led the NAIA in rebounding in both the 1984–1985 and 1985–1986 seasons. In three seasons at the school (1983–1986), he averaged 25.7 points and 15.7 rebounds and twice led the NAIA in rebounding. At a pre-draft camp, he caught the attention of the Detroit Pistons. Rodman was inducted into the Naismith Memorial Basketball Hall of Fame in 2011 after an NBA career with the Detroit Pistons, San Antonio Spurs, Chicago Bulls, Los Angeles Lakers, and Dallas Mavericks. (Courtesy of Southeastern Oklahoma State University.)

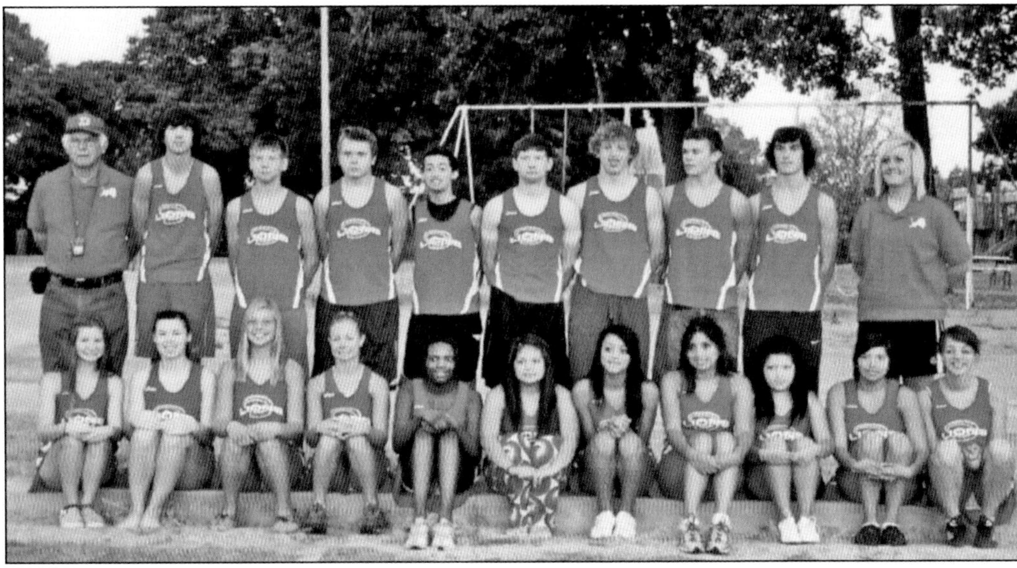

Durant High School Athletes. Pictured here are student athletes from Durant High School. (Courtesy of Durant High School.)

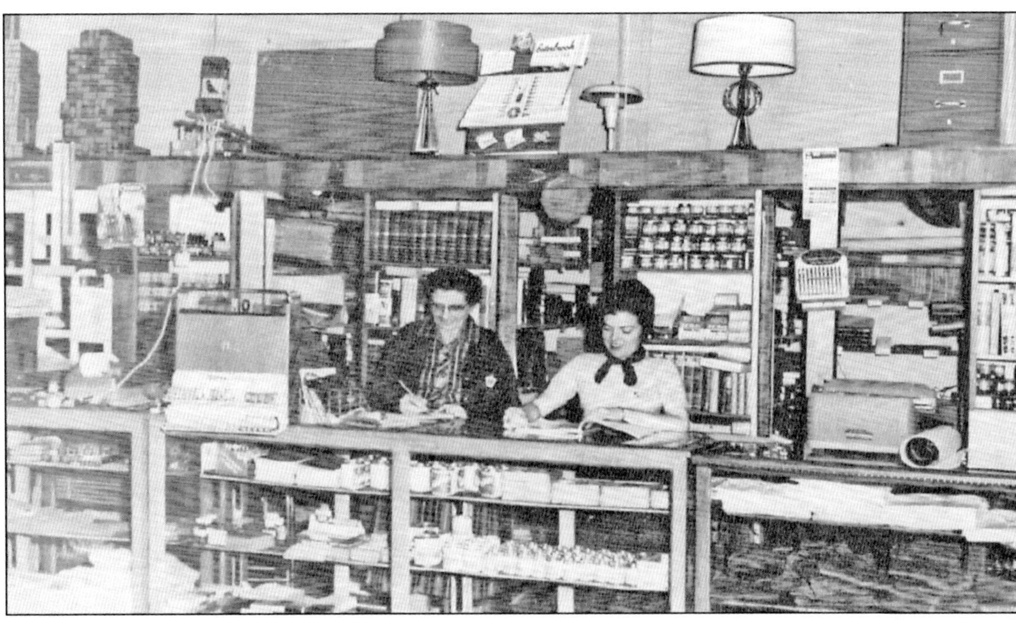

Thompson Book & Supply Company. Two employees of the Thompson Book & Supply Company at Southeastern State College are shown here. (Courtesy of Southeastern Oklahoma State University.)

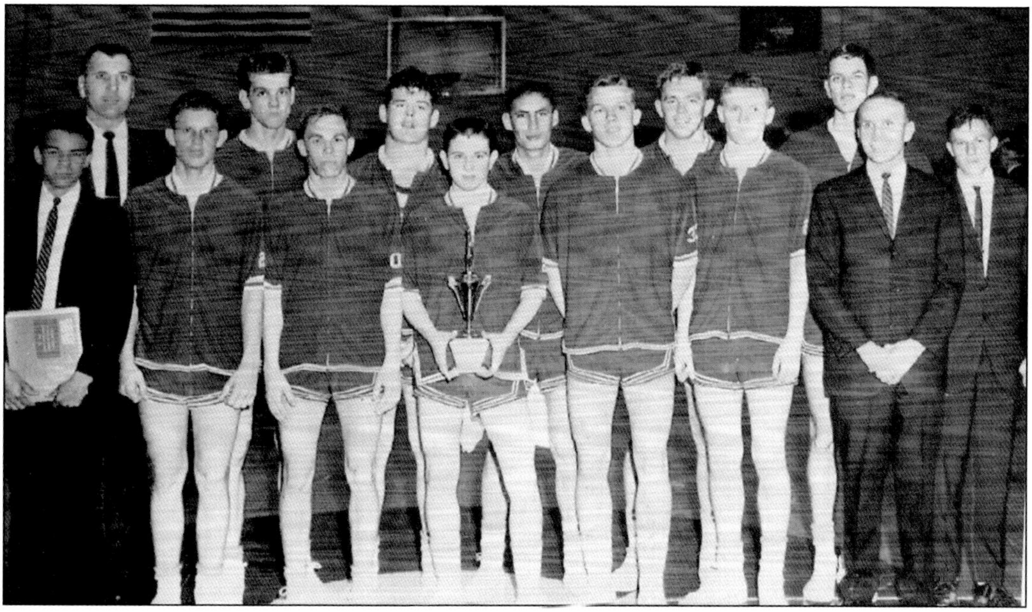

Durant Lions "A" Team Championships. The Lions are pictured here with the championship trophy they won at Southeastern State College Invitational Tournament. Seen with the team are coach John Gecks and assistant coach B.W. Smith. (Courtesy of the *Durant High School Lion.*)

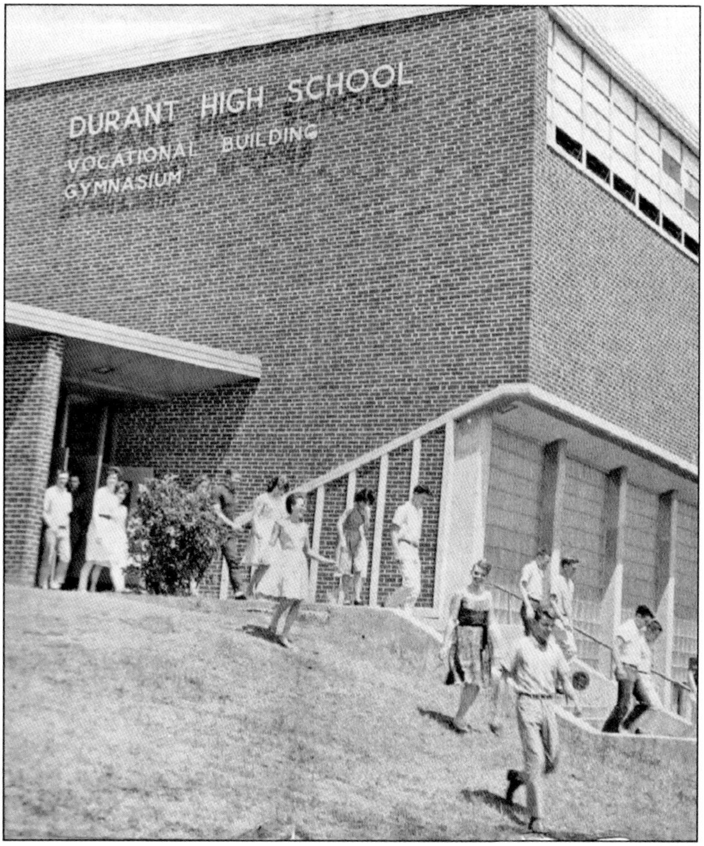

Durant High School. Students are shown in front of the Vocational Building/Gymnasium. (Courtesy of the *Durant High School Lion.*)

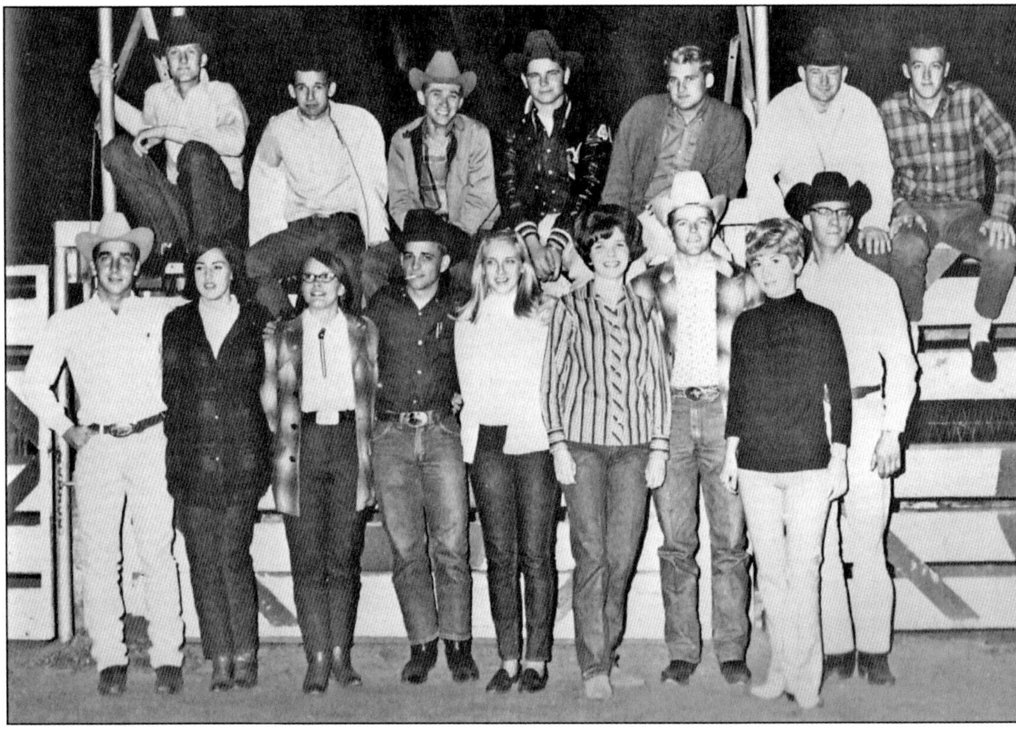

SOUTHEASTERN'S LITTLE "D" RODEO CLUB. Pictured here are, from left to right, (first row) Jerry Pebsworth, Deborah Shelby, Estell Wilson, Buddy Enis, Alicia Brents, Mary Winters, Joe Ben Nance, Sharon Williams, and Steve Davis; (second row), Ronnie Sharrock, Ronald Stoke, Donald Brents, Thomas Howard, Sammy Bene, Weldon Brown, and Eddie White. (Courtesy of the *Southeastern Oklahoma State College Savage.*)

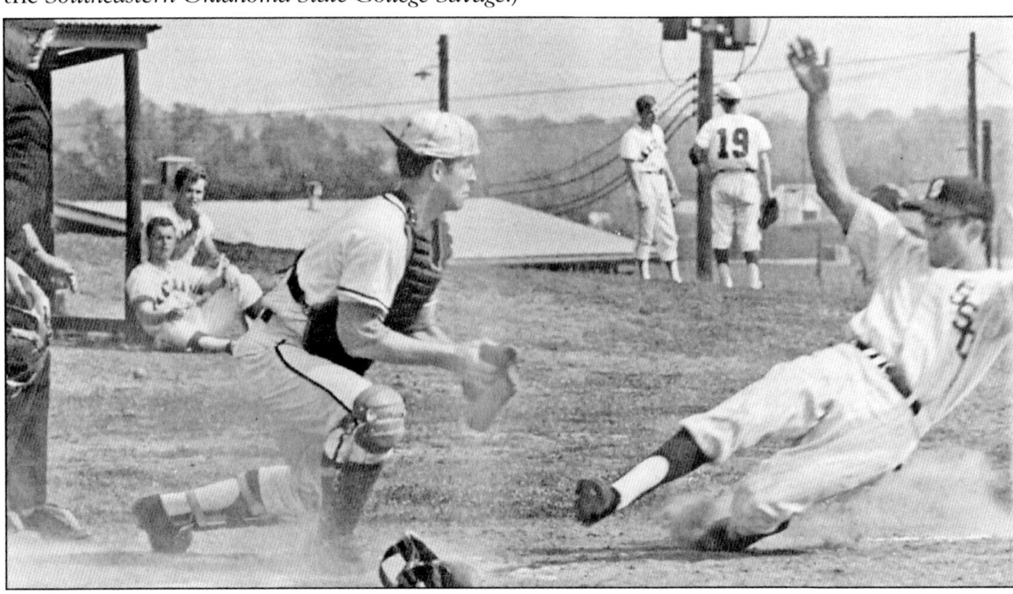

SOUTHEASTERN VERSUS AUGUSTANA, ILLINOIS. Southeastern player Tommy Pratt slides into home plate while avoiding a tag from the catcher from Augustana, Illinois. The teams each won a game this day in 1968. (Courtesy of Southeastern Oklahoma State University.)

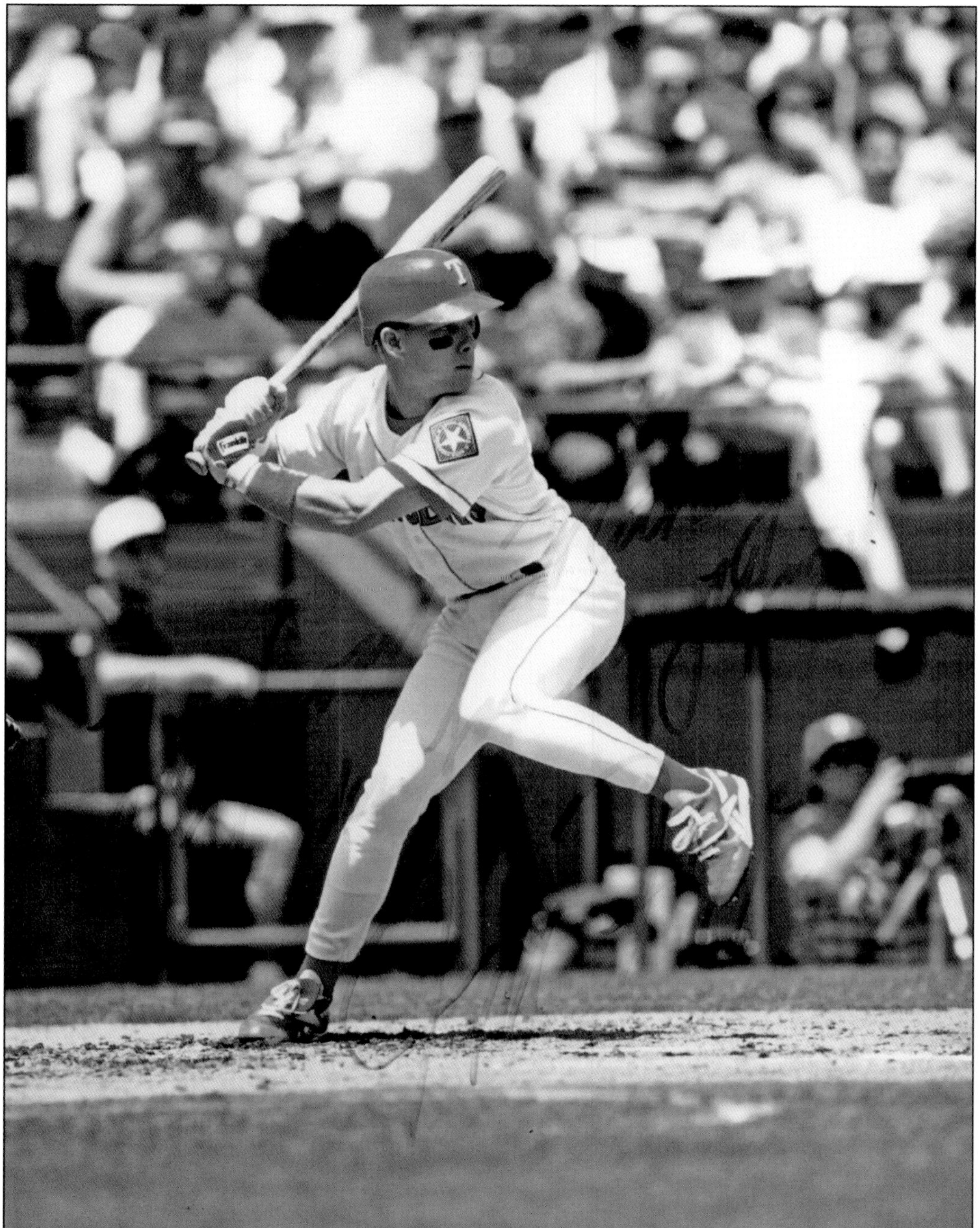

Jeff Frye. Frye attended Southeastern, where he became an outstanding second baseman for coach Mike Metheny. He set an SOSU record by hitting .455 in 1988, and his .420 career batting average is the second highest in the school's history. Frye, an NAIA All-American, was drafted by the Texas Rangers; he later played for the Boston Red Sox, Toronto Blue Jays, and Colorado Rockies. SOSU honored him with membership in the Southeastern Athletic Hall of Fame in 1998. (Courtesy of SOSU and Mike Metheny.)

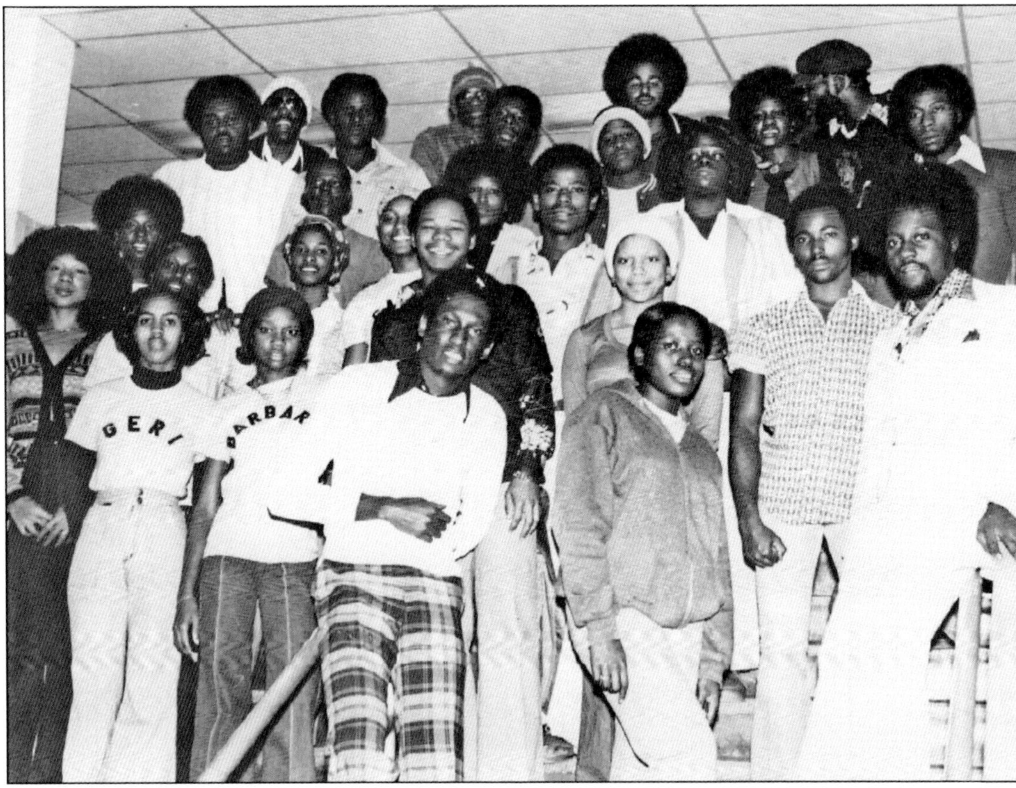

AFRO-AMERICAN STUDENT ORGANIZATION. This student organization at Southeastern State College sponsored an annual heritage event and did charity work in Durant to help needy families. (Courtesy of Southeastern Oklahoma State University.)

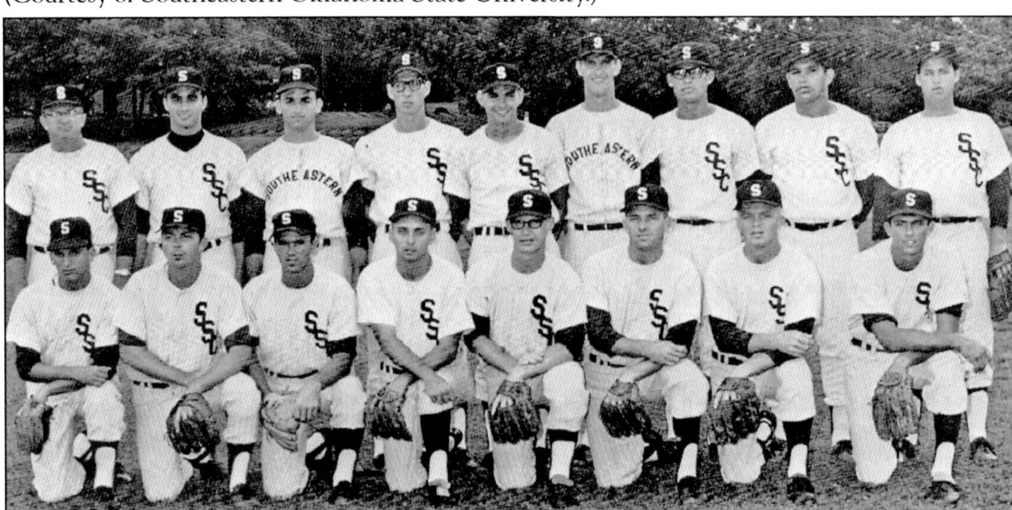

SOUTHEASTERN STATE COLLEGE CHAMPIONS, 1968. This was the first team in the school's history to win the Oklahoma Collegiate Conference title in baseball. The team had a 22-8 record, and six players—Danny Hubbell, Jim Godsby, Robert Drew, Jerry Hulme, Gary Clements, and Trent Baulch— received conference honors. Baulch received the Bloomer Sullivan Award for top athlete. (Courtesy of Southeastern Oklahoma State University.)

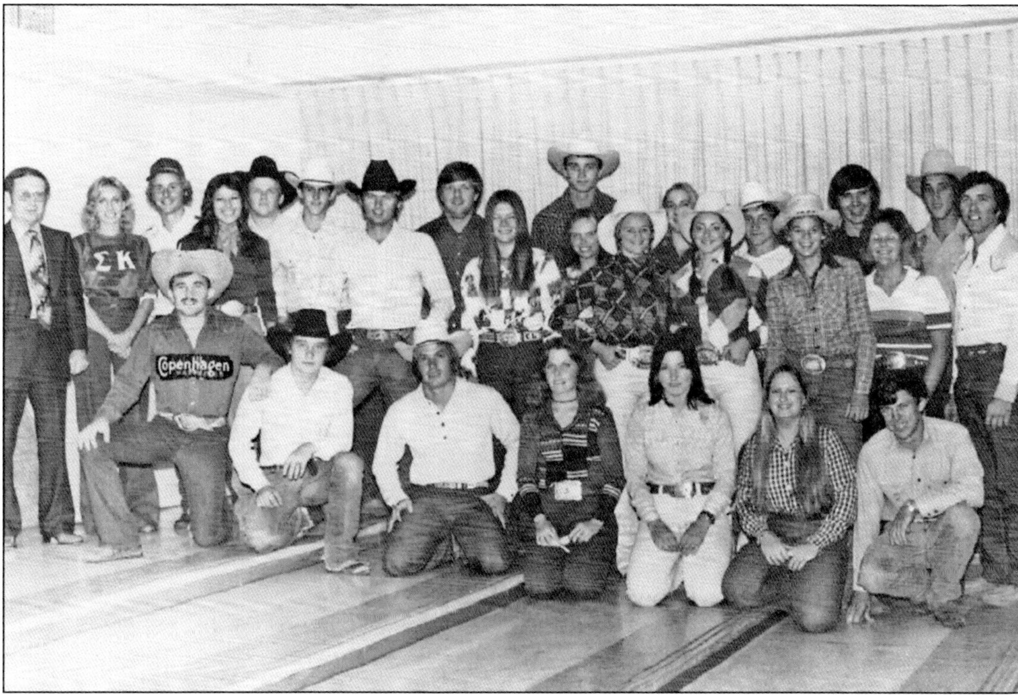

Southeastern Rodeo Club. It was big news for the rodeo club when Roy Cooper competed in the National Finals and became a world champion calf roper. Cooper, an SOSU student and alumnus, was involved in professional rodeo for more than 35 years. He won eight World Titles and qualified for the National Finals Rodeo 32 times, winning the NFR title (aggregate score) eight times. He was inducted into the Pro Rodeo Hall of Fame in 1979. (Courtesy of Southeastern Oklahoma State University.)

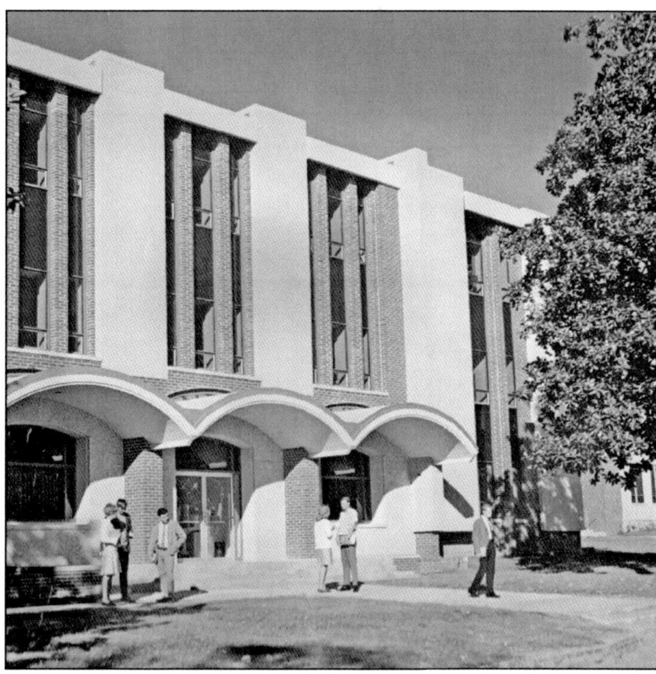

Southeastern State College, Durant. Southeastern State students are pictured here around 1969. (Courtesy of Southeastern Oklahoma State University.)

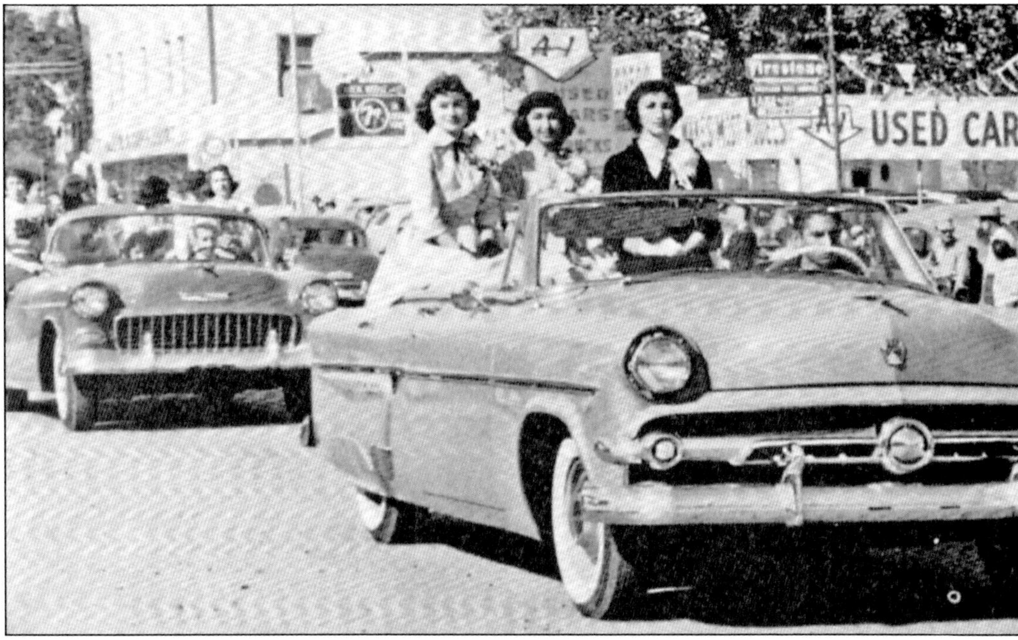

Parade in Durant. These Durant High School students are participating in a downtown parade. The car in front is a 1954 Ford Crestline Sunliner convertible. (Courtesy of the *Durant High School Lion*.)

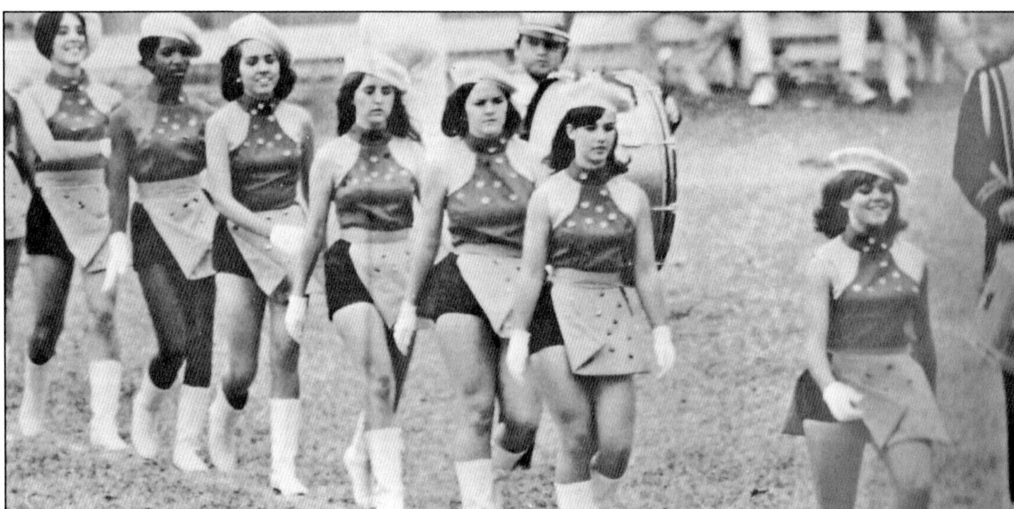

Southeastern State College Drill Team, 1969. Members of the team included Joy Phillips, Billie Brewer, Debbie Shelby, Kathi Stansel, Molly Walker, Rebecca Williams, Joyce Reed, Wanda Burnett, Mona Lombard, Lujane Kitchens, Retta Martin, Charlotte Young, La Chrica Coyle (captain), Pat Tatum, Belinda Martin, Rita Van Cleave, Margaret Nofire, Clommer Ellis, Betty Mahana, Glenda McCord, Debbie Moran, Kathi McCombs. The managers were Jon Livingston, Jim Slaughter, and Rodney Avant. (Courtesy of Southeastern Oklahoma State University.)

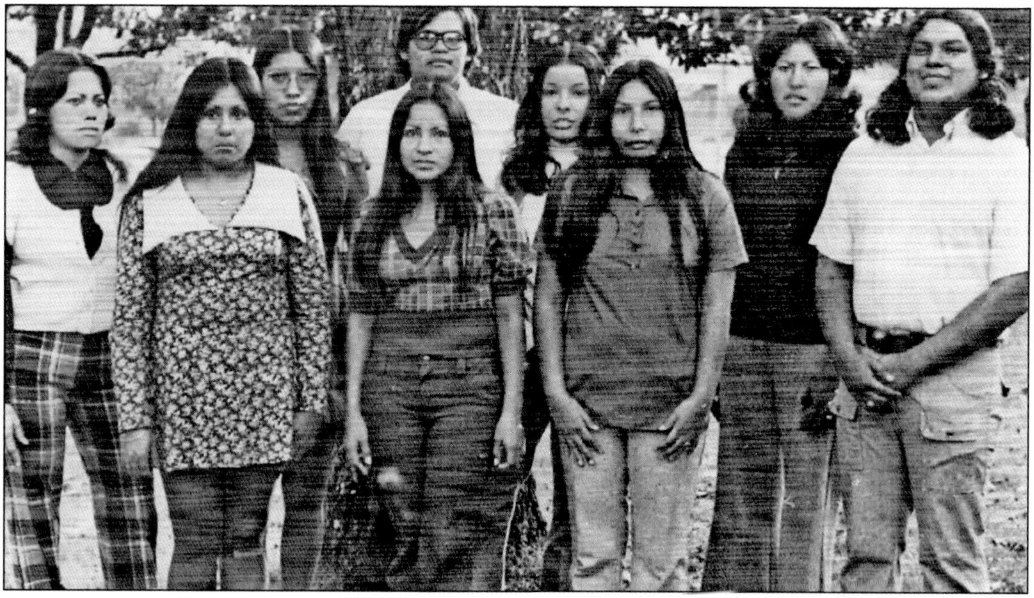

SOUTHEASTERN STATE COLLEGE INDIAN HERITAGE CLUB, AROUND 1973. The members pictured here are, from left to right, (first row) Connie White, Roberta Green, and Carol Wesley; (second row) Ann Wade, Pat Miller, Glen Billy, Bettie Deere, Sue Folsum, and Doyle Tubby. (Courtesy of Southeastern Oklahoma State University.)

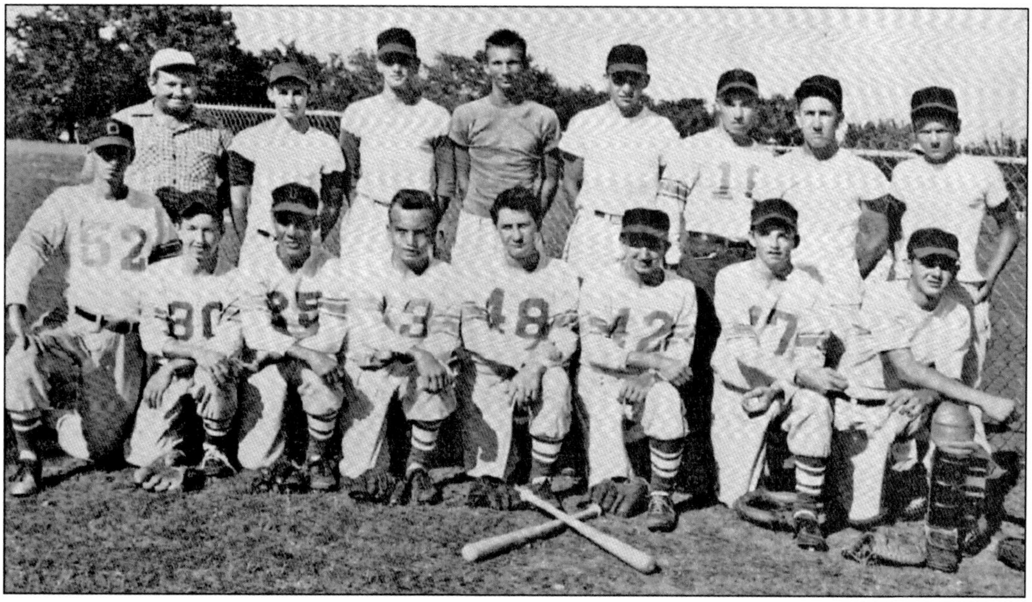

DURANT HIGH SCHOOL BASEBALL TEAM, 1956. The team members pictured here are, from left to right, (first row) Willy Hill, Wayne Mitchell, Larry Dane, Jim Butler, Harold Grundy, T.J. Roberts, Junior Manners, and Pat Phelps; (second row) coach Pigg, Tommy Davenport, Donald Skaggs, Mike Robinson, Ronnie Parker, Benny Martin, Odis Massey, and Earnist Rickman. (Courtesy of the *Durant High School Lion*.)

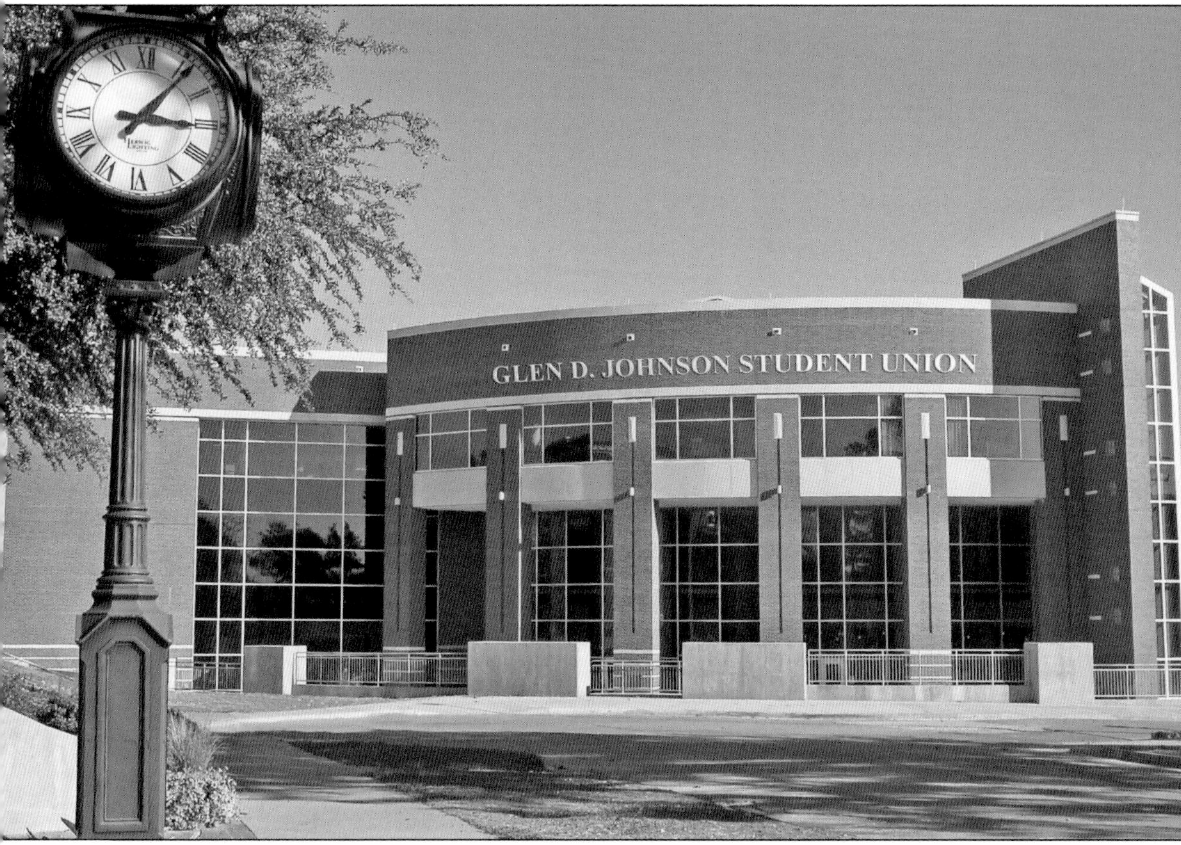

GLEN D. JOHNSON STUDENT UNION, SOSU. This new student union building at Southeastern is named for Dr. Glen D. Johnson, who became the eighth chancellor of the Oklahoma State System of Higher Education in 2007. Prior to this position, he served as the 16th president of Southeastern Oklahoma State University for 10 years. (Courtesy of Southeastern Oklahoma State University.)

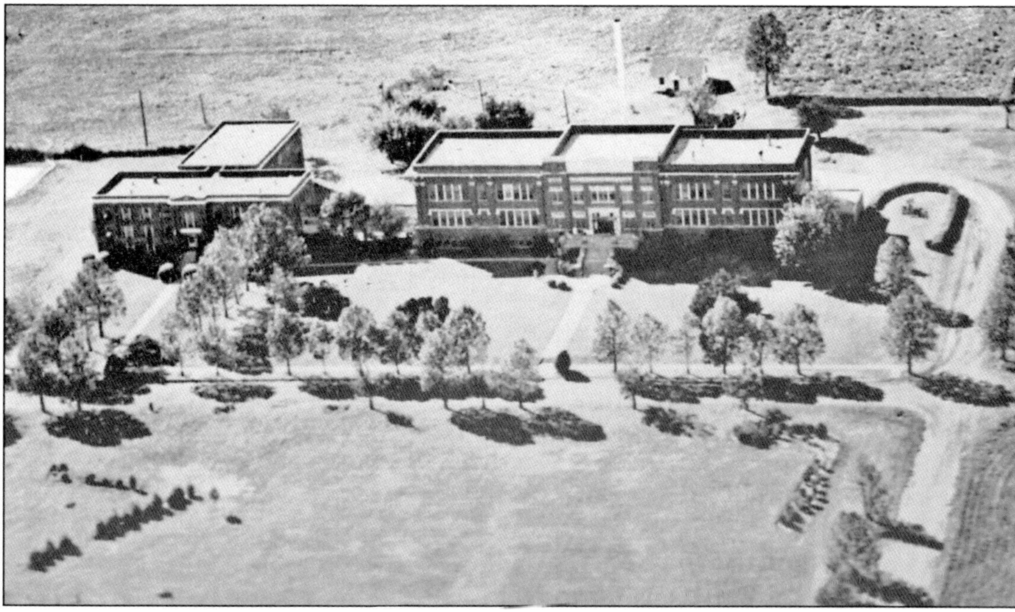

Oklahoma Presbyterian College. This is an aerial view from 1955 of the Oklahoma Presbyterian College in 1955. The facility currently serves as the headquarters of the Choctaw Nation of Oklahoma. (Courtesy of Southeastern Oklahoma State University.)

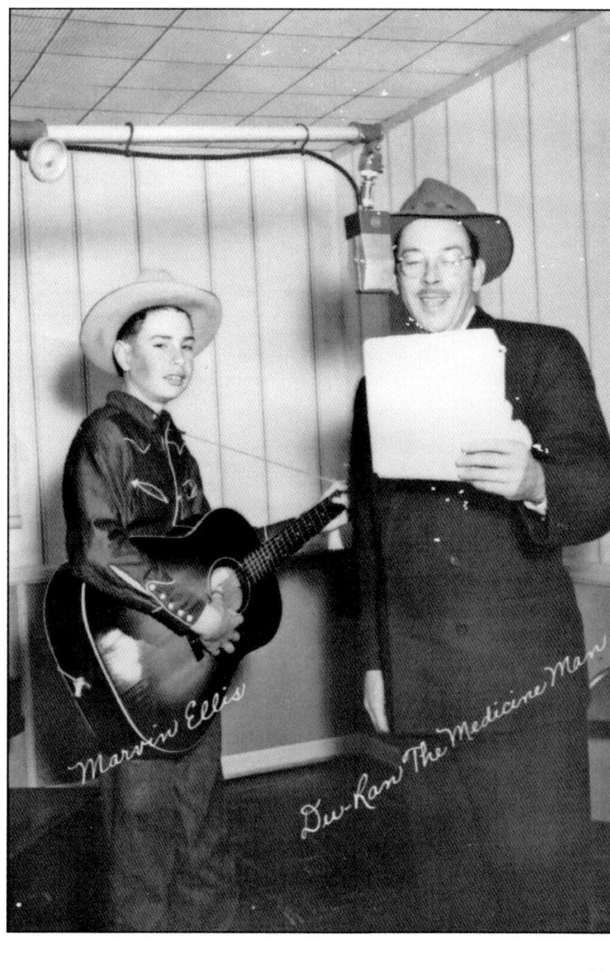

Marvin Ellis and Dew Ran "The Medicine Man." Ellis (left) is pictured with Dew Ran "The Medicine Man," a local celebrity. (Courtesy of Don Parker.)

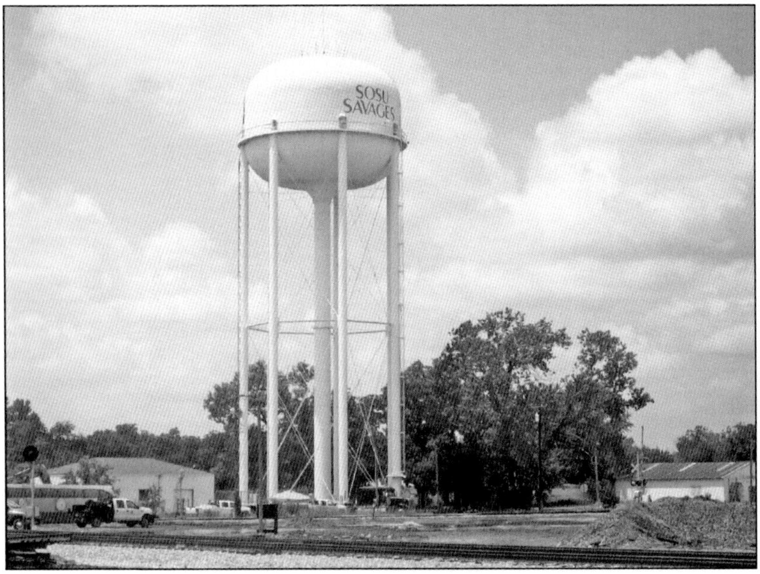

Downtown Durant Water Tower. This structure is located in downtown Durant. (Author's collection.)

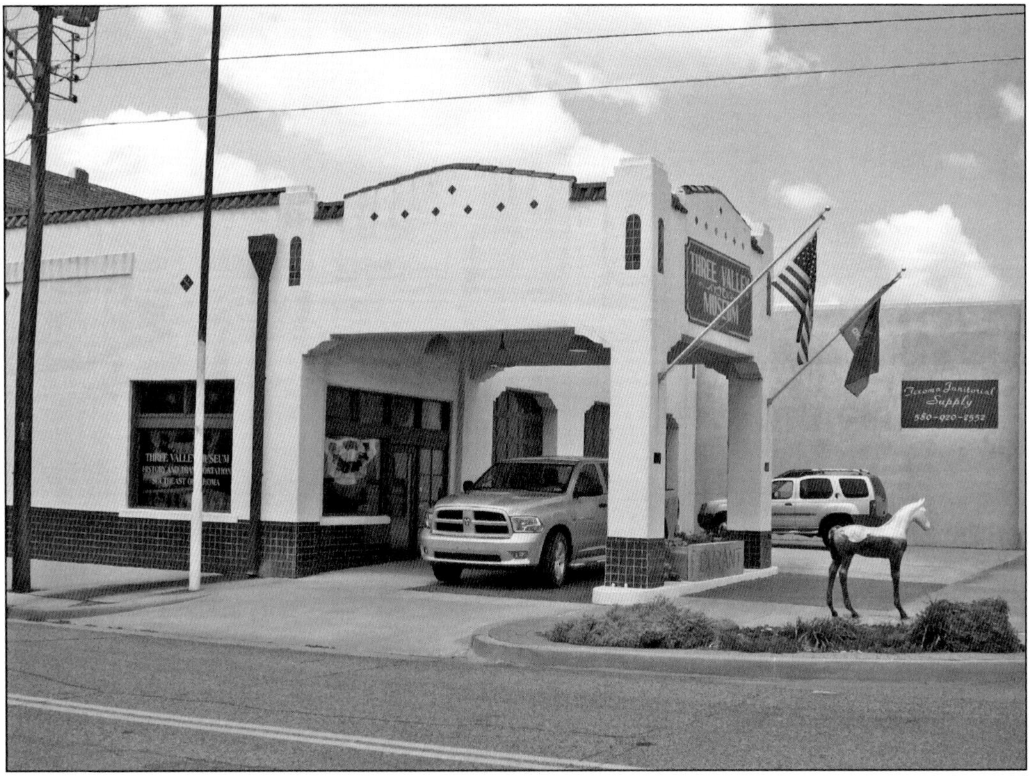

Three Valley Museum. The museum opened at this site (formerly the location of the Old Carpenter Machine Shop) in 2003. The Three Valley Museum began in 1976, taking its name from *Queen of Three Valleys* by Henry McCreary. The book is a history of Durant, and its title references the area's location in the heart of the Red, Blue, and Washita River valleys. (Author's collection.)

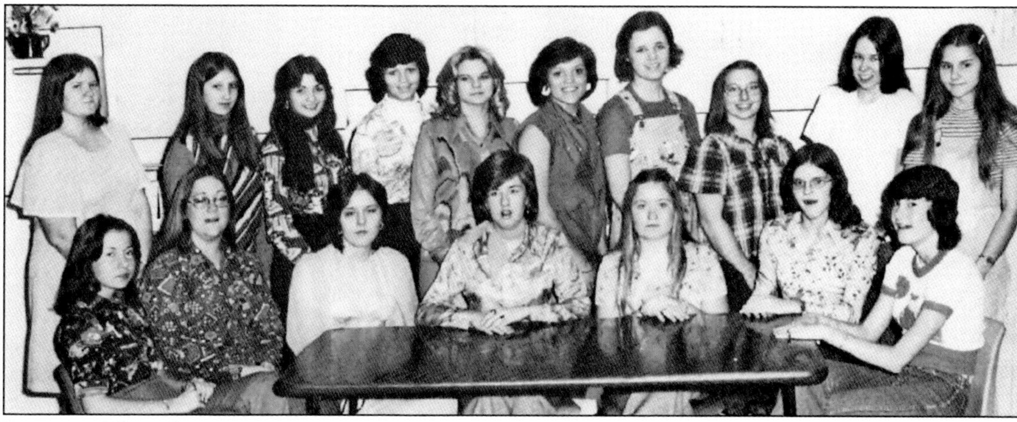

DURANT HIGH SCHOOL FUTURE HOMEMAKERS OF AMERICA, LATE 1960S. Pictured here are, from left to right, (first row) Sheri Cleveland, Gina Nelson, Sherri Rodgers, LoAnn Potter, Miriam Crawford, Emma Robinson, and Debbie Laymon; (second row) Bonnie Crawford, Carla Ridings, Celia Cleveland, Cindy Spradling, Tammy Smith, Debi Boaen, Kim Francies, LuAnn Thomas, Brenda Jeffreys, and Candy Dobbs. (Courtesy of the *Durant High School Lion*.)

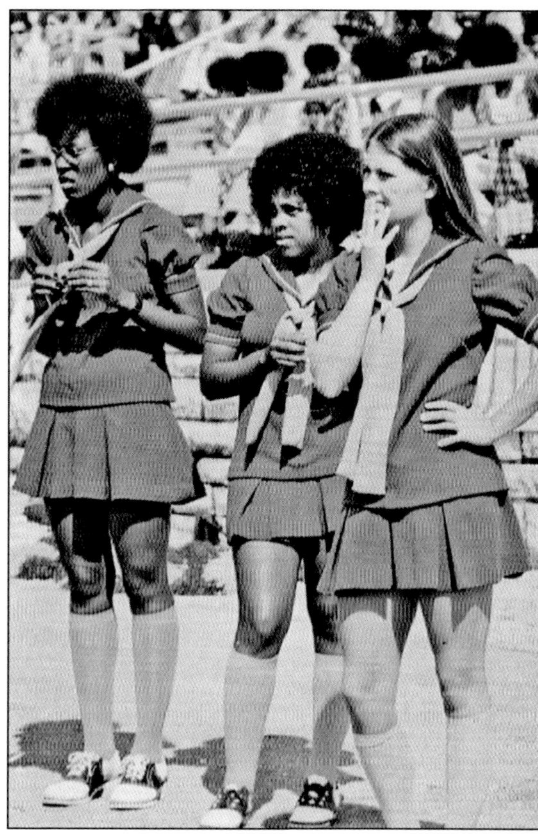

SOUTHEASTERN CHEERLEADERS. Three Southeastern cheerleaders are shown here at the college football and track stadium. (Courtesy of Southeastern Oklahoma State University.)

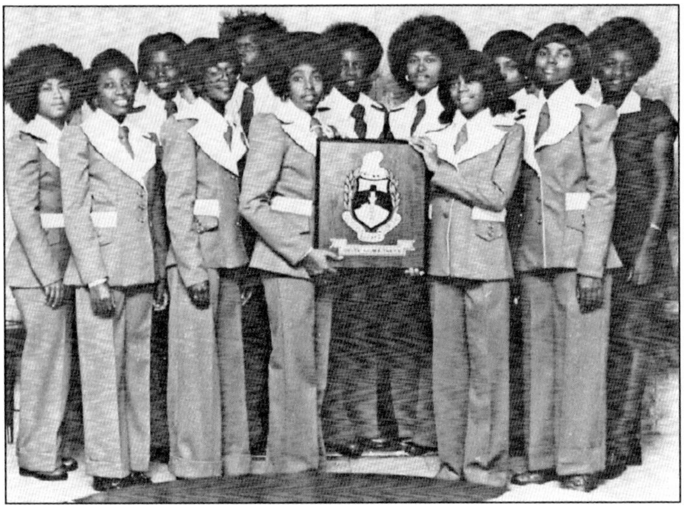

SOUTHEASTERN DELTA SIGMA THETA, 1973–1974. Pictured are, from left to right, (first row) Brenda Wiggins, Billie McCutcheon, LaVerne Howard, Carol King, Vicky Jarvis, and Lincolnette Edwards; (second row) Paula Watkins, Pamela Watkins, Wanda Huckaby, Thelma Benson, Terri Gathron, and Beatrice McDaniel. (Courtesy of Southeastern Oklahoma State University.)

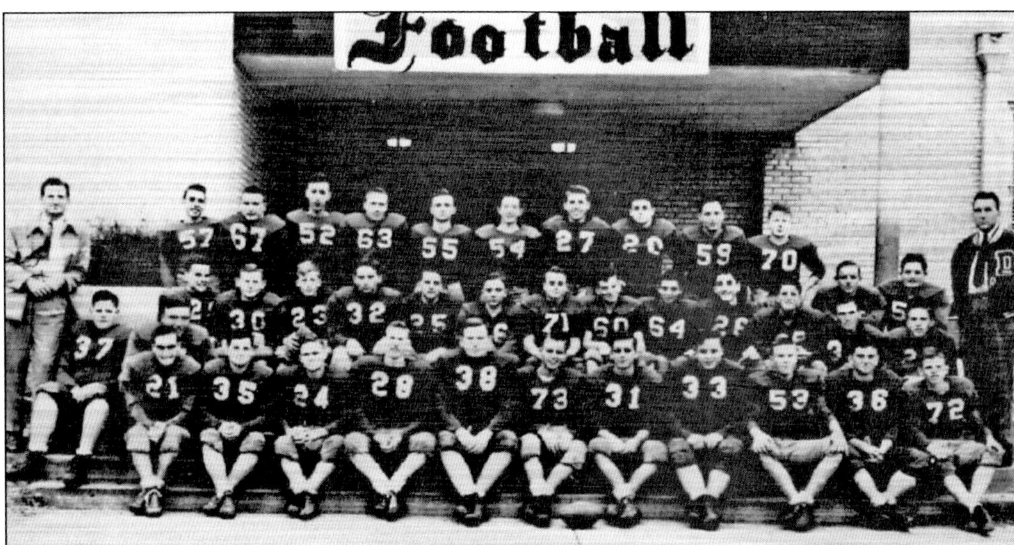

DURANT HIGH SCHOOL FOOTBALL TEAM, 1948. Team members pictured here include James Attaway, Charles Potts, Zeina Craig, James Miller, Richard Harrison, Wallace Riddle, Dale Norwood, Bill Johnson, Pat Cole, Garlan Gibson, Bill Rodgers, assistant coach J.M. Carey, Ralph Mills, Bob Hodge, Bobby Gowen, Paul Johnson, Calvin Wylie, Buddy Tomme, Bobby Nichols, James Davis, Jimmy Ely, Earl Hughes, Dwain Hiberd, Clyde Juett, Donald Elliott, Don Herron, Billy Wayne Smith, head coach Lynn Marsh, Jim Ed Meeker, Rame Moody, Bob Grafa, Frank Vanderbilt, Glenn Potter, Bobby England, Harry Lee, James Kennamer, Bill Atherton, and Roy Paul. (Courtesy of the *Durant High School Lion.*)

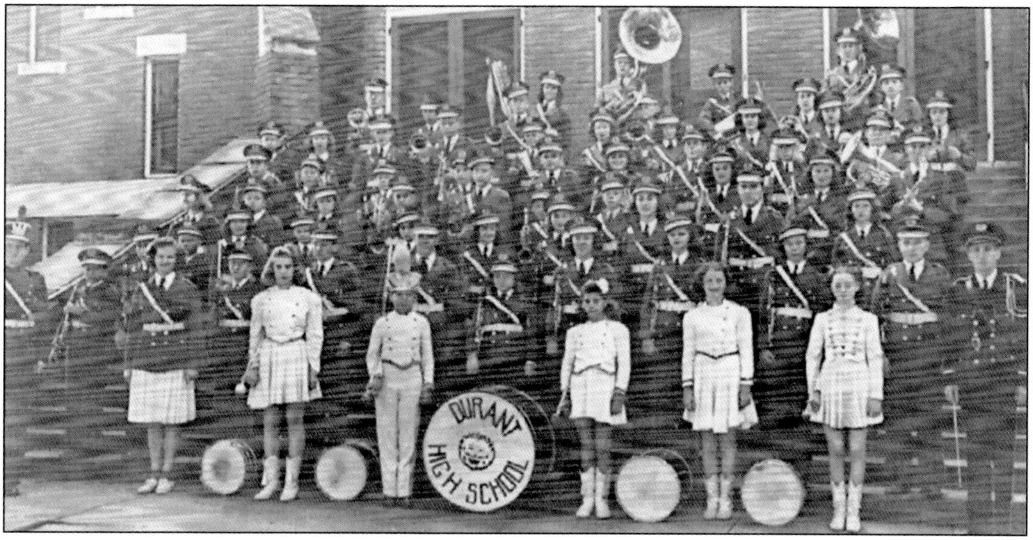

DURANT HIGH SCHOOL BAND. Posing here around 1945 are 65 student musicians in their uniforms. (Courtesy of David L. Crouch and the *Durant Daily Democrat*.)

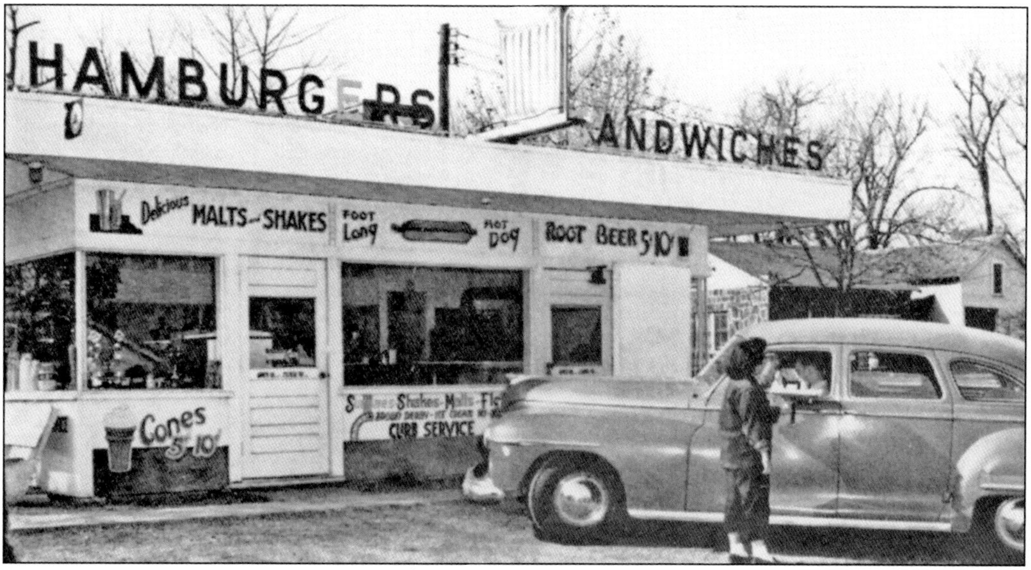

PETE'S DRIVE-IN. Pete's Drive-In has been a landmark in Durant since it opened in 1947. The owner was George Bryant, and at one point it became Geo's Drive-In. The business, located at 1301 North First Avenue, is presently owned by Paul Lovan. (Courtesy of Southeastern Oklahoma State University.)

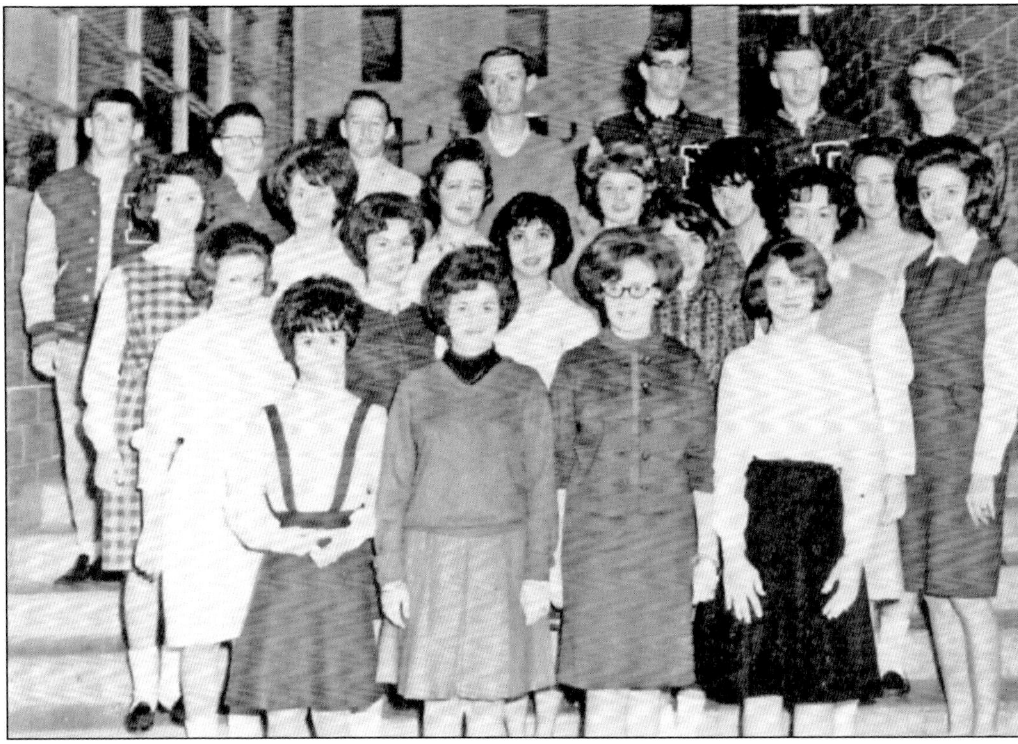

National Honor Society, Durant High School. Pictured here are National Honor Society members Kay Turley, Betty Ford, Paula Sterling, Sharon Cobb, Susie Smith, Toni Uselding, Alice Baker, Kathy Bowlby, Sue Jackson, Beth Doxsee, Linda Gann, Susan Seeley, Judith Steakley, Marilyn Mueller, Betty Mahana, Susan Gantrell, John Haskins, Richard McLean, Gary Lancaster, Larry Vaden, Bill Gentry, Arthur Tidwell, Steve Freeman; not pictured is Jim Slaughter. (Courtesy of the *Durant High School Lion*.)

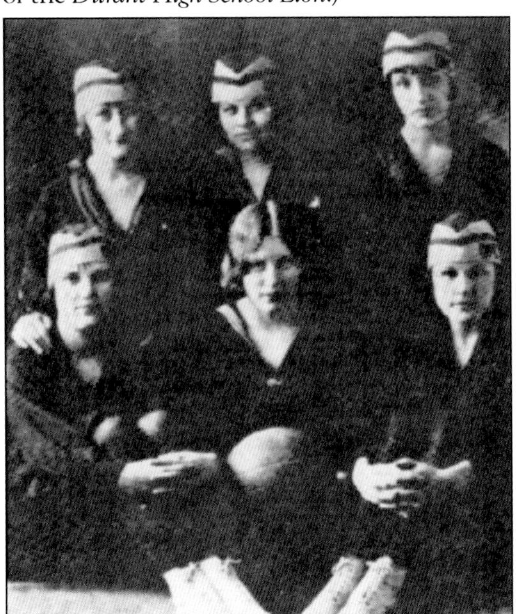

Oklahoma Presbyterian College Cardinals. The 1924 OPC Cardinals are, from left to right, (first row) Delores Allen, Loretta Cowling, and Reta Franklin (Newman); (second row) Alyce Pollack, Rose Fowler, and Ethel Hunter. Bible school and summer revivals were held, and ponds were used for baptizing. (Courtesy of Bryan County Archives.)

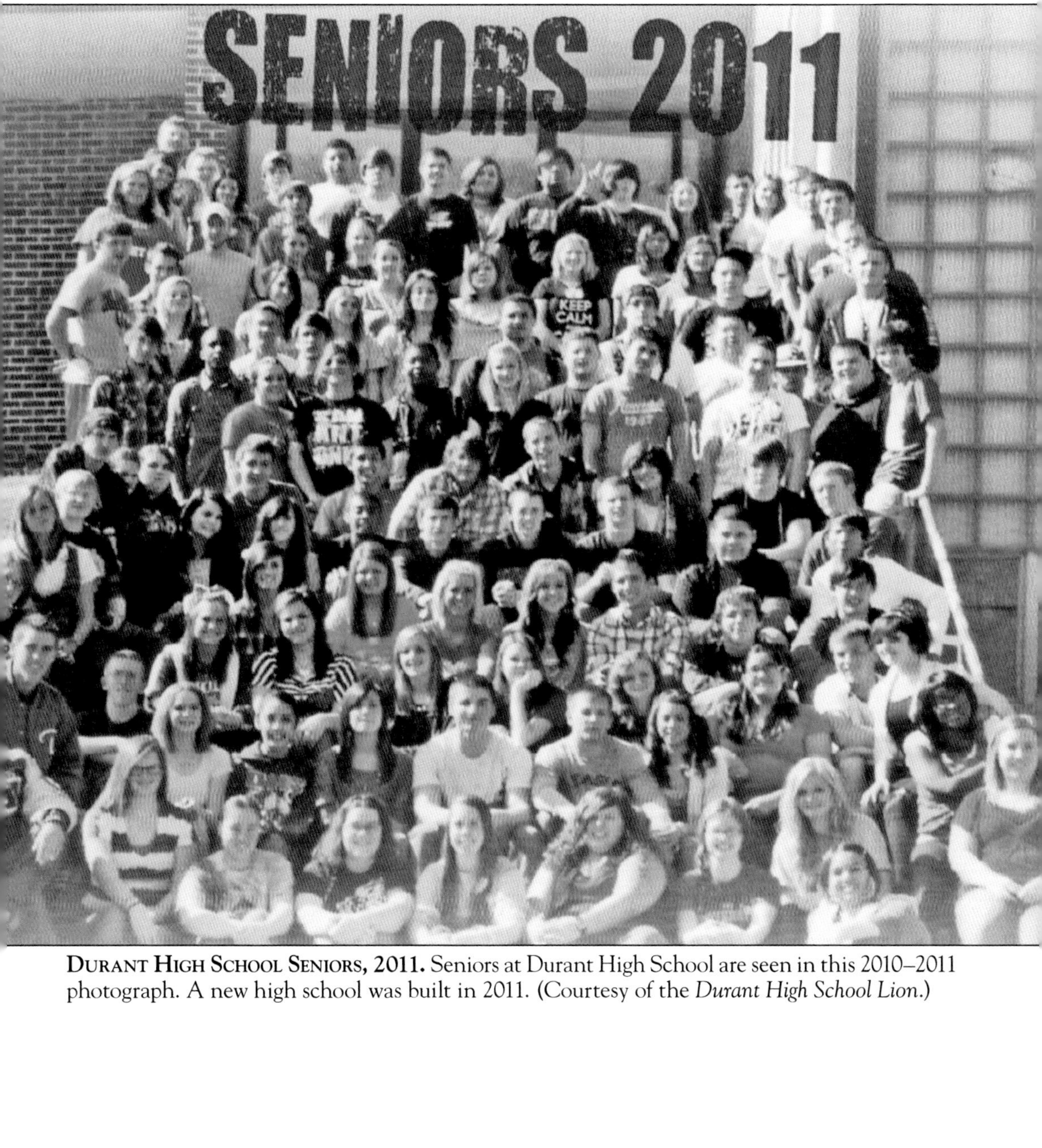

Durant High School Seniors, 2011. Seniors at Durant High School are seen in this 2010–2011 photograph. A new high school was built in 2011. (Courtesy of the *Durant High School Lion*.)

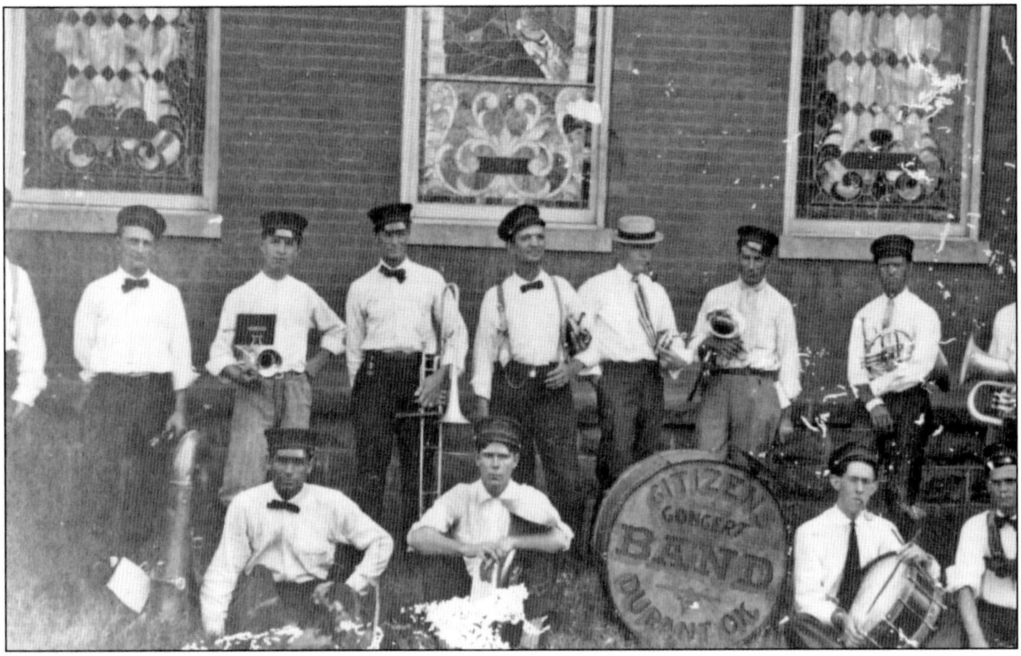

Citizens Concert Band. The drum identifies this group as the Citizens Concert Band of Durant, Oklahoma. (Courtesy of Marion Downs.)

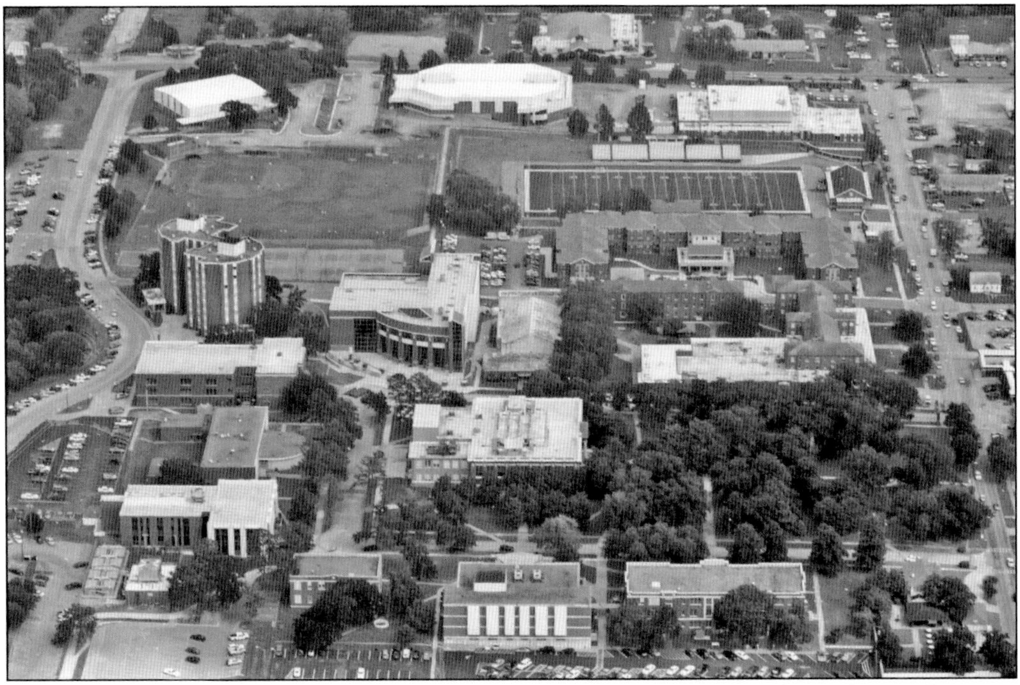

Aerial View of Southeastern Oklahoma State University Campus. This is the Southeastern campus as viewed from the west. The first sessions of Southeastern Normal were held in temporary quarters. In 1910, the Normal School Building, later called Morrison Hall, was constructed on Dr. J.L. Schuler's peach orchard. Southeastern's original purpose was the education of teachers for the public schools of Oklahoma. (Courtesy of Southeastern Oklahoma State University.)

Four

Durant, City of Magnolias

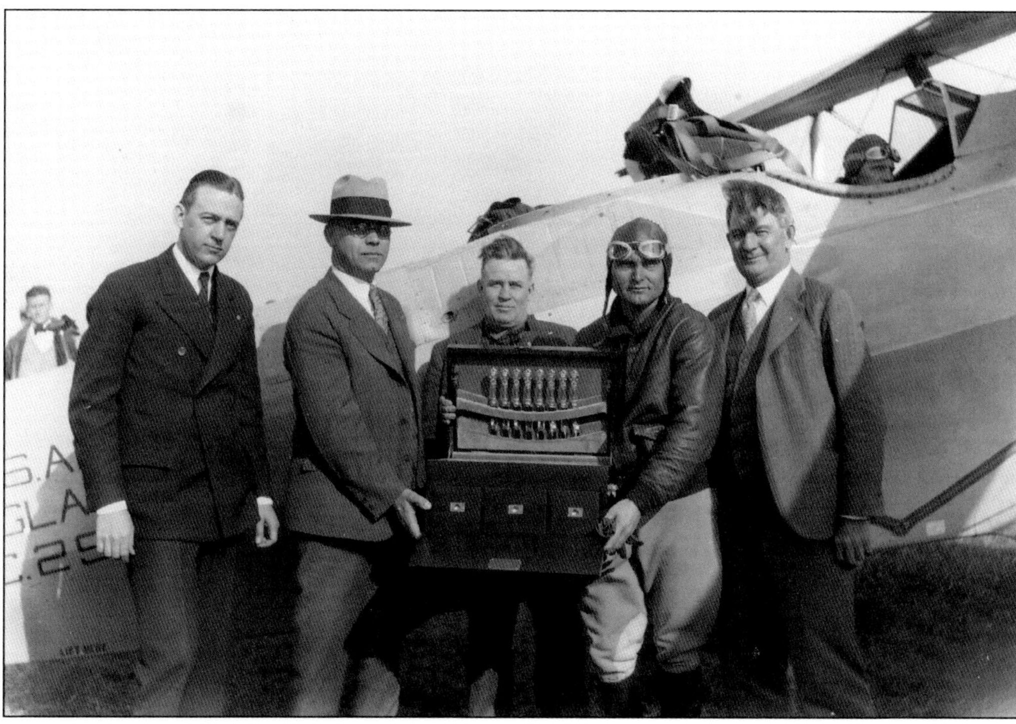

Ira C. Eaker Arrives in Durant, around 1930. Pictured here are, from left to right, Harry Kimbrel (druggist), Eugene Briggs (Southeastern Teachers College president), Harry Haigh (civil engineer), Ira C. Eaker, and Paul Laird (Southeastern Teachers College coach). Eaker, for whom Durant's airport is named, was commanding general of the 8th Air Force in Europe during World War II. (Courtesy of Southeastern Oklahoma State University.)

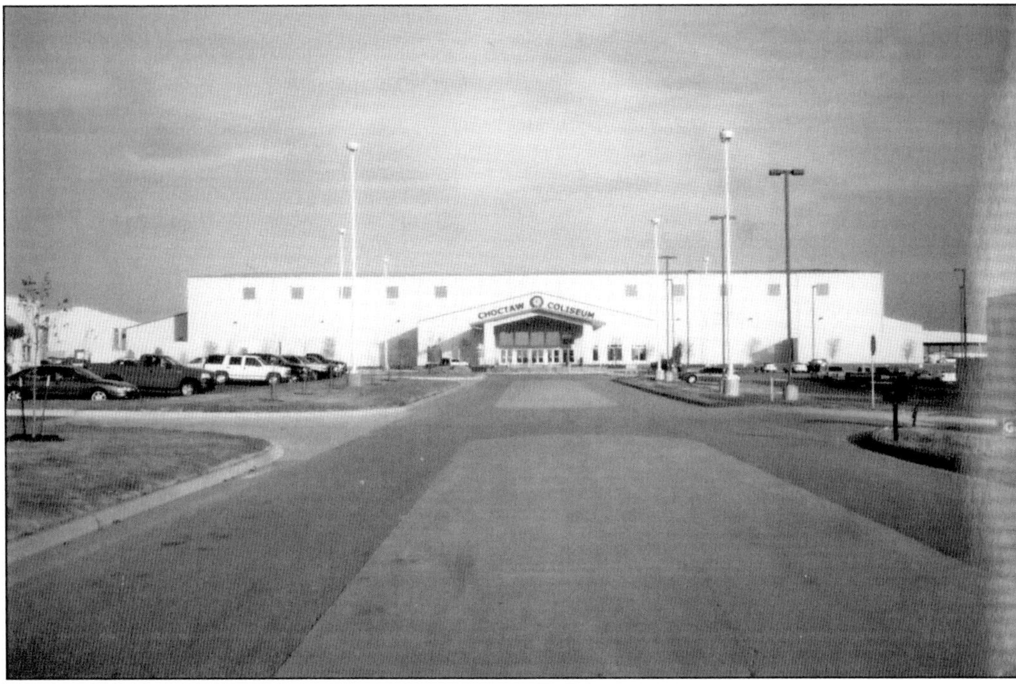

Choctaw Bingo. Pictured here, the Choctaw Bingo & Casino is owned and operated by the Choctaw Nation of Oklahoma. (Author's collection.)

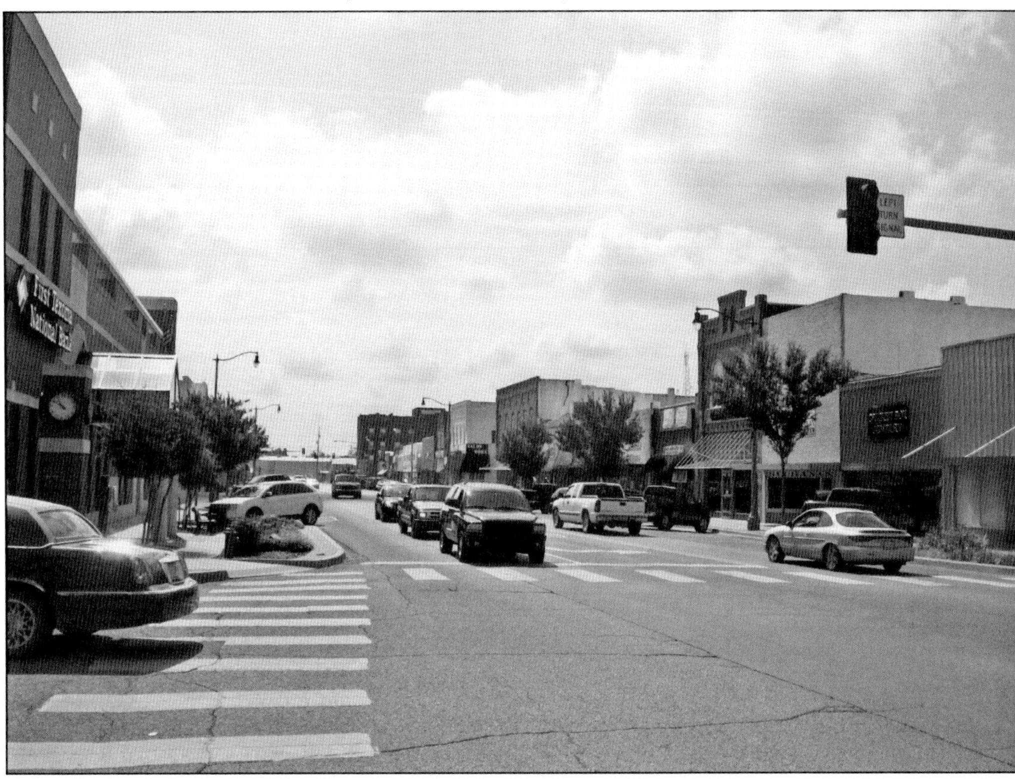

Downtown Durant. This present-day scene looks to the east. (Author's collection.)

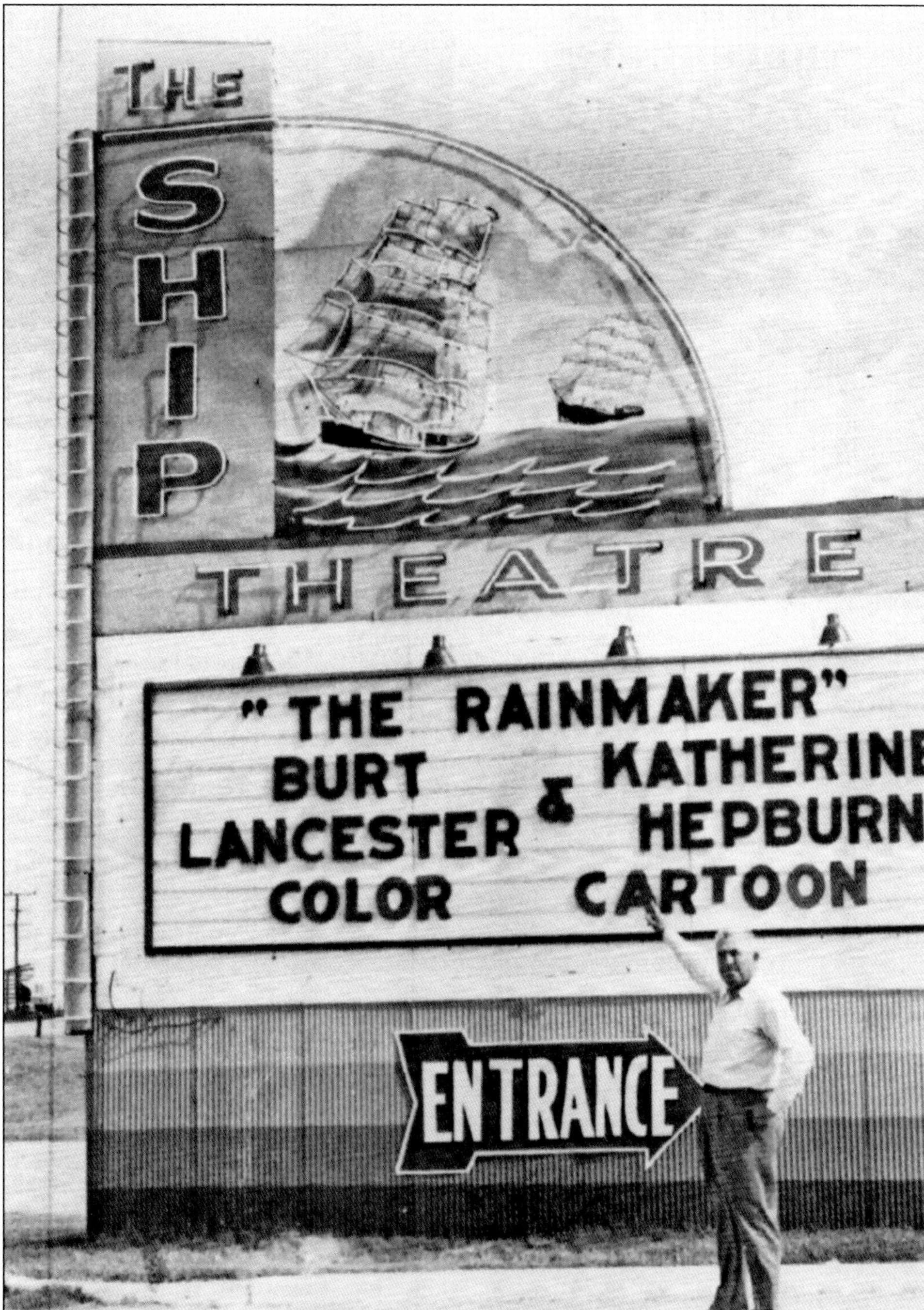

The Ship Drive-In Theatre. Owner Shipman Bullard is pictured in front of the marquee of his movie theater, which opened north of Durant in 1952. He is pointing to the title of the movie *The Rainmaker* (and a misspelling of actor Burt Lancaster's name), which was showing at the time. Earlier theaters included the Colonial, which opened in 1915, and later The Queen, Metro, Savage, New Plaza Theatre, and The Plaza (renamed State). The Ship Drive-in itself was originally known as the Sky-Vu Drive-In. (Courtesy of Bryan County Archives.)

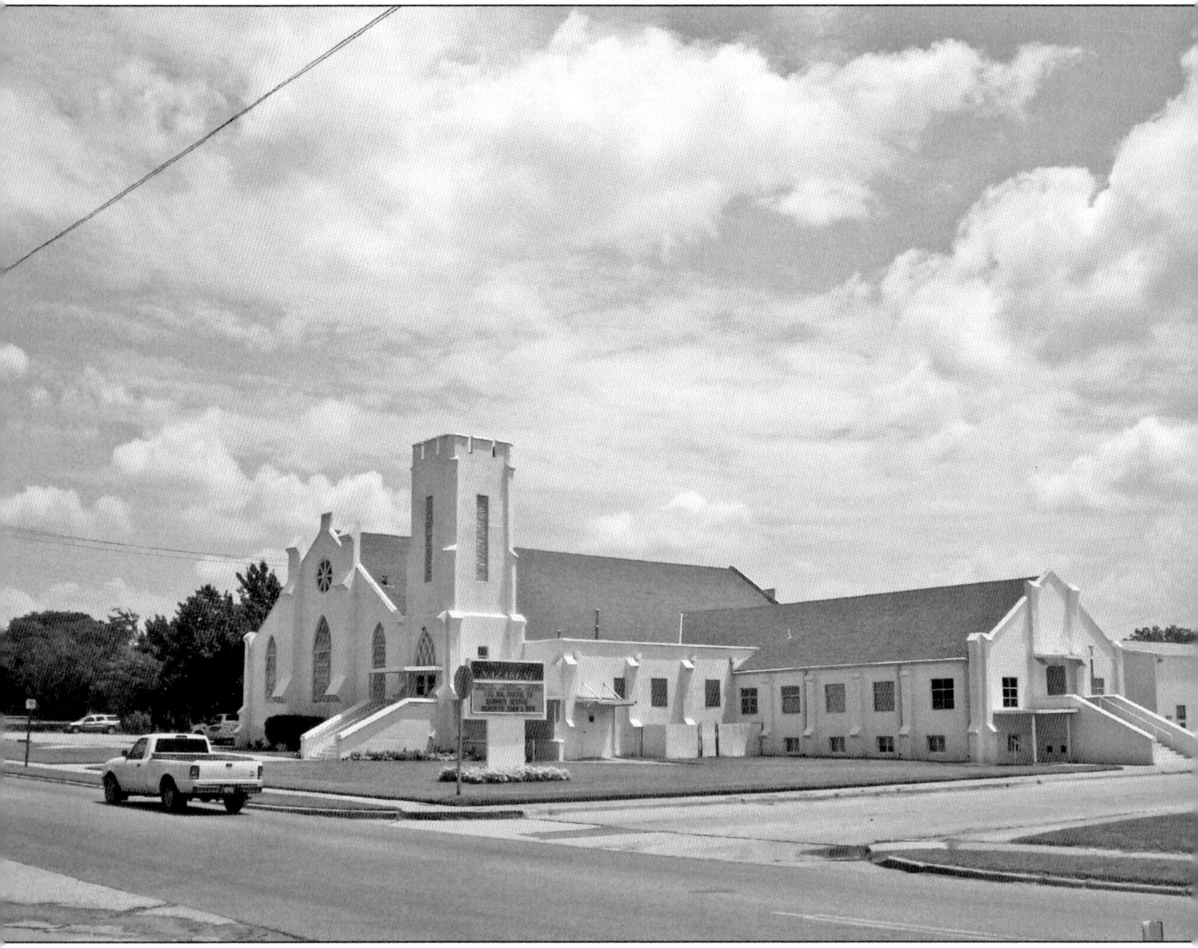

FIRST CHURCH OF THE NAZARENE. This church is located at 724 West Texas Street in Durant. It began its ministry over 100 years ago and has been in this location since the 1940s. (Author's collection.)

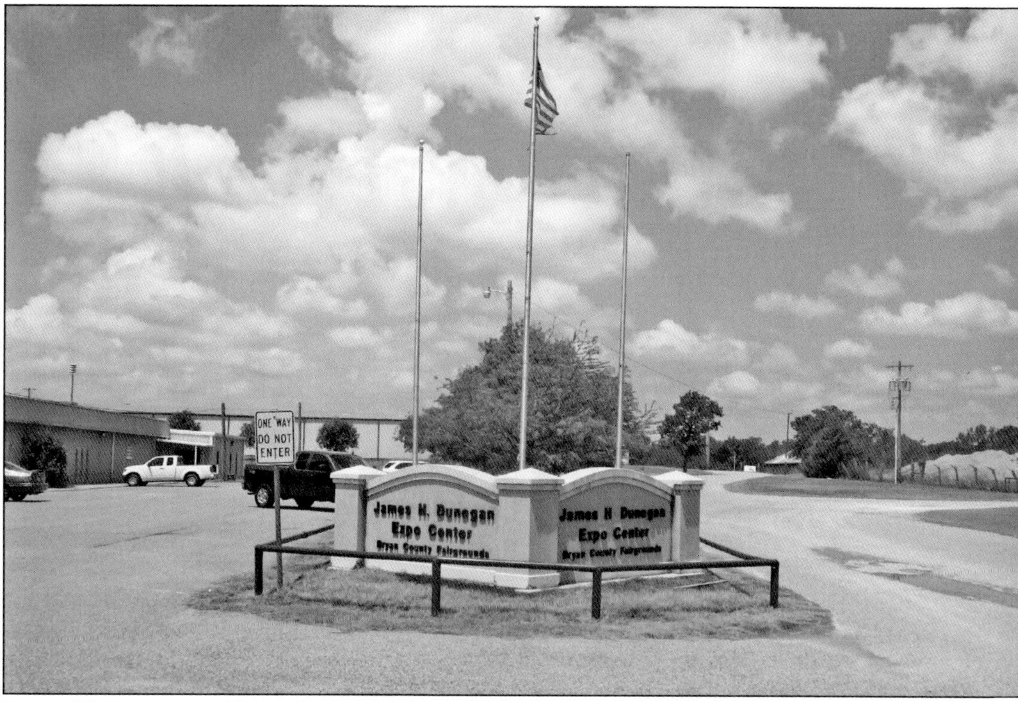

James H. Dunegan Expo Center. This exposition center was named for James H. Dunegan, a former state legislator (1990–2002) and present city manager of Durant (since 2006). The Clay Jones Community Center & Fair Grounds of Bryan County is also located here. Gov. Brad Henry appointed Dunegan to the Oklahoma Transportation Commission from 2003 to 2011. In 2001, he received the Oklahoma Public Employees Association's Legislator of the Year distinction, and the Bryan County Fairgrounds dedicated the James H. Dunegan Expo Center in his name. In 2002, he received the Oklahoma State Troopers Association and Legislator of the Year in 2003. He is chairman of the Durant Magnolia Festival and serves as the 1st vice president of the Durant Area Chamber of Commerce. James and his wife, Sandra, have five children: Mike, Steve, Lori, Diane, and Tammy. (Author's collection.)

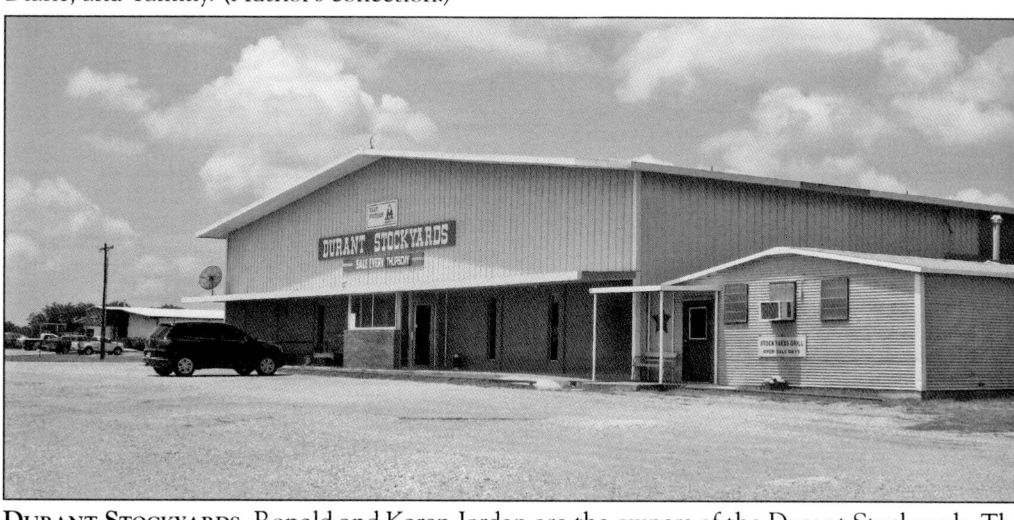

Durant Stockyards. Ronald and Karen Jordan are the owners of the Durant Stockyards. The highway in this area is named for Durant city councilman Leon Sherrer. (Author's collection.)

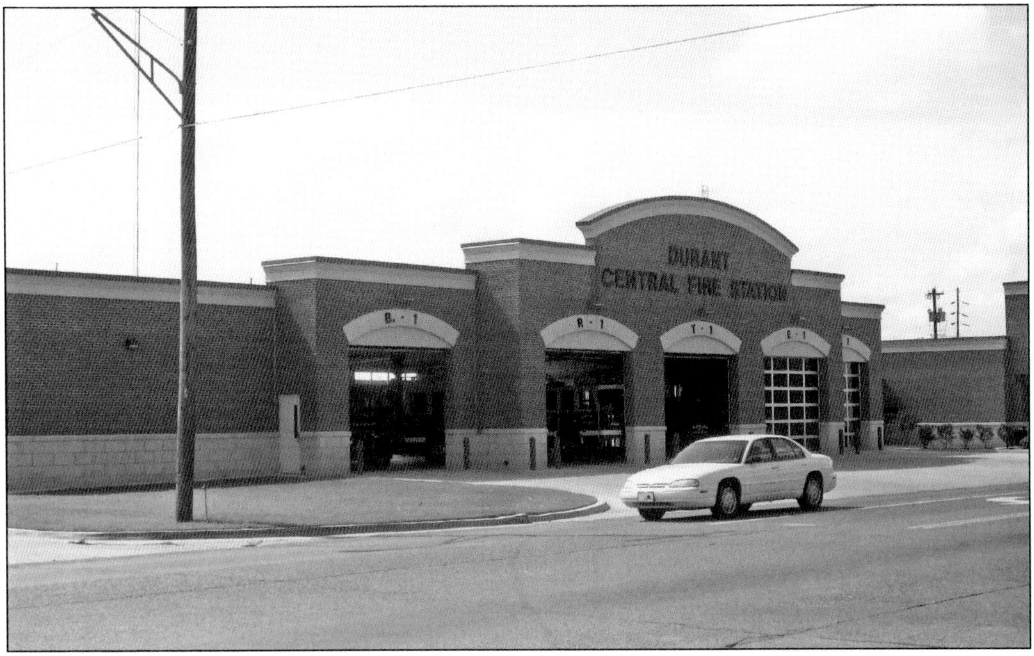

Durant Central Fire Station. This fire station was completed in 2010 across from Market Square. It was formerly located at the west end of Durant City Hall. (Author's collection.)

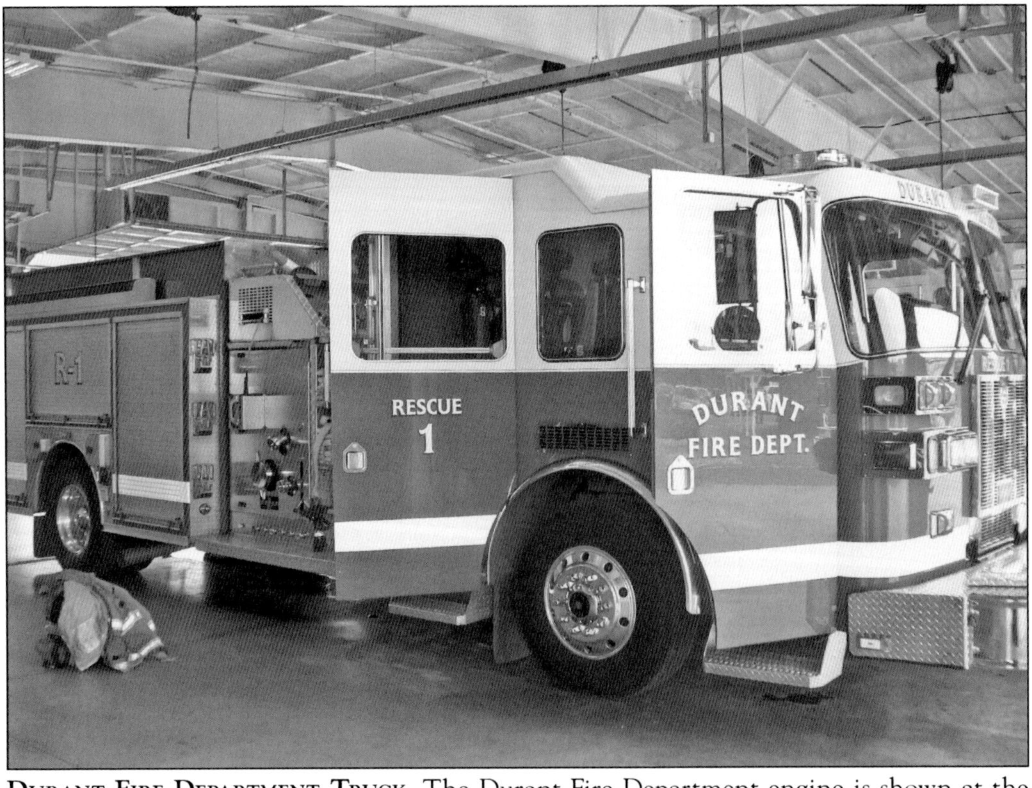

Durant Fire Department Truck. The Durant Fire Department engine is shown at the department's new location. (Author's collection.)

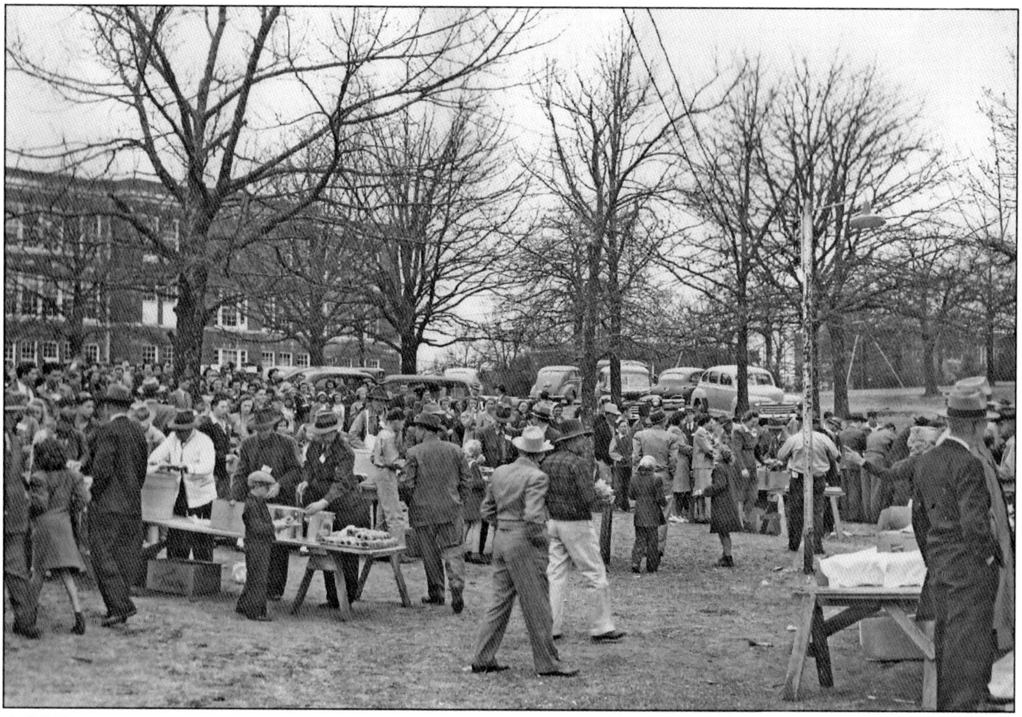

4-H Barbeque. Between 1,600 and 1,700 people attended the 4-H barbeque of March 29, 1947. They were guests of Durant businessmen Dr. W.K. Haynie and Rector Swearengin, and the event featured 900 pounds of beef that included two prize-winning calves from the 4-H, FFA, and FHA. The barbeque followed a 45-minute program at Southeastern honoring the boys and girls. (Courtesy of Matt Swearengin.)

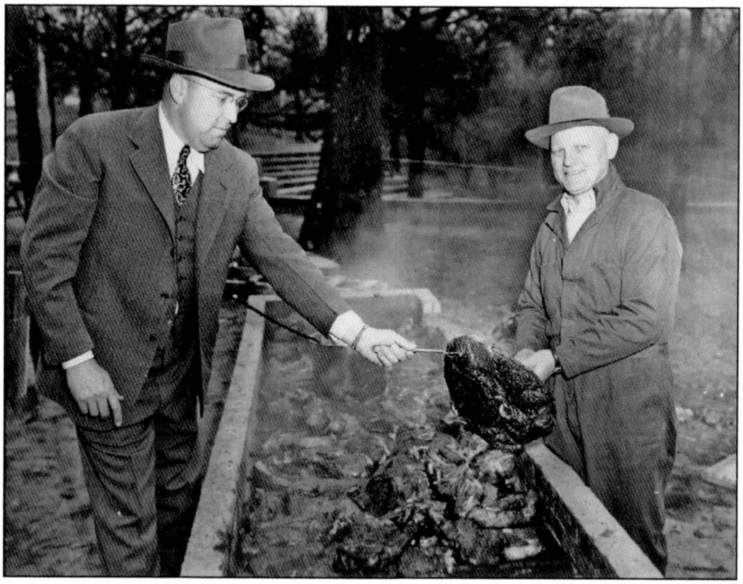

Durant 4-H Barbecue. This 4-H barbecue was held on March 29, 1947. Standing over the barbeque pit are Dr. W.K. Haynie (left) and Rector Swearengin. It was the generosity of these two community business leaders that made the event possible. Lat Lutes prepared the barbeque, and chamber of commerce officers and members served the people. (Courtesy of Matt Swearengin.)

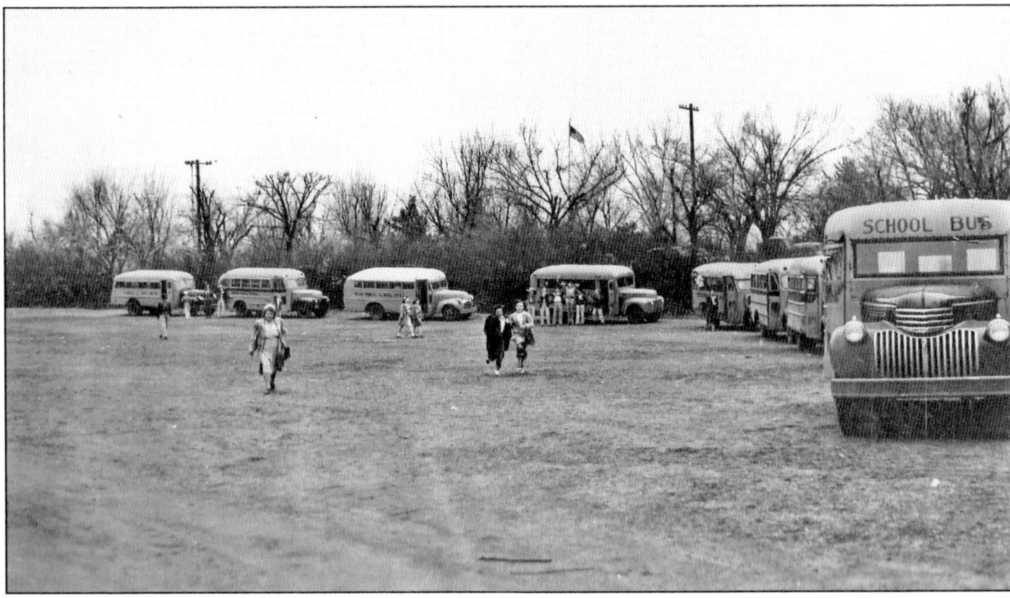

Busing Students to 4-H Barbecue. These buses are bringing students into the Durant 4-H barbecue on March 29, 1947. This noon barbeque was held to honor 1,600 local 4H, FFA, FHA club members. In addition to these youths, the event was attended by parents, coaches, and teachers. (Courtesy of Matt Swearengin.)

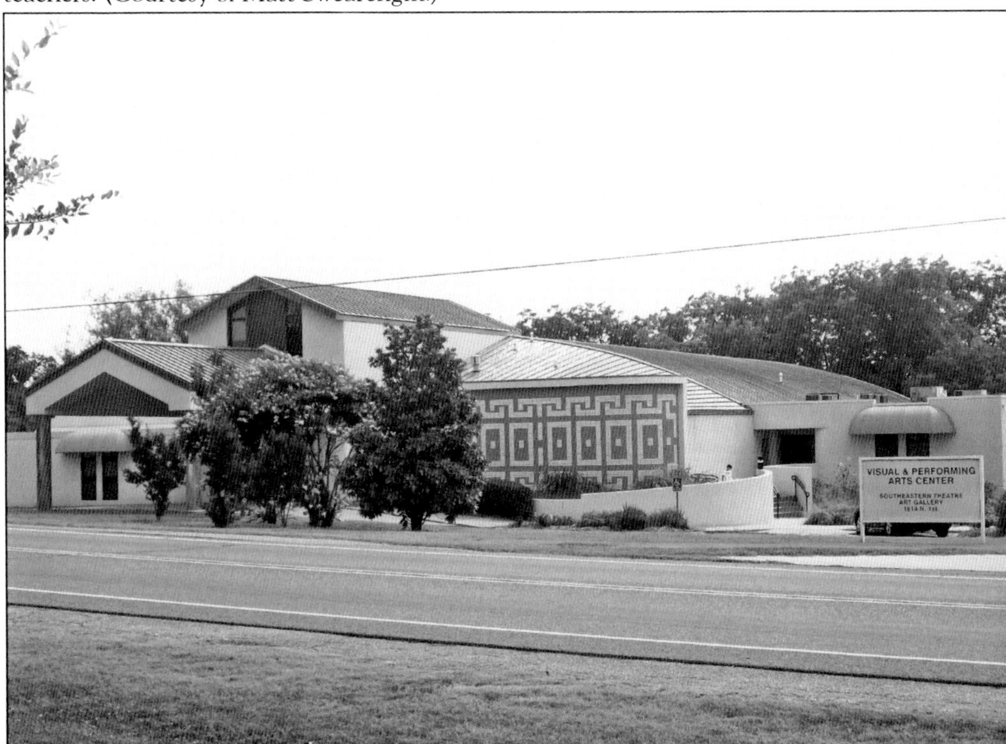

Visual & Performing Arts Center, SOSU. This is the Visual & Performing Arts Center, Southeastern Theatre Art Gallery. (Author's collection.)

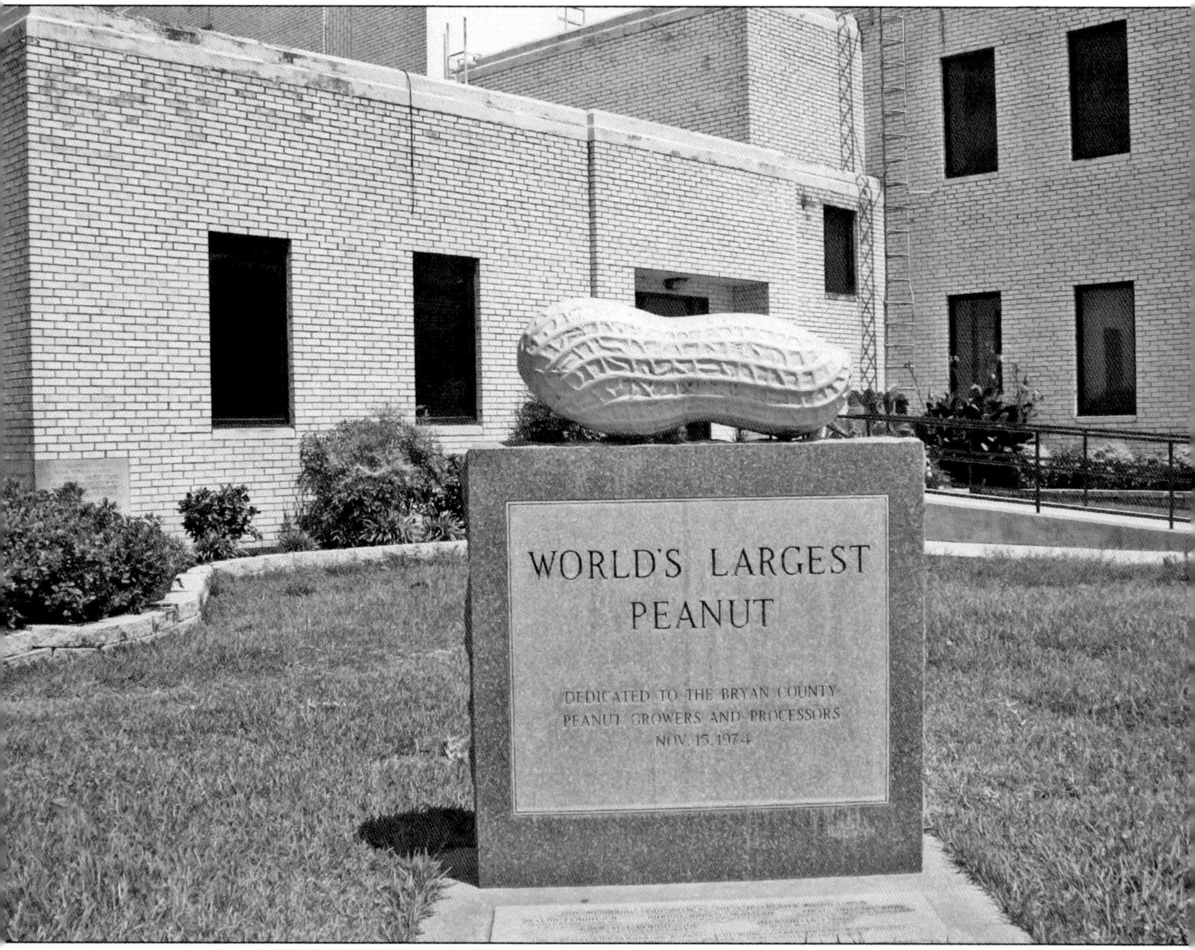

World's Largest Peanut. This peanut is displayed in front of Durant City Hall, dedicated to the Bryan County peanut growers and processors on November 15, 1974. On June 16, 1973, a time capsule commemorating Durant's centennial celebration was buried 30 inches in front of this marker; it will be opened in June 2023. (Author's collection.)

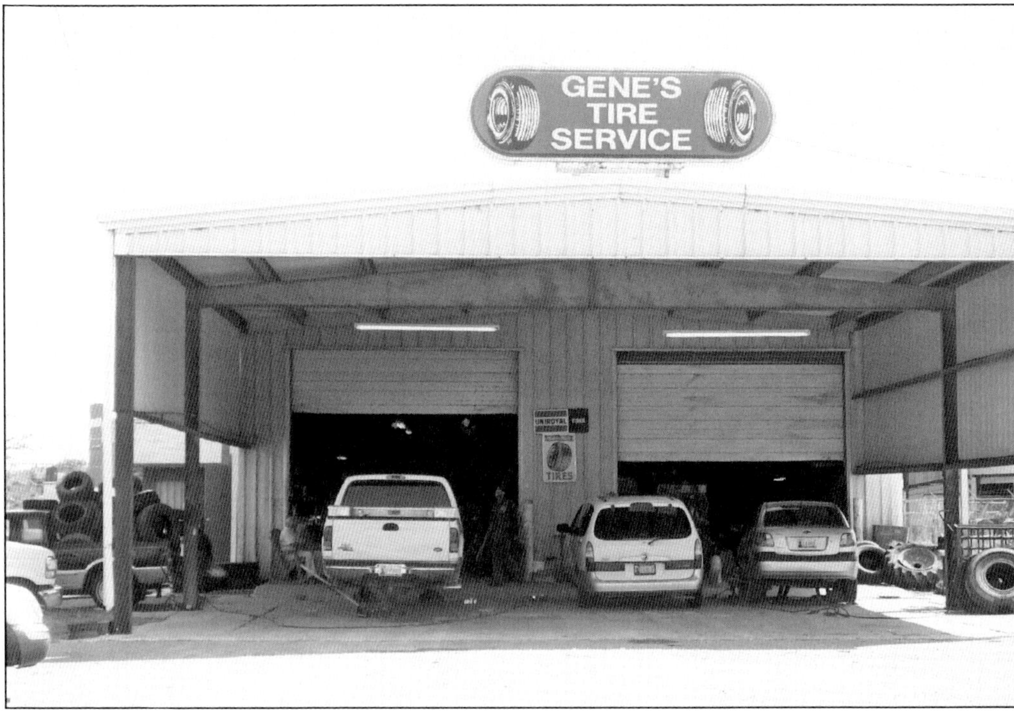

GENE'S TIRE SERVICE. Gene's Tire Service stays busy fixing cars, trucks, and farm vehicles. Owner Rick Munholland succeeded his father in operating the business. (Author's collection.)

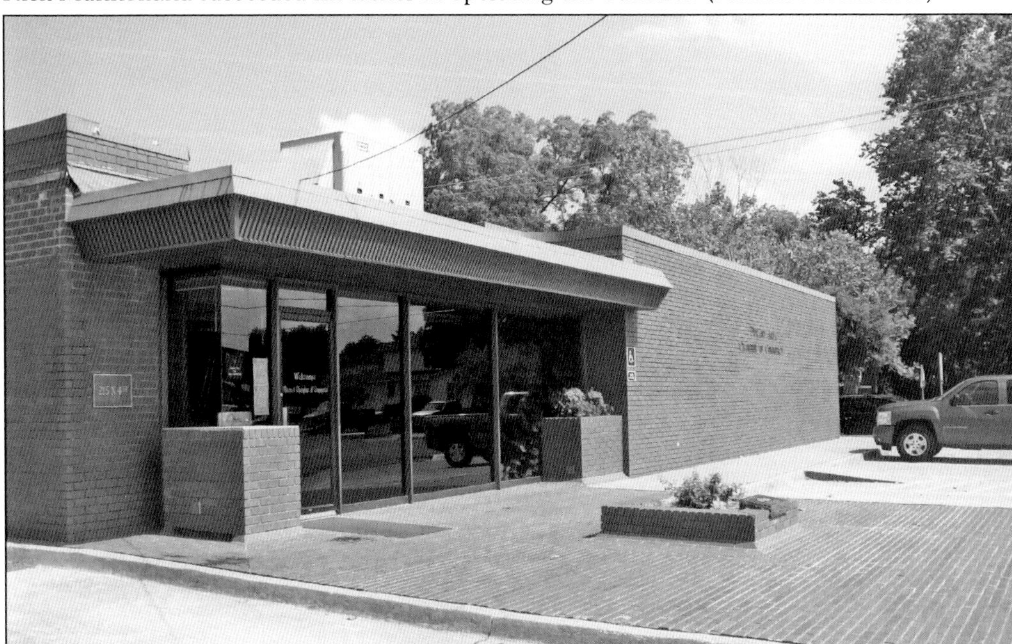

DURANT AREA CHAMBER OF COMMERCE. Durant is located 90 miles from Dallas, Texas, and 150 miles from both Tulsa and Oklahoma City, Oklahoma. Currently, Janet Reed is the executive director, Jennifer Brewer is the administrative assistant, and Malorie Estes is the manager. The chamber of commerce is located at 215 North Fourth Avenue. (Author's collection.)

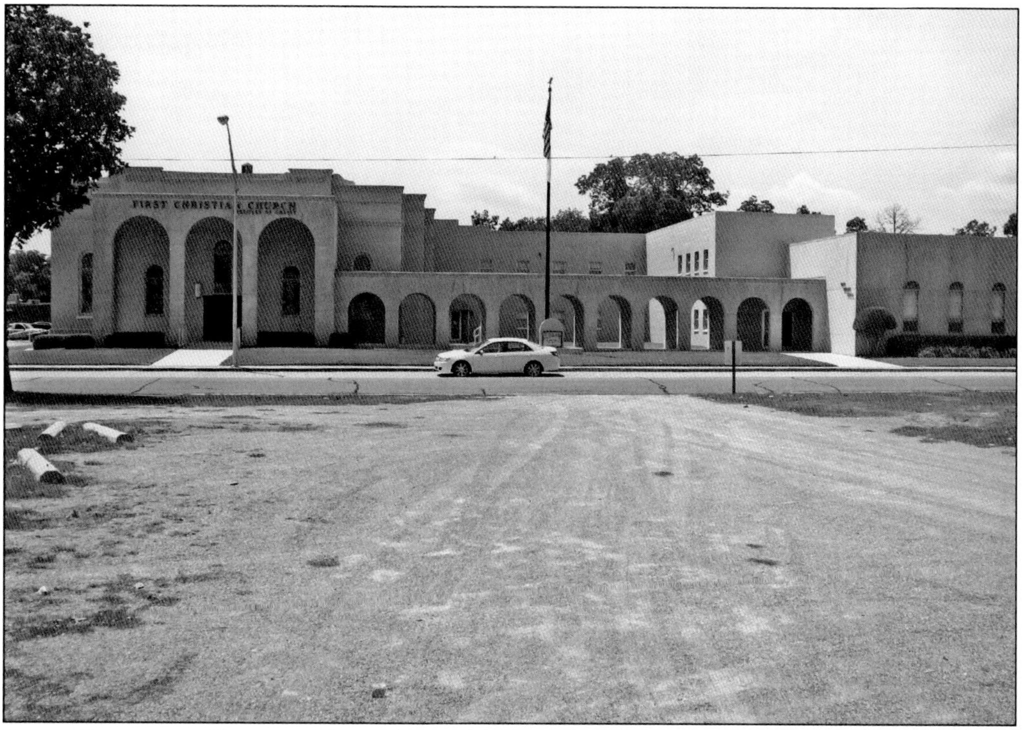

First Christian Church. First Christian Church is located at 301 North Third Avenue in Durant and was founded in 1900. It has been in operation since then at this location. (Author's collection.)

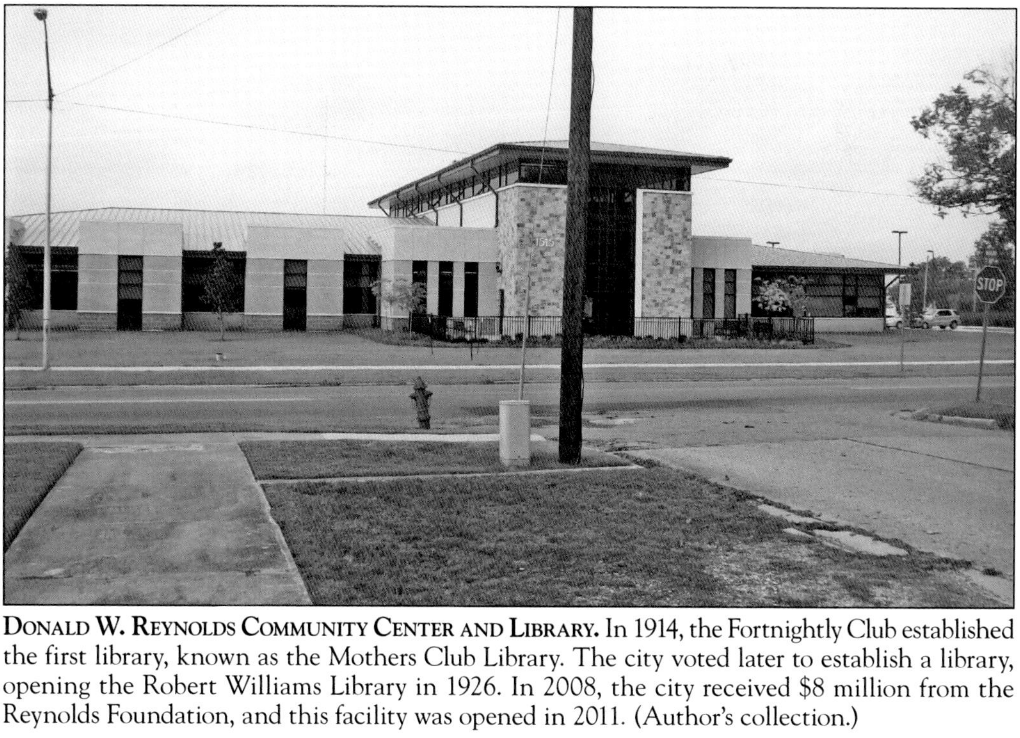

Donald W. Reynolds Community Center and Library. In 1914, the Fortnightly Club established the first library, known as the Mothers Club Library. The city voted later to establish a library, opening the Robert Williams Library in 1926. In 2008, the city received $8 million from the Reynolds Foundation, and this facility was opened in 2011. (Author's collection.)

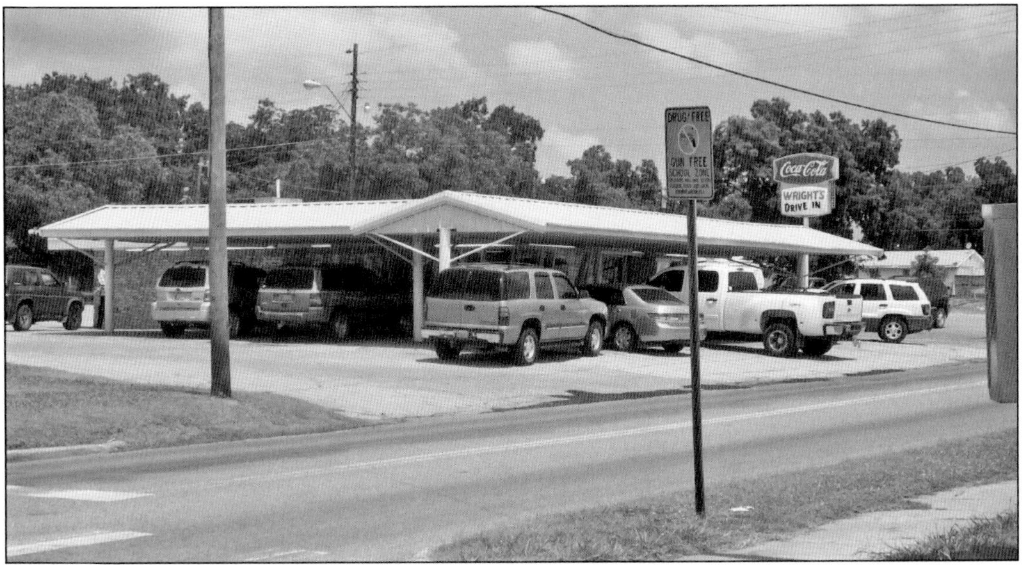

WRIGHT'S DRIVE-IN. This business on South Ninth Avenue first opened in 1949 as Emrick's Drive In. It became Wright's Drive-In in the early 1960s, and present owner Jesse Holder purchased the business in 1979. Holder retained the Wright's Drive-In name, and the establishment remains a popular establishment. (Author's collection.)

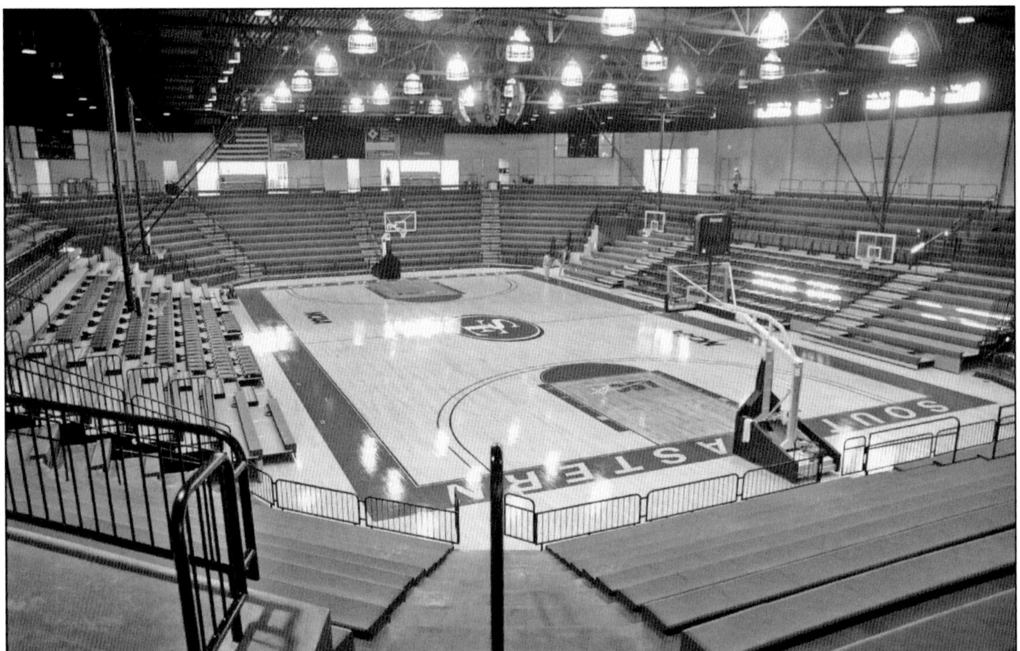

BLOOMER SULLIVAN ARENA, SOSU. The gymnasium at Southeastern Oklahoma State University is named for Bloomer Sullivan, one of the nation's great college basketball coaches. Sullivan, who was NAIA Coach of the Year in 1957, won 662 college games and 13 Oklahoma Collegiate Conference Championships. He was inducted as a charter member of the SOSU Athletic Hall of Fame in 1977. He joined the Southeastern faculty in 1930. (Courtesy of Southeastern Oklahoma State University.)

JUANITA ESTES. Juanita Estes, the daughter of John Dunn and Susie Thompson of Talihina, was born in Durant in 1920. She taught beadwork, loom work, and turquoise, silver, and ceramic work. Juanita and her husband, Haskell Estes, have both passed away. Their children are Johnny Ray (died at seven months), Mary Sue, Melba Rose, and Charlotte. Juanita's grandmother was Vina Ellington, and her great-great-great grandmother was Betsy McCoy. (Author's collection.)

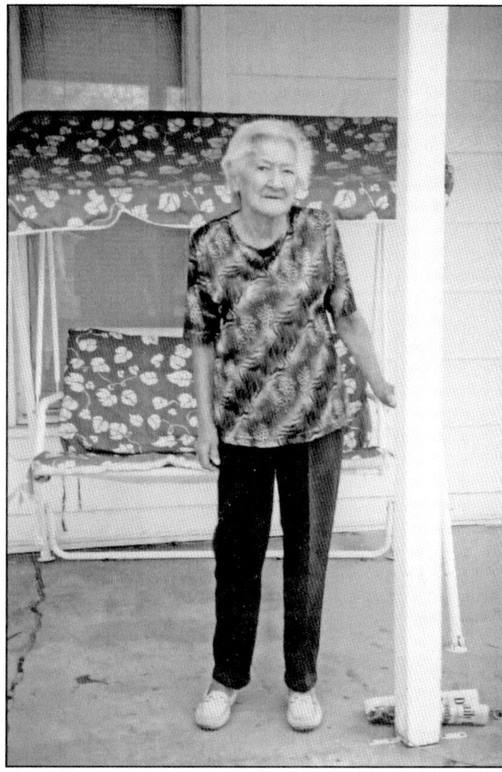

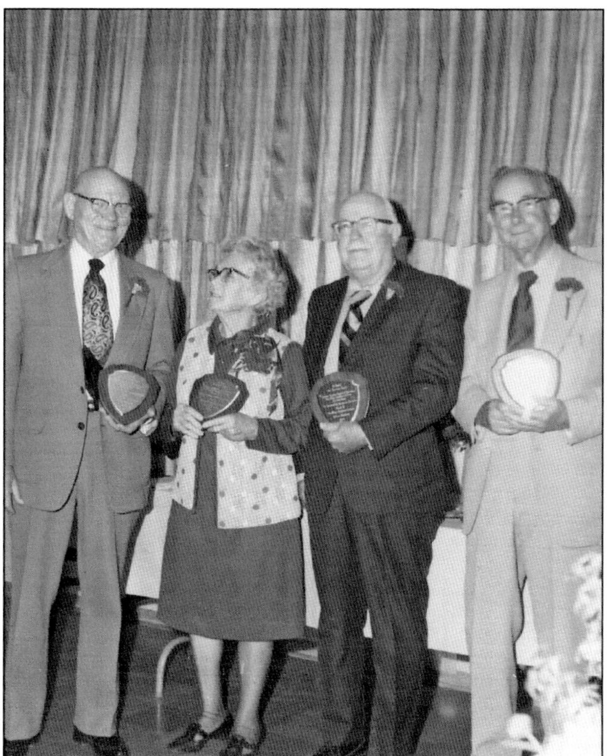

KING'S DAUGHTERS AND SONS RECEPTION. Standing are, from left to right, Rector Swearengin, Dora Gates, B. Story, and John Steakley. This 1973 reception honored the original board of the non-profit nursing home. (Courtesy of Matt Swearengin.)

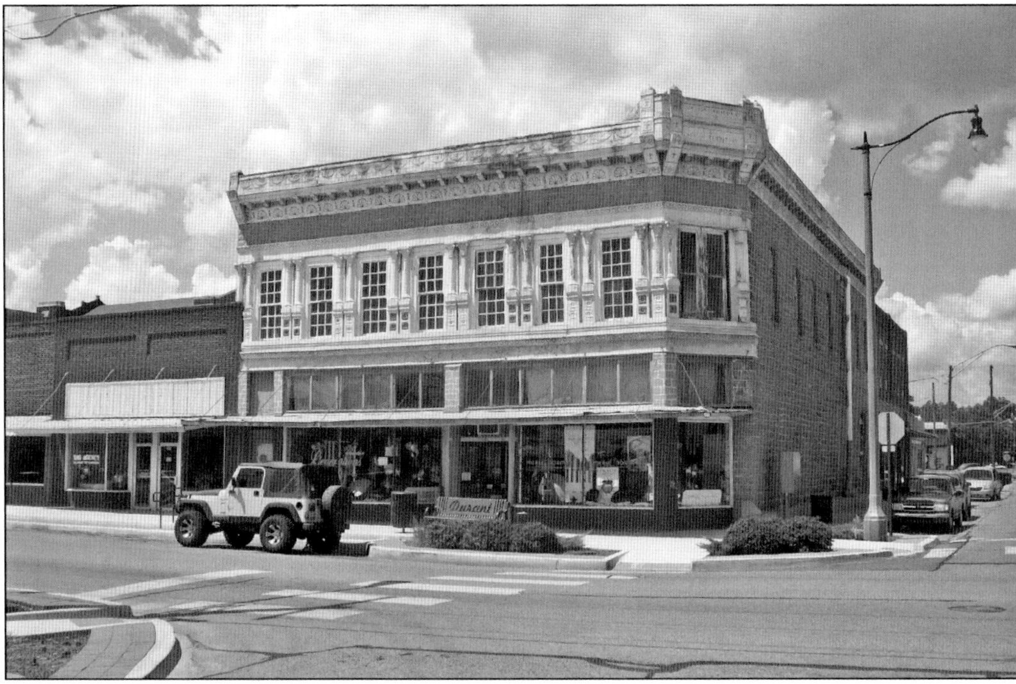

J.L. Wilson Building. This structure, also known as the Durant Opera House, dates back to around 1898. With the rise of motion pictures, the opera house began to decline in popularity. Today, the lower level of the building is occupied by Fortenberry Furniture. (Author's collection.)

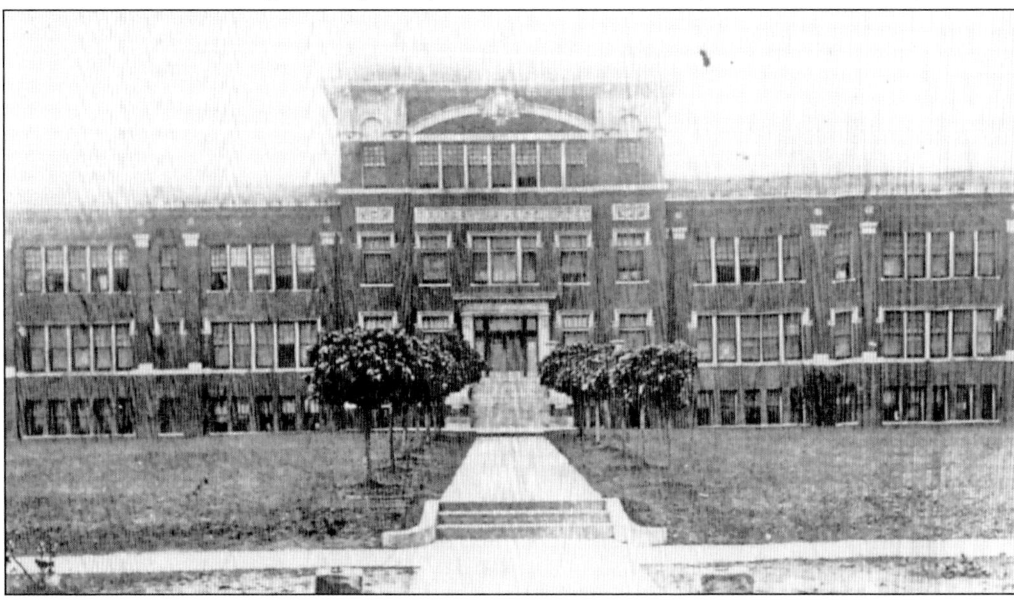

Oklahoma Presbyterian College. This college evolved from Haskell Institute and Durant College. When this c. 1925 photograph was taken, the top floor served as the school gym. The college was built in 1910 for $80,000 on a one-acre tract given by the Durant Area Chamber of Commerce. A 1941 fire destroyed the interior of the building, but the structure was restored, and the school continued until 1965. It was purchased in an auction by the chamber of commerce and given by prearrangement to the Choctaw Nation. (Courtesy of Durant Area Chamber of Commerce.)

Bibliography

Bryan County History, 1983.

Durant, Randle. *Footsteps of a Durant Choctaw*. Self-published, 1999.

Freeny, John Ellis. *Whuppin' and Spurrin' Through Choctaw Country*. Edmond, OK: self-published, 1998.

Kidwell, Clara Sue, and Charles Roberts. *The Choctaws: A Critical Bibliography*. Indiana University Press, 1980.

Littlejohn, Joseph E., ed. *I Remember When*, vol. 1. Durant, OK: Three Valley Museum, 2006.

MacCreary, Henry. *A Story of Durant: Queen of Three Valleys*. Durant, OK: The Democrat Printing Company, 1946.

Milligan, James C., and David L. Norris. *Morrison's Social History of the Choctaw Nation: 1865–1907*. Abilene, TX: H.V. Chapman and Sons, 2005.

———, ———, and Ann Vanmeter. *Durant: 1872–1990*. Durant, OK: Bryan County Heritage Association, 1990.

Norris, L. David. *Southeastern Oklahoma State University since 1909, Vol. 1*. Durant, OK: Mesa Publishing Co., 1986.

Peterson, Robert, ed. *Reflections of Durant and Bryan County, Oklahoma*, vols. 1 and 2. Marceline, MO: D-Books Publishing, 1994.

Samuels, Wesley and Charleen. *Life and Times of the Choctaw Original Enrollees*. Self-published, 1997.

Sprague, Donovin. *Choctaw Nation of Oklahoma*. Charleston, SC: Arcadia Publishing, 2007.

INDEX